BROTHERS DRACUL

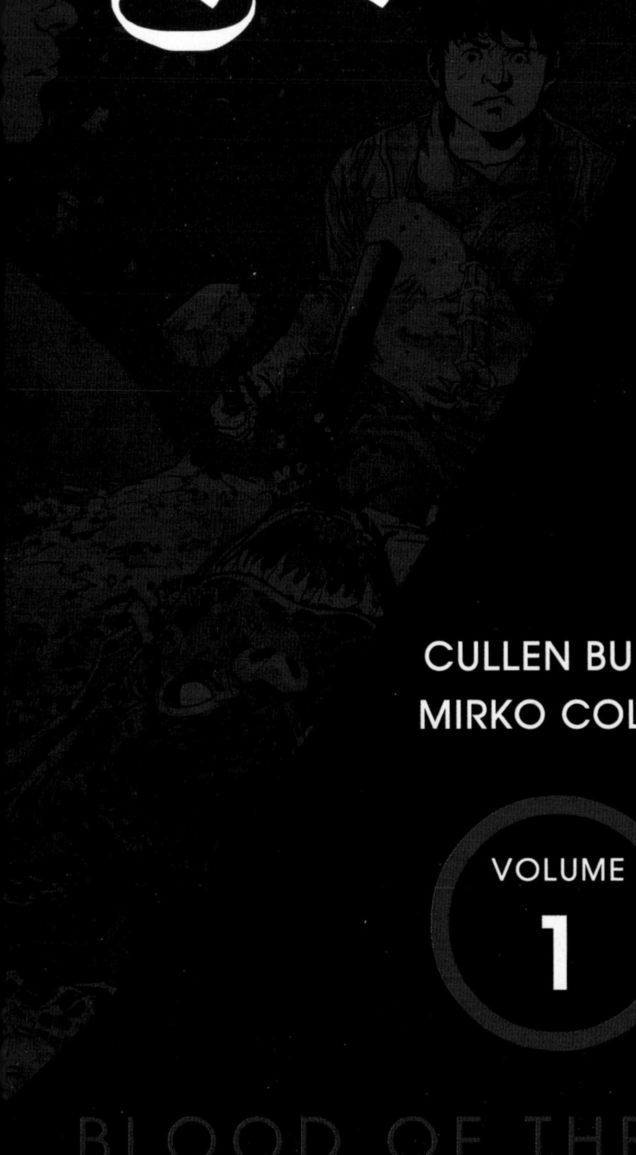

CULLEN BUNN

MIRKO COLAK

VOLUME

1

BLOOD OF THE DRAGON

MARIA SANTAOLALLA

SIMON BOWLAND

AFTERSHOCK

BROTHERS

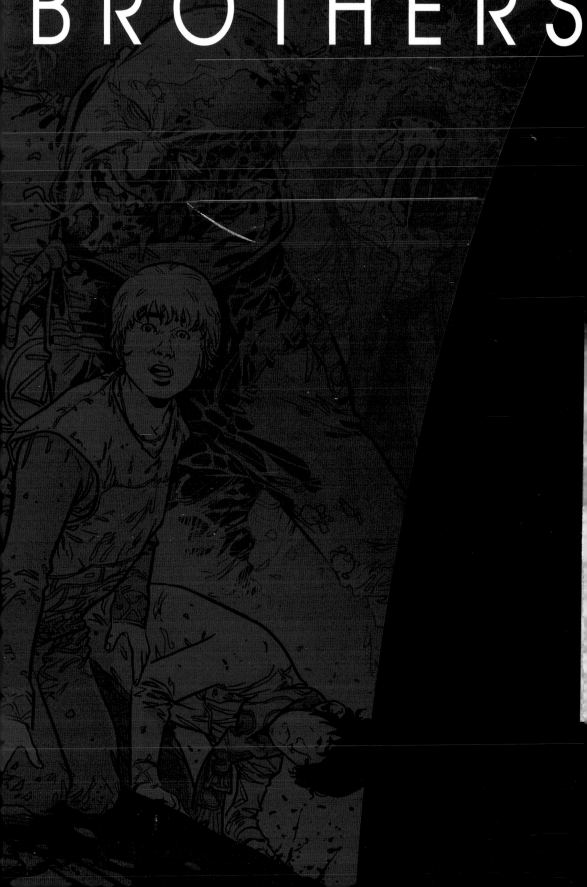

DRACUL™

VOLUME 1

BLOOD OF THE DRAGON

CULLEN BUNN creator & writer

MIRKO COLAK artist

MARIA SANTAOLALLA colorist

SIMON BOWLAND letterer

MIRKO COLAK w/ MARIA SANTAOLALLA front cover & original covers

FRANCESCO FRANCAVILLA, SZYMON KUDRANSKI, MARCO RUDY & DALIBOR TALAJIĆ variant covers

JARED K. FLETCHER logo designer

COREY BREEN book designer

MIKE MARTS editor

AFTERSHOCK™

MIKE MARTS - Editor-in-Chief • JOE PRUETT - Publisher/CCO • LEE KRAMER - President • JON KRAMER - Chief Executive Officer
STEVE ROTTERDAM - SVP, Sales & Marketing • LISA Y. WU - Retailer/Fan Relations Manager
CHRISTINA HARRINGTON - Managing Editor • JAY BEHLING - Chief Financial Officer • JAWAD QURESHI - SVP, Investor Relations
AARON MARION - Publicist • CHRIS LA TORRE - Sales Associate • LISA MOODY - Finance
CHARLES PRITCHETT - Comics Production • COREY BREEN - Collections Production • TEDDY LEO - Editorial Assistant
STEPHANIE CASEBIER & SARAH PRUETT - Publishing Assistants

AfterShock Logo Design by COMICRAFT
Publicity: contact AARON MARION (aaron@publichausagency.com) & RYAN CROY (ryan@publichausagency.com) at PUBLICHAUS
Special thanks to: IRA KURGAN, STEPHAN NILSON & JULIE PIFHER

First Printing: September 2018. 10 9 8 7 6 5 4 3 2 1

AFTERSHOCKCOMICS.COM Follow us on social media

Artist Mirko Colak and I had just wrapped up work on UNHOLY GRAIL, my twisted, horrific version of the King Arthur myth, and we were discussing how we might be able to continue working together. Mirko sent me a quick e-mail that basically said, "Hey...you know what I've always liked? That nasty ol' bloodsucker, Dracula!" (Only this was said in Mirko's own much more eloquent way.) "Maybe we should do a vampire story!"

Now, I'm no stranger to vampire yarns, and I've been fascinated by tales of Vlad Dracul ever since I stumbled onto an ad for "real soil" from Dracula's Castle in the back of a *Famous Monsters* magazine. I thought, though, that it might be a good idea to do something a little different with Vlad.

An idea smacked me upside the head very quickly. Within minutes, I e-mailed Mirko back, saying "Hey...Vlad and his brother Radu were held prisoner by the Ottoman Empire when they were teens. What if they were trained to be vampire killers during that time?" (Only I was far less eloquent, as is my way.)

Okay, okay. My inspiration might have been the Frog Brothers from *Lost Boys*. Or maybe I drew my ideas from the rich (although somewhat sketchy) historical notes about Vlad and Radu. Or I might have been inspired by my relationship with my own brother. If so, this is an idealized version of that brotherhood, because if ever a vampir stalked the two of us, I would have tripped my brother, essentially handing him over to the undead fiend so I could make my escape.

I kid, of course. I love my brother dearly. I regret that he was taken by the vampir.

So, this story started from humble beginnings, but I hope you enjoy where we've taken it. Is there more story to be told? Of course there is! But from humble beginnings, great and terrible things are born.

Thanks for reading!

Writing from somewhere under a pile of *Famous Monsters* magazines,

CULLEN BUNN
August 2018

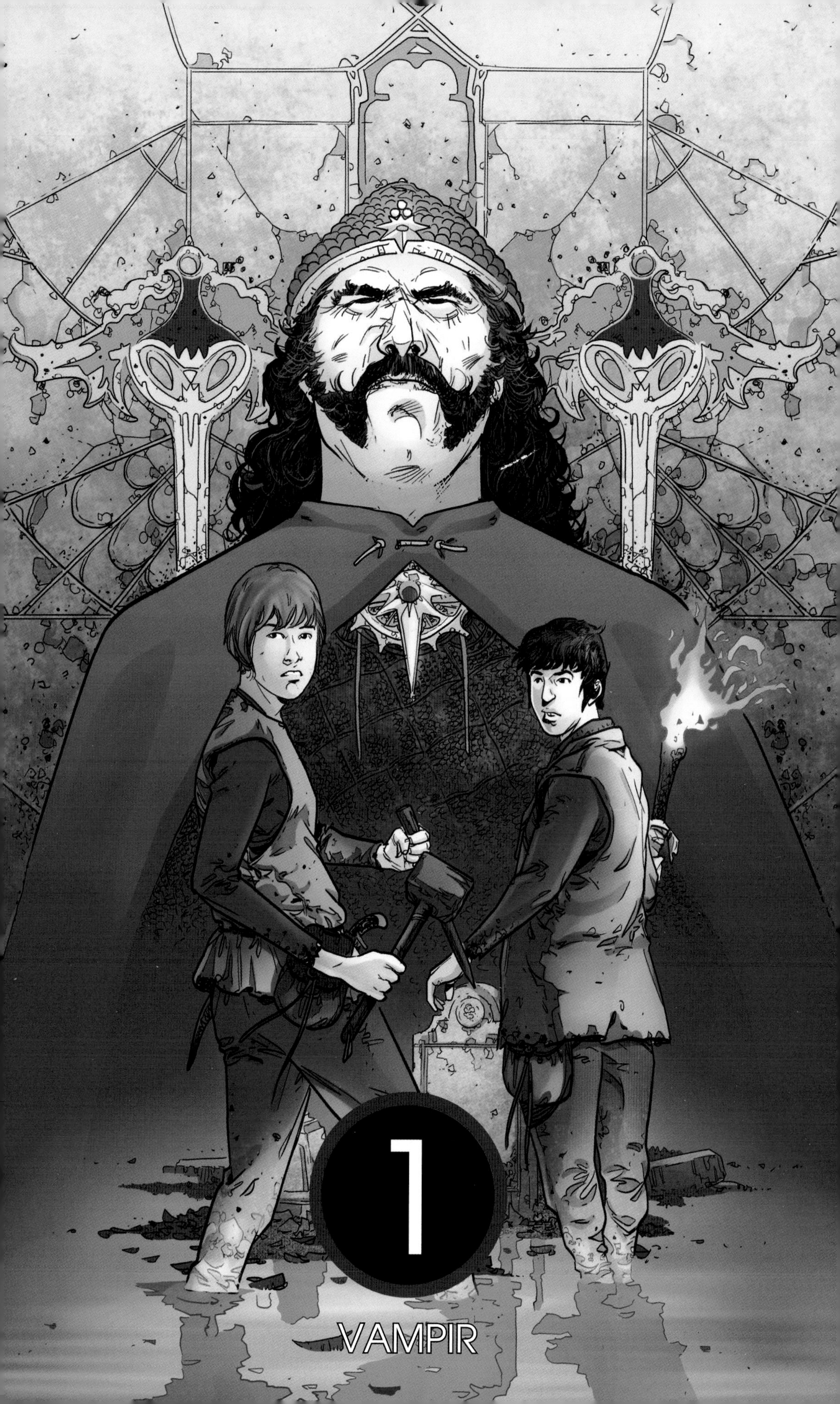
1
VAMPIR

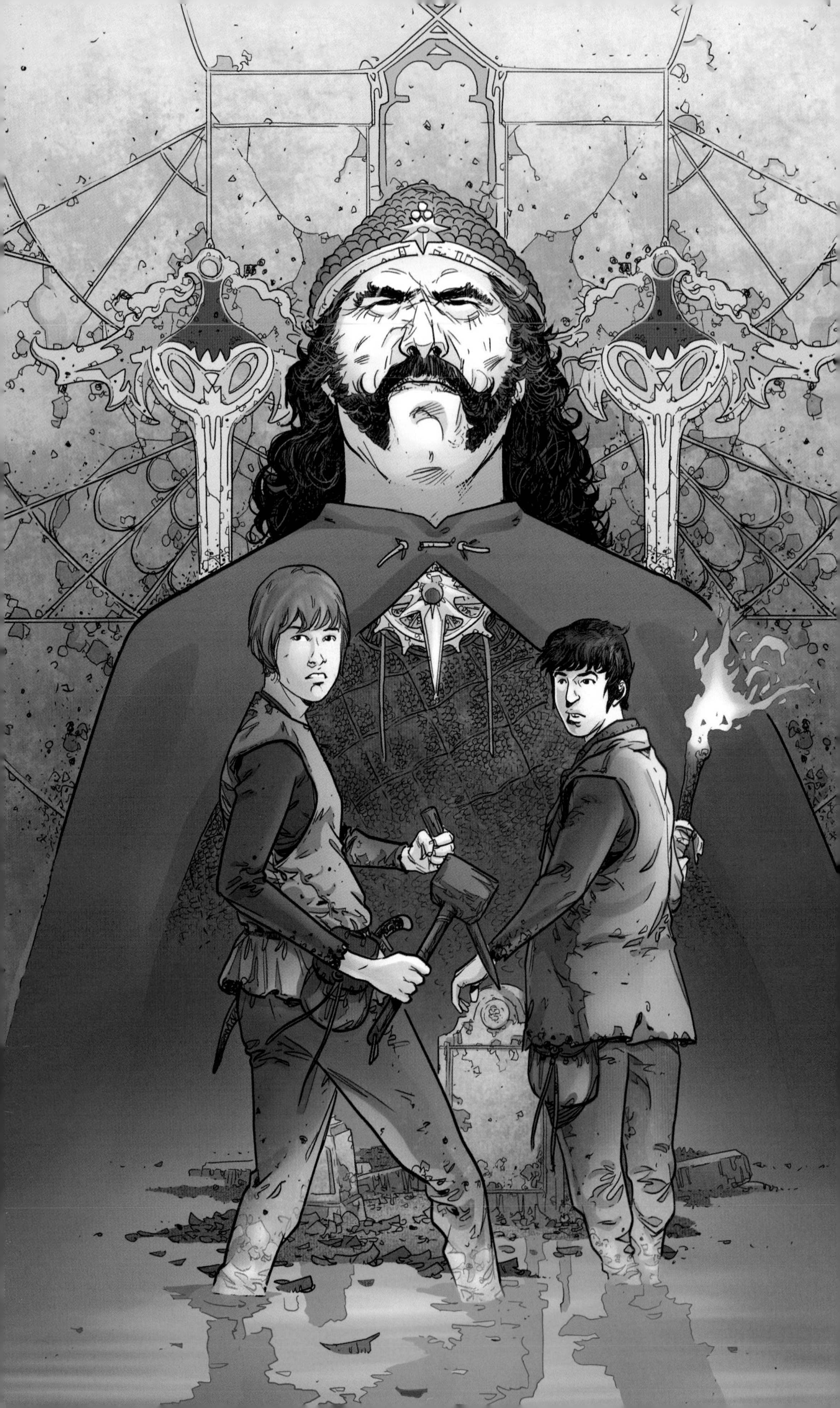

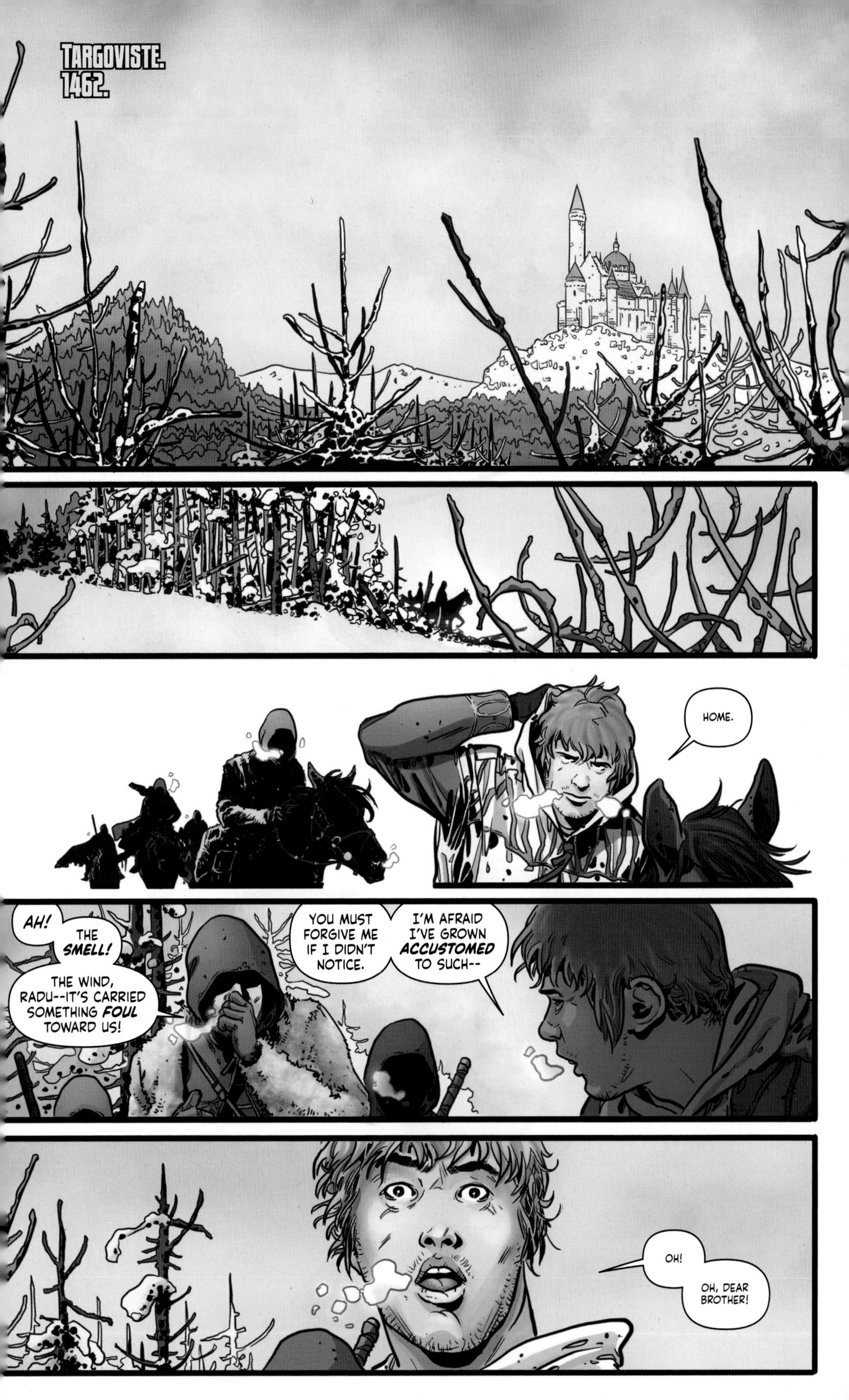
TARGOVISTE.
1462.
HOME.
AH!
THE SMELL!
THE WIND, RADU--IT'S CARRIED SOMETHING FOUL TOWARD US!
YOU MUST FORGIVE ME IF I DIDN'T NOTICE.
I'M AFRAID I'VE GROWN ACCUSTOMED TO SUCH--
OH!
OH, DEAR BROTHER!

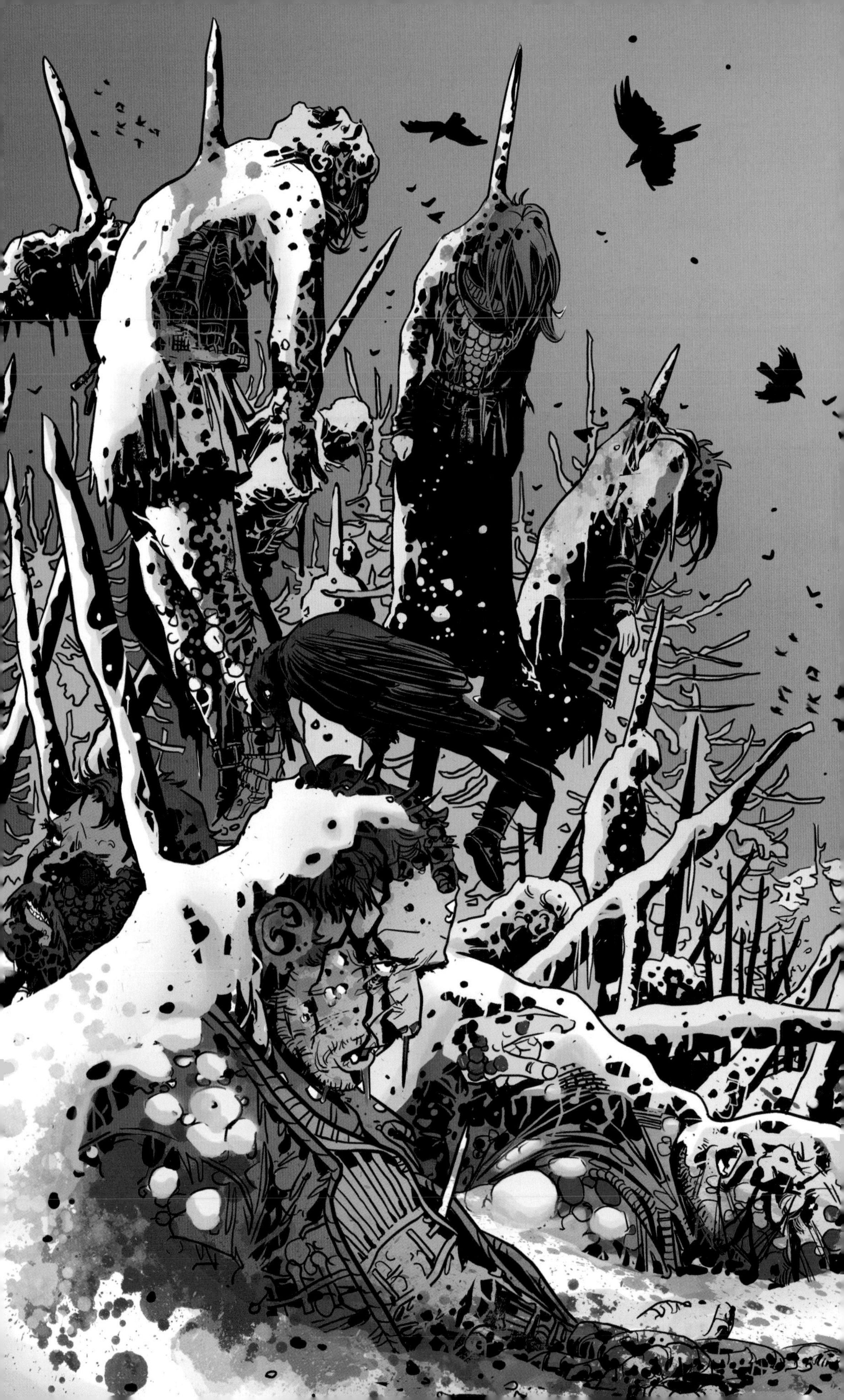

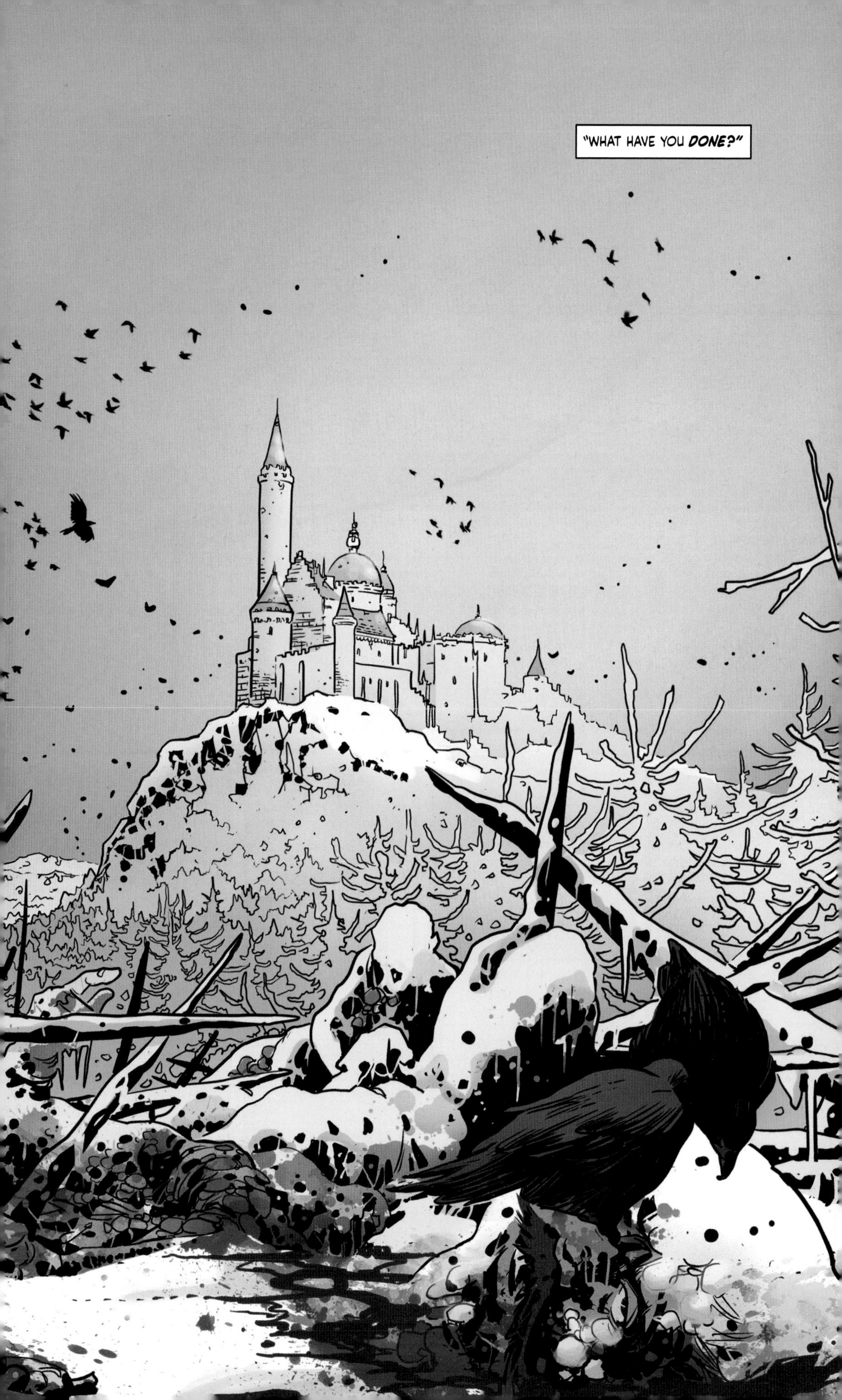
"WHAT HAVE YOU DONE?"

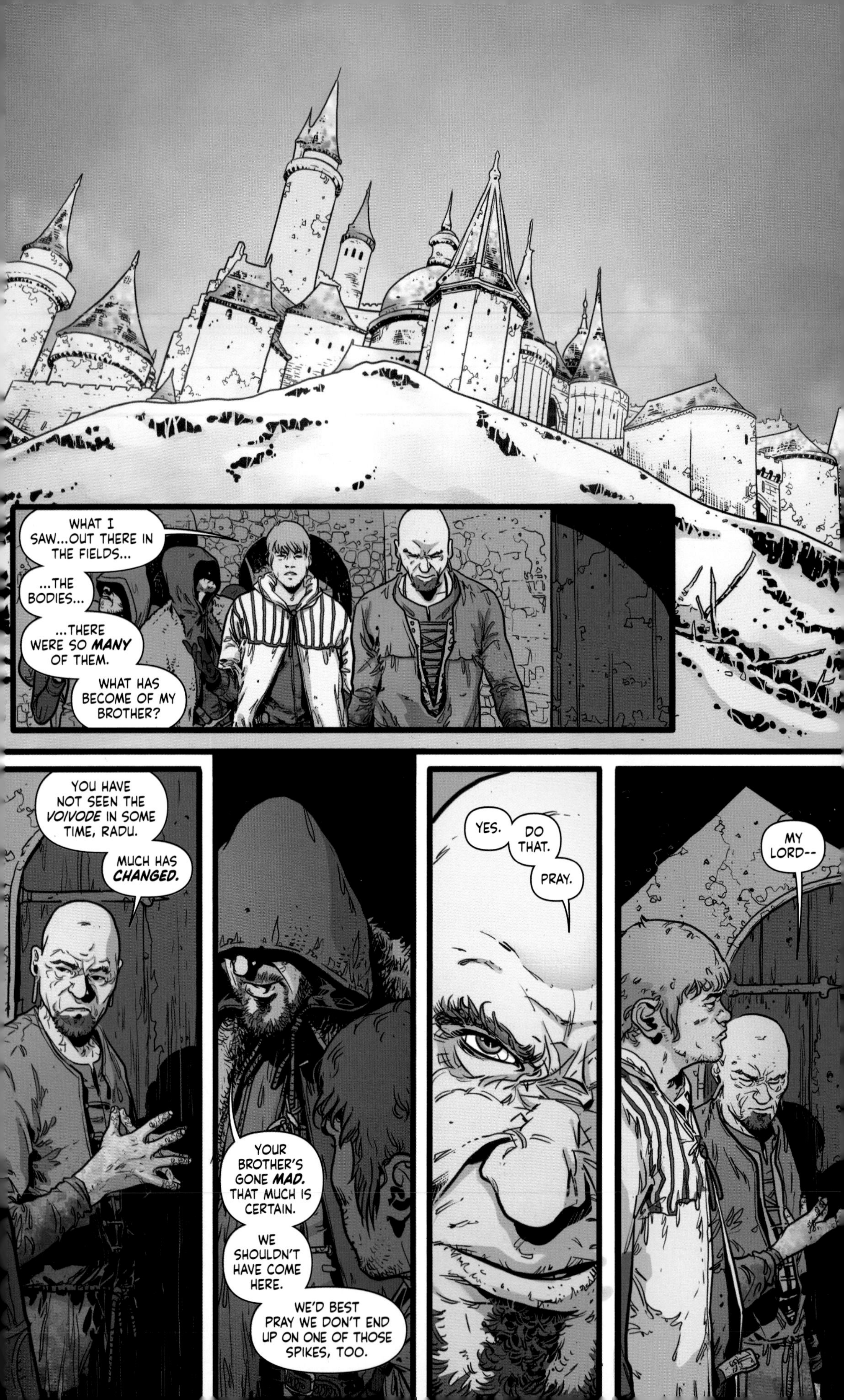

WHAT I SAW...OUT THERE IN THE FIELDS...
...THE BODIES...
...THERE WERE SO MANY OF THEM.
WHAT HAS BECOME OF MY BROTHER?
YOU HAVE NOT SEEN THE VOIVODE IN SOME TIME, RADU.
MUCH HAS CHANGED.
YOUR BROTHER'S GONE MAD. THAT MUCH IS CERTAIN.
WE SHOULDN'T HAVE COME HERE.
WE'D BEST PRAY WE DON'T END UP ON ONE OF THOSE SPIKES, TOO.
YES.
DO THAT.
PRAY.
MY LORD--

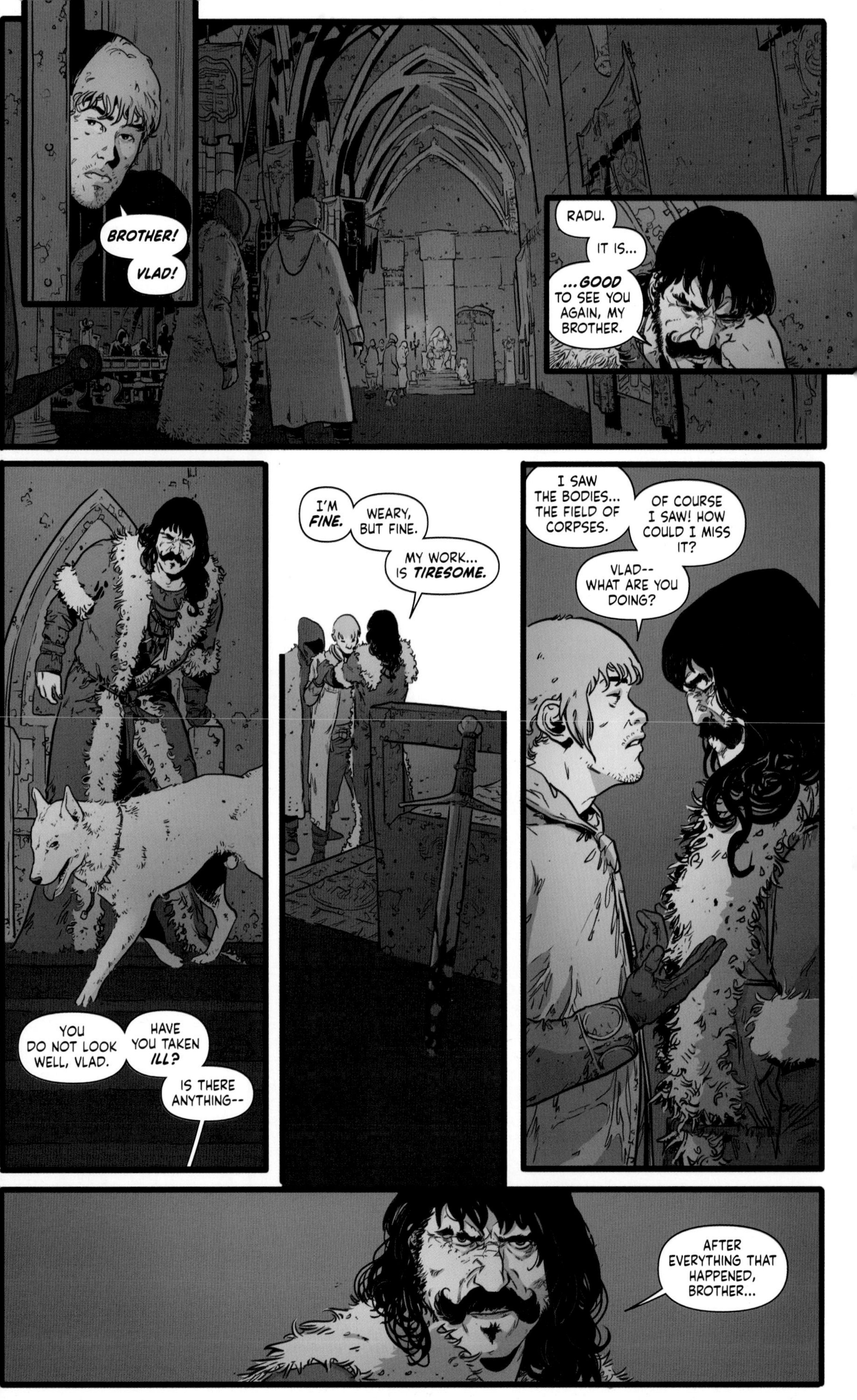
BROTHER!
VLAD!
RADU.
IT IS...
...GOOD TO SEE YOU AGAIN, MY BROTHER.
YOU DO NOT LOOK WELL, VLAD.
HAVE YOU TAKEN ILL?
IS THERE ANYTHING--
I'M FINE.
WEARY, BUT FINE.
MY WORK... IS TIRESOME.
I SAW THE BODIES... THE FIELD OF CORPSES.
OF COURSE I SAW! HOW COULD I MISS IT?
VLAD-- WHAT ARE YOU DOING?
AFTER EVERYTHING THAT HAPPENED, BROTHER...

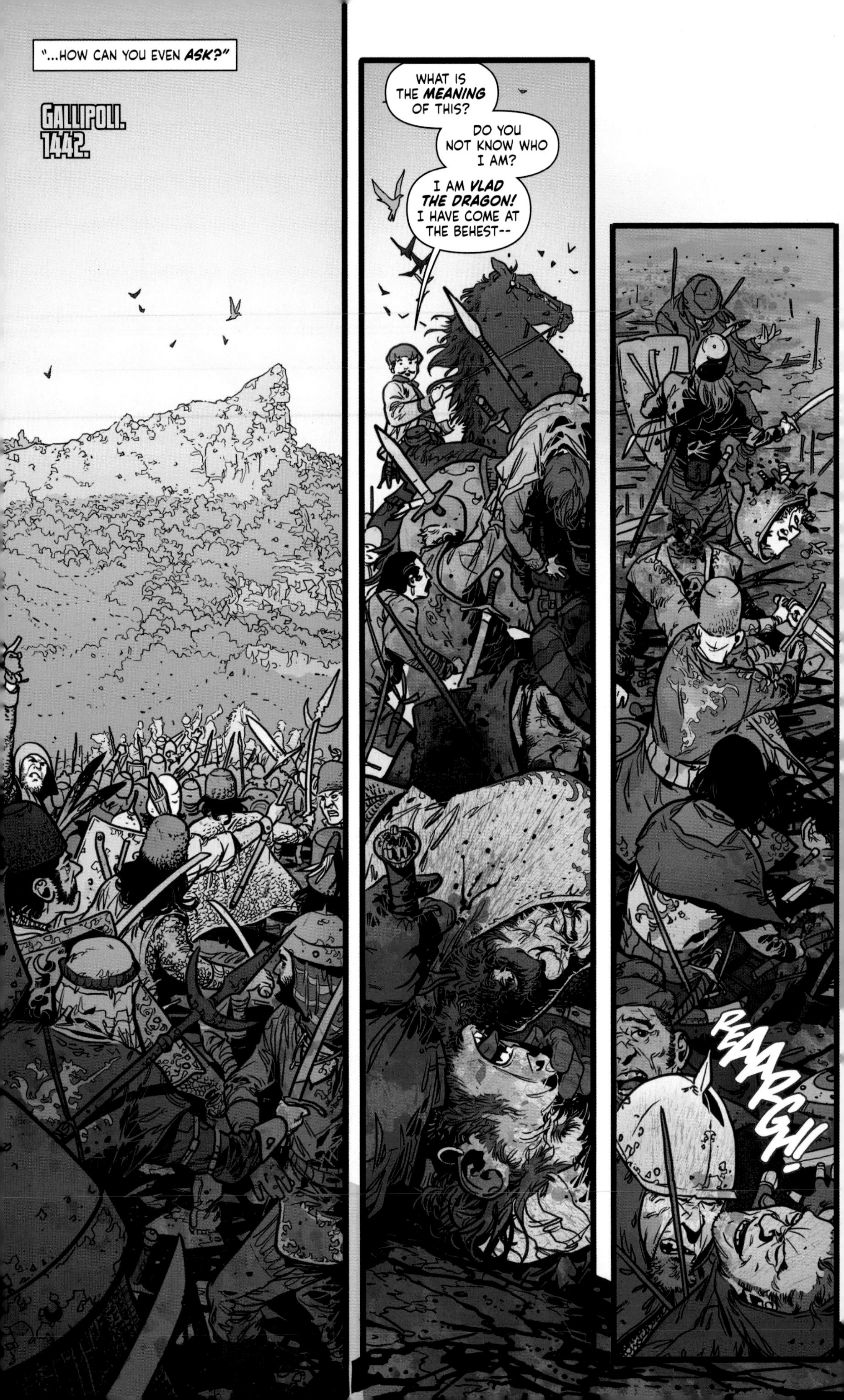

"...HOW CAN YOU EVEN ***ASK?***"
GALLIPOLI. 1442.
WHAT IS THE ***MEANING*** OF THIS?
DO YOU NOT KNOW WHO I AM?
I AM ***VLAD THE DRAGON!*** I HAVE COME AT THE BEHEST--
REAAARGH!!

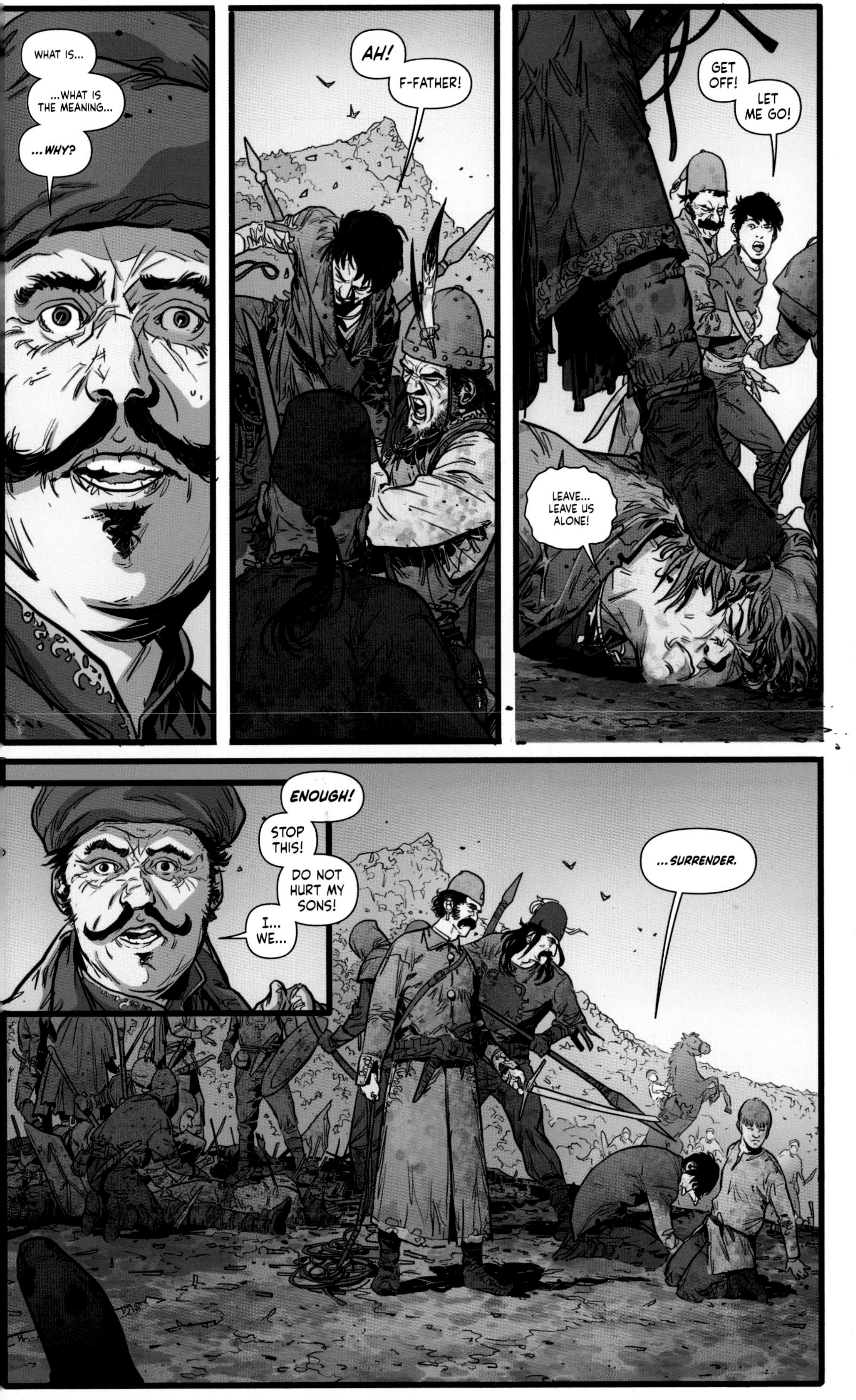
WHAT IS...
...WHAT IS THE MEANING...
...WHY?
AH!
F-FATHER!
GET OFF!
LET ME GO!
LEAVE... LEAVE US ALONE!
ENOUGH!
STOP THIS!
DO NOT HURT MY SONS!
I... WE...
...SURRENDER.

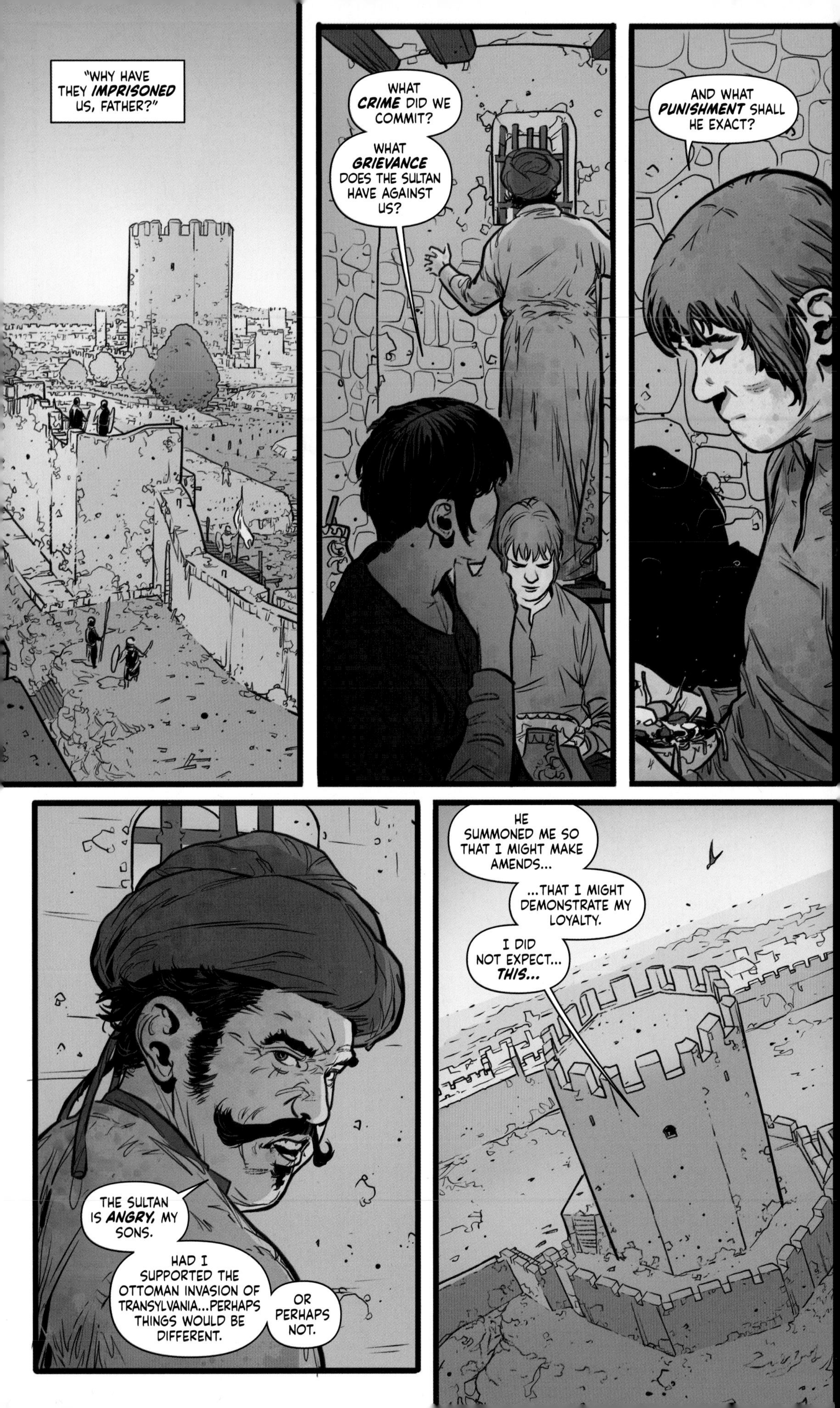
"WHY HAVE THEY *IMPRISONED* US, FATHER?"
WHAT *CRIME* DID WE COMMIT?
WHAT *GRIEVANCE* DOES THE SULTAN HAVE AGAINST US?
AND WHAT *PUNISHMENT* SHALL HE EXACT?
THE SULTAN IS *ANGRY,* MY SONS.
HAD I SUPPORTED THE OTTOMAN INVASION OF TRANSYLVANIA...PERHAPS THINGS WOULD BE DIFFERENT.
OR PERHAPS NOT.
HE SUMMONED ME SO THAT I MIGHT MAKE AMENDS...
...THAT I MIGHT DEMONSTRATE MY LOYALTY.
I DID NOT EXPECT... *THIS...*

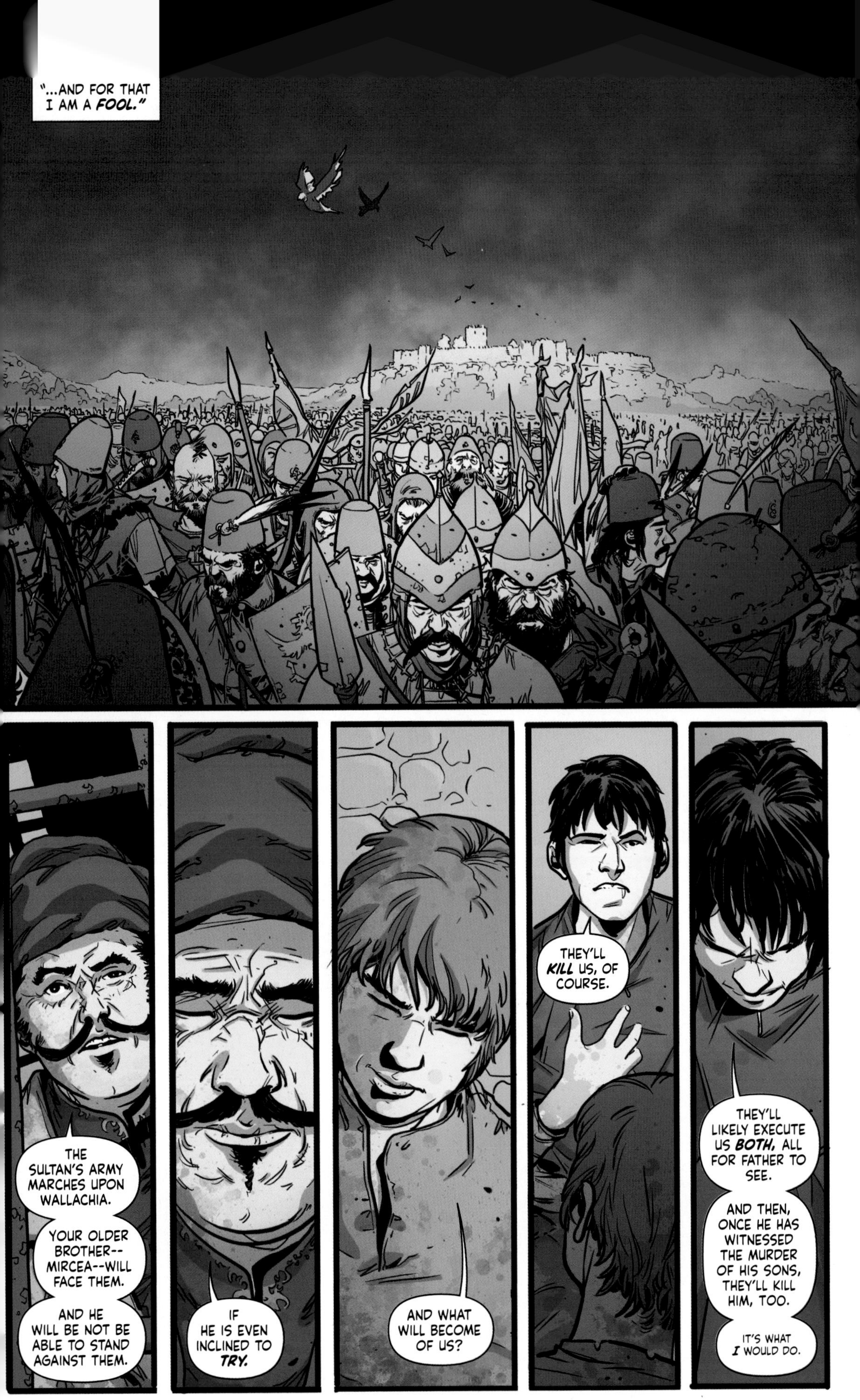
"...AND FOR THAT I AM A FOOL."
THE SULTAN'S ARMY MARCHES UPON WALLACHIA.
YOUR OLDER BROTHER--MIRCEA--WILL FACE THEM.
AND HE WILL BE NOT BE ABLE TO STAND AGAINST THEM.
IF HE IS EVEN INCLINED TO TRY.
AND WHAT WILL BECOME OF US?
THEY'LL KILL US, OF COURSE.
THEY'LL LIKELY EXECUTE US BOTH, ALL FOR FATHER TO SEE.
AND THEN, ONCE HE HAS WITNESSED THE MURDER OF HIS SONS, THEY'LL KILL HIM, TOO.
IT'S WHAT I WOULD DO.

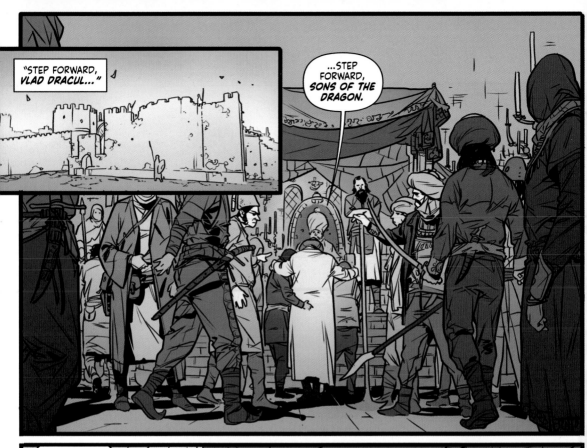

"STEP FORWARD, *VLAD DRACUL...*"

...STEP FORWARD, *SONS OF THE DRAGON.*

STAND BEFORE ME AND LET'S HAVE A LOOK AT YOU.

LET'S SEE IF YOUR TIME AS MY PRISONERS HAS TAUGHT YOU SOME *HUMILITY.*

HUMILITY, MY SULTAN, YES.

I WAS... *WRONG.*

AND I THANK YOU FOR YOUR MERCY... FOR THE GENEROSITY OF YOUR LESSONS...FOR SHOWING MY SONS AND I THE *ERROR* OF OUR WAYS.

INDEED?

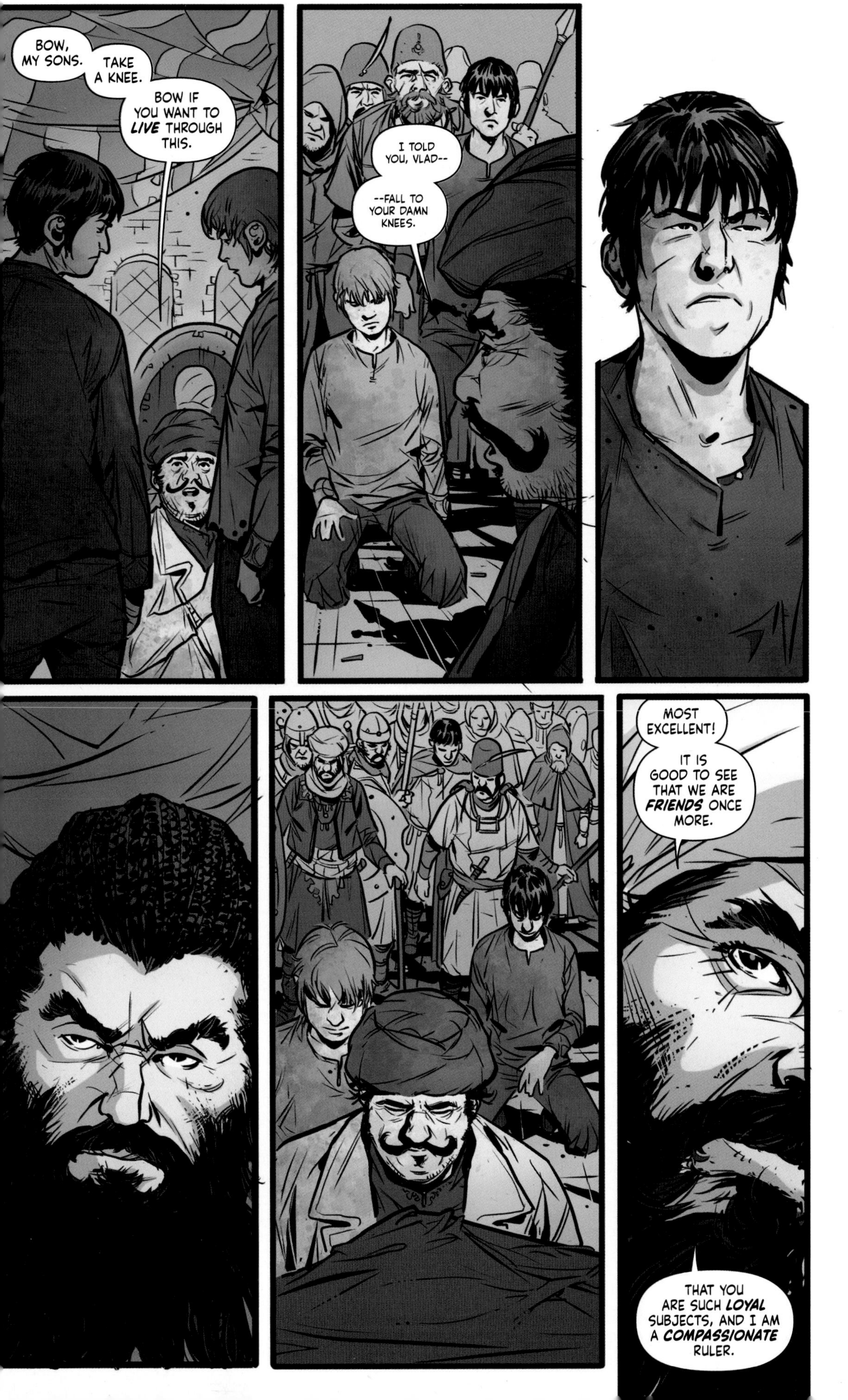
BOW, MY SONS.
TAKE A KNEE.
BOW IF YOU WANT TO LIVE THROUGH THIS.
I TOLD YOU, VLAD--
--FALL TO YOUR DAMN KNEES.
MOST EXCELLENT!
IT IS GOOD TO SEE THAT WE ARE FRIENDS ONCE MORE.
THAT YOU ARE SUCH LOYAL SUBJECTS, AND I AM A COMPASSIONATE RULER.

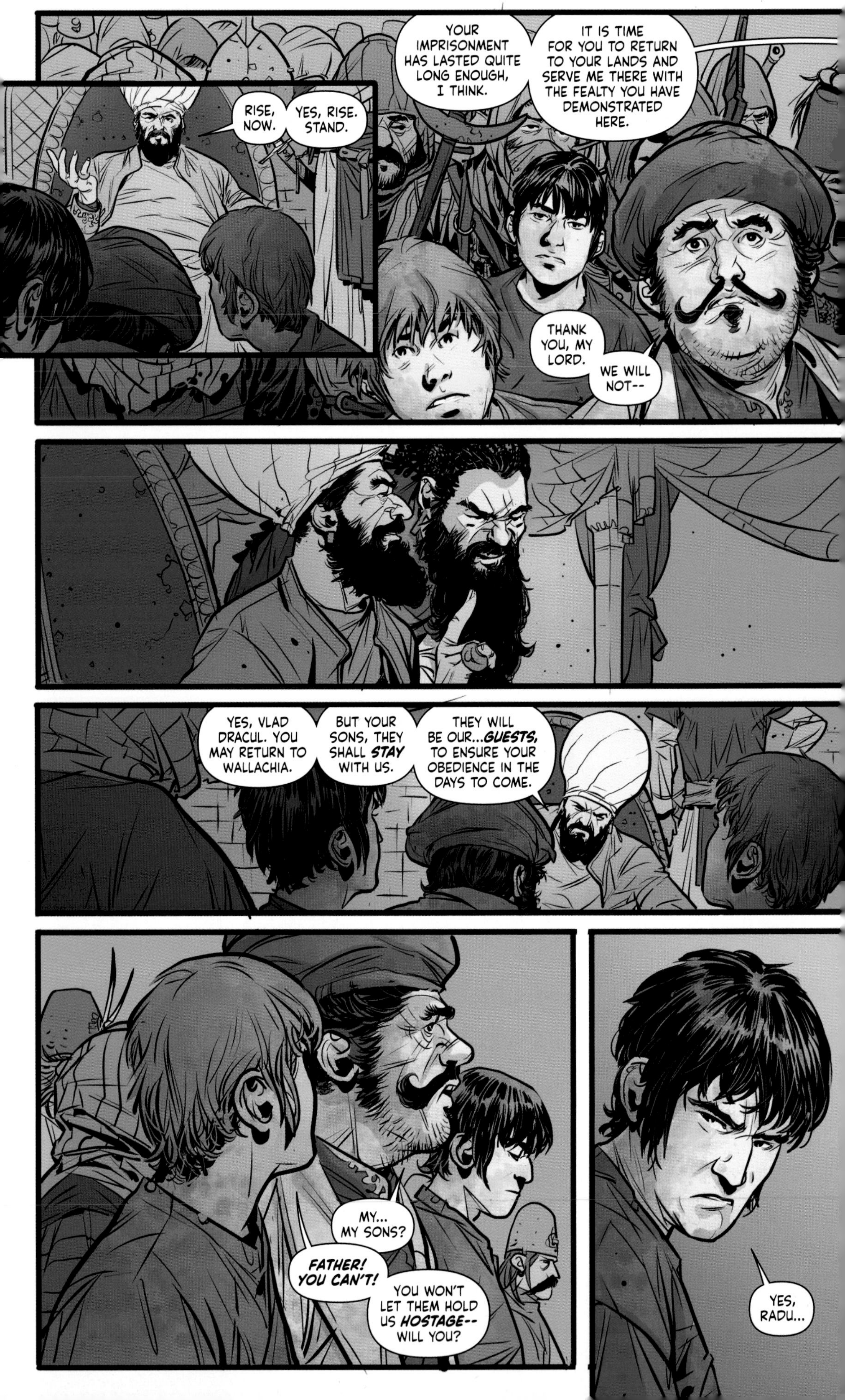
RISE, NOW.
YES, RISE. STAND.
YOUR IMPRISONMENT HAS LASTED QUITE LONG ENOUGH, I THINK.
IT IS TIME FOR YOU TO RETURN TO YOUR LANDS AND SERVE ME THERE WITH THE FEALTY YOU HAVE DEMONSTRATED HERE.
THANK YOU, MY LORD.
WE WILL NOT--
YES, VLAD DRACUL. YOU MAY RETURN TO WALLACHIA.
BUT YOUR SONS, THEY SHALL *STAY* WITH US.
THEY WILL BE OUR...*GUESTS,* TO ENSURE YOUR OBEDIENCE IN THE DAYS TO COME.
MY... MY SONS?
FATHER! YOU CAN'T!
YOU WON'T LET THEM HOLD US *HOSTAGE--* WILL YOU?
YES, RADU...

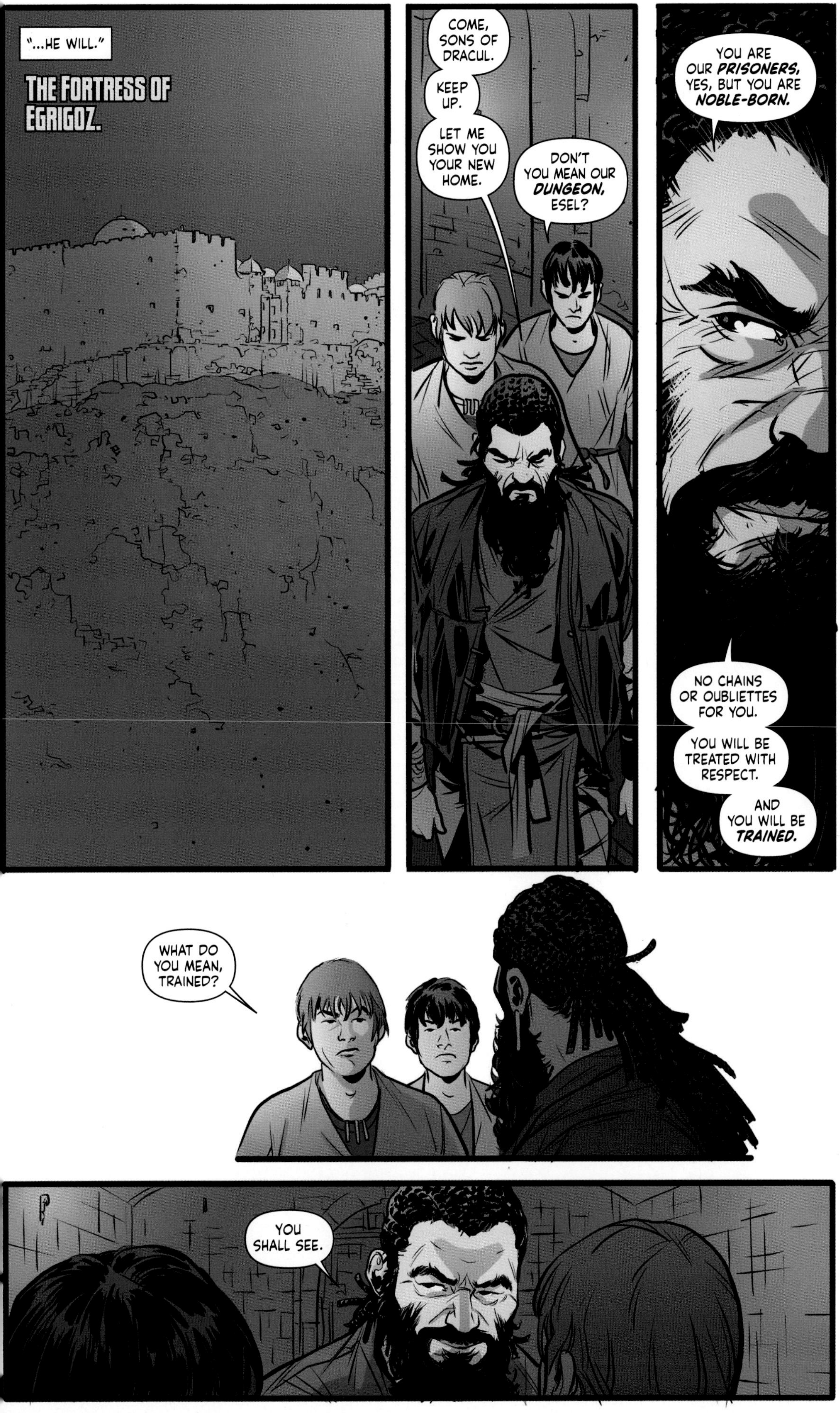
"...HE WILL."
THE FORTRESS OF EGRIGOZ.
COME, SONS OF DRACUL.
KEEP UP.
LET ME SHOW YOU YOUR NEW HOME.
DON'T YOU MEAN OUR DUNGEON, ESEL?
YOU ARE OUR PRISONERS, YES, BUT YOU ARE NOBLE-BORN.
NO CHAINS OR OUBLIETTES FOR YOU.
YOU WILL BE TREATED WITH RESPECT.
AND YOU WILL BE TRAINED.
WHAT DO YOU MEAN, TRAINED?
YOU SHALL SEE.

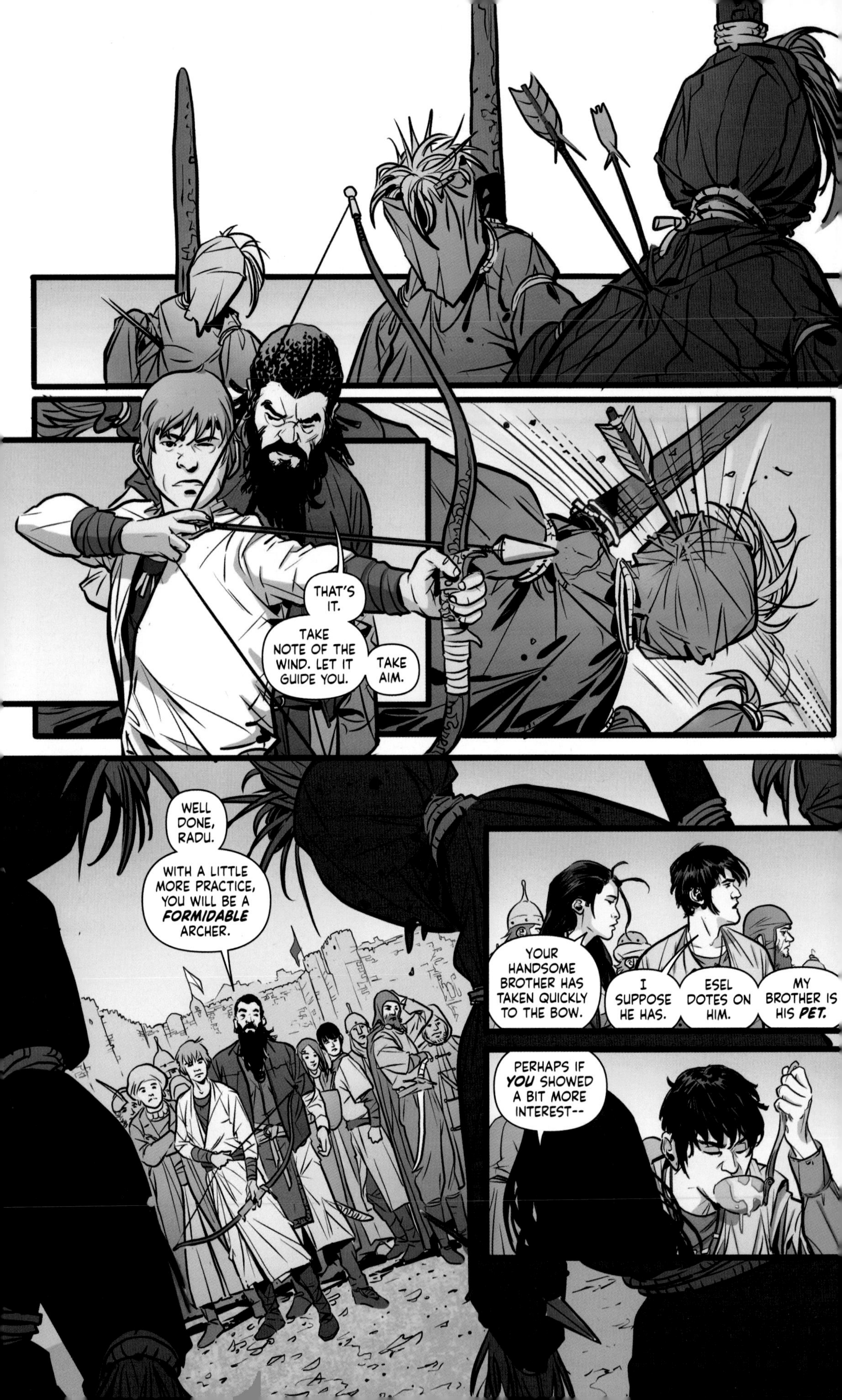
THAT'S IT.
TAKE NOTE OF THE WIND. LET IT GUIDE YOU.
TAKE AIM.
WELL DONE, RADU.
WITH A LITTLE MORE PRACTICE, YOU WILL BE A ***FORMIDABLE*** ARCHER.
YOUR HANDSOME BROTHER HAS TAKEN QUICKLY TO THE BOW.
I SUPPOSE HE HAS.
ESEL DOTES ON HIM.
MY BROTHER IS HIS ***PET.***
PERHAPS IF ***YOU*** SHOWED A BIT MORE INTEREST--

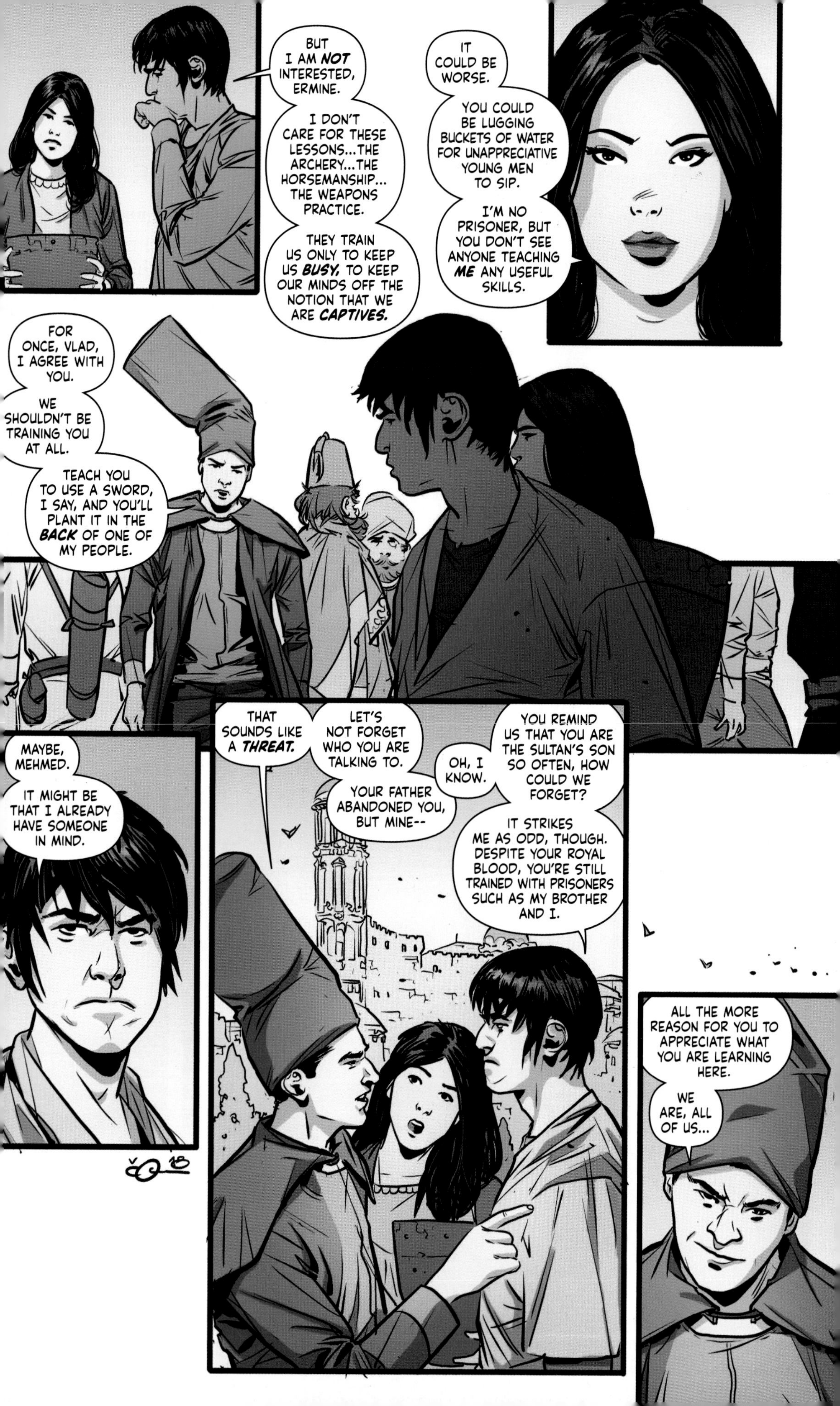

BUT I AM NOT INTERESTED, ERMINE.
I DON'T CARE FOR THESE LESSONS...THE ARCHERY...THE HORSEMANSHIP... THE WEAPONS PRACTICE.
THEY TRAIN US ONLY TO KEEP US BUSY, TO KEEP OUR MINDS OFF THE NOTION THAT WE ARE CAPTIVES.
IT COULD BE WORSE.
YOU COULD BE LUGGING BUCKETS OF WATER FOR UNAPPRECIATIVE YOUNG MEN TO SIP.
I'M NO PRISONER, BUT YOU DON'T SEE ANYONE TEACHING ME ANY USEFUL SKILLS.
FOR ONCE, VLAD, I AGREE WITH YOU.
WE SHOULDN'T BE TRAINING YOU AT ALL.
TEACH YOU TO USE A SWORD, I SAY, AND YOU'LL PLANT IT IN THE BACK OF ONE OF MY PEOPLE.
MAYBE, MEHMED.
IT MIGHT BE THAT I ALREADY HAVE SOMEONE IN MIND.
THAT SOUNDS LIKE A THREAT.
LET'S NOT FORGET WHO YOU ARE TALKING TO.
YOUR FATHER ABANDONED YOU, BUT MINE--
OH, I KNOW.
YOU REMIND US THAT YOU ARE THE SULTAN'S SON SO OFTEN, HOW COULD WE FORGET?
IT STRIKES ME AS ODD, THOUGH. DESPITE YOUR ROYAL BLOOD, YOU'RE STILL TRAINED WITH PRISONERS SUCH AS MY BROTHER AND I.
ALL THE MORE REASON FOR YOU TO APPRECIATE WHAT YOU ARE LEARNING HERE.
WE ARE, ALL OF US...

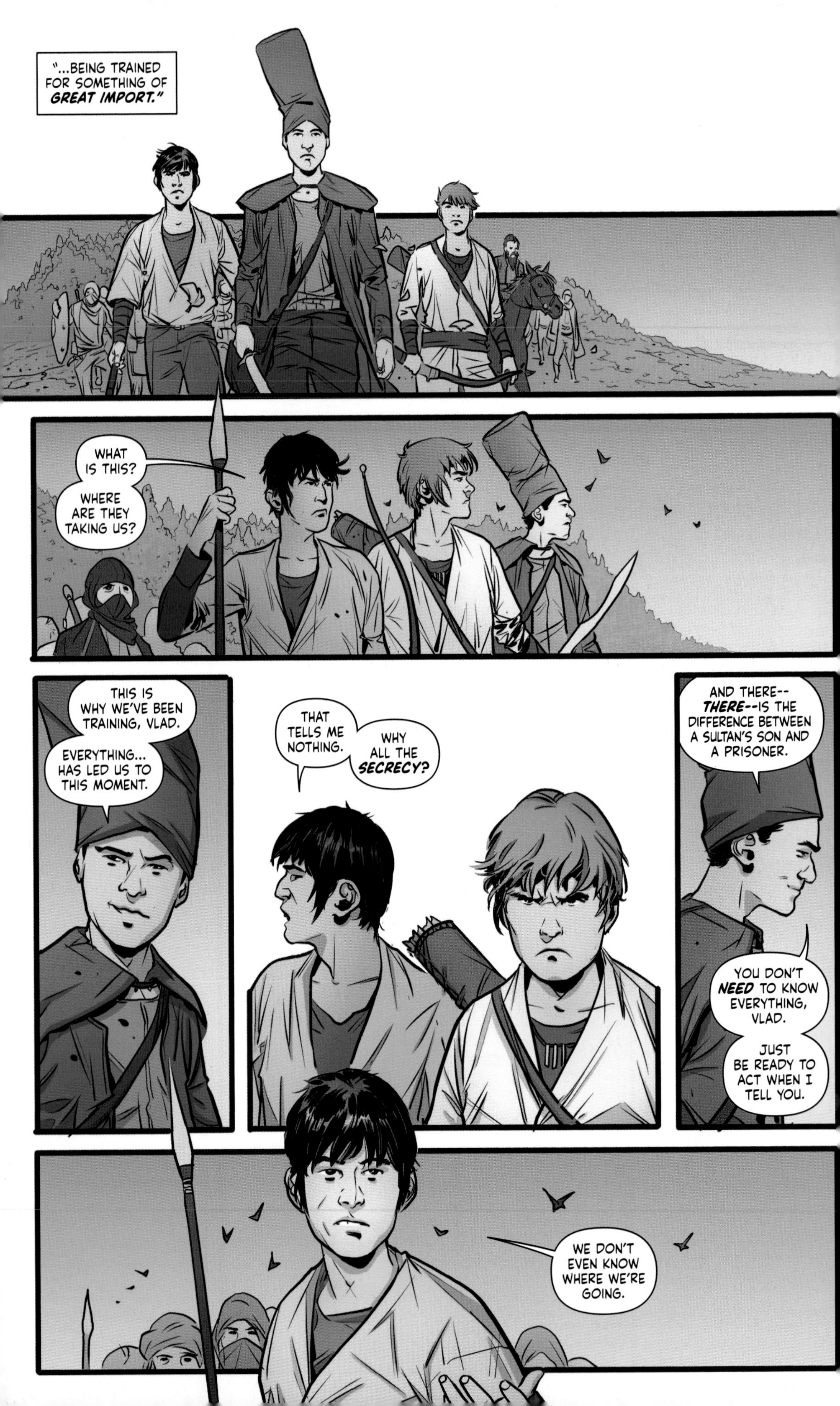
"...BEING TRAINED FOR SOMETHING OF GREAT IMPORT."
WHAT IS THIS?
WHERE ARE THEY TAKING US?
THIS IS WHY WE'VE BEEN TRAINING, VLAD.
EVERYTHING... HAS LED US TO THIS MOMENT.
THAT TELLS ME NOTHING.
WHY ALL THE SECRECY?
AND THERE-- THERE--IS THE DIFFERENCE BETWEEN A SULTAN'S SON AND A PRISONER.
YOU DON'T NEED TO KNOW EVERYTHING, VLAD.
JUST BE READY TO ACT WHEN I TELL YOU.
WE DON'T EVEN KNOW WHERE WE'RE GOING.

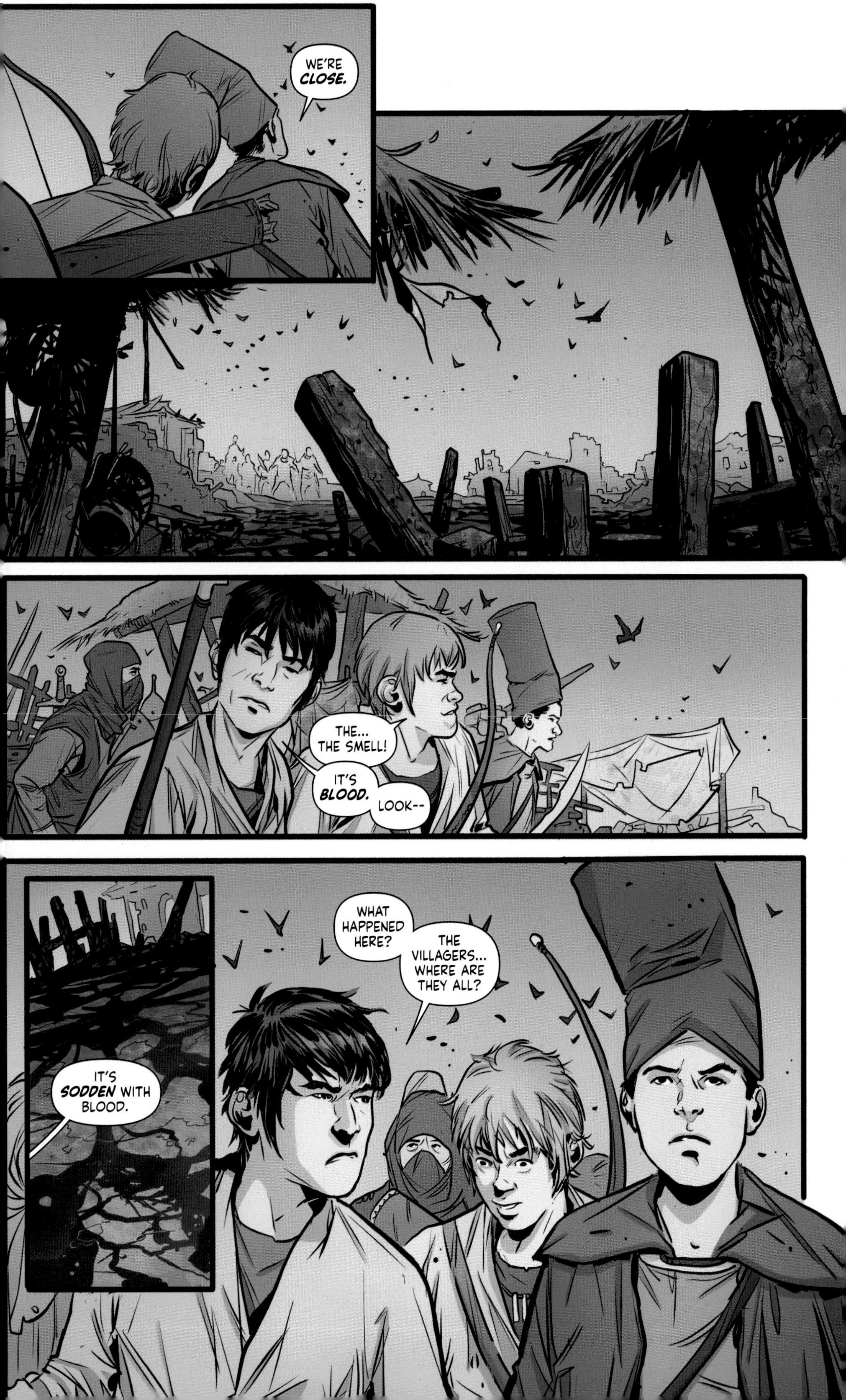
WE'RE CLOSE.
THE... THE SMELL!
IT'S BLOOD.
LOOK--
WHAT HAPPENED HERE?
THE VILLAGERS... WHERE ARE THEY ALL?
IT'S SODDEN WITH BLOOD.

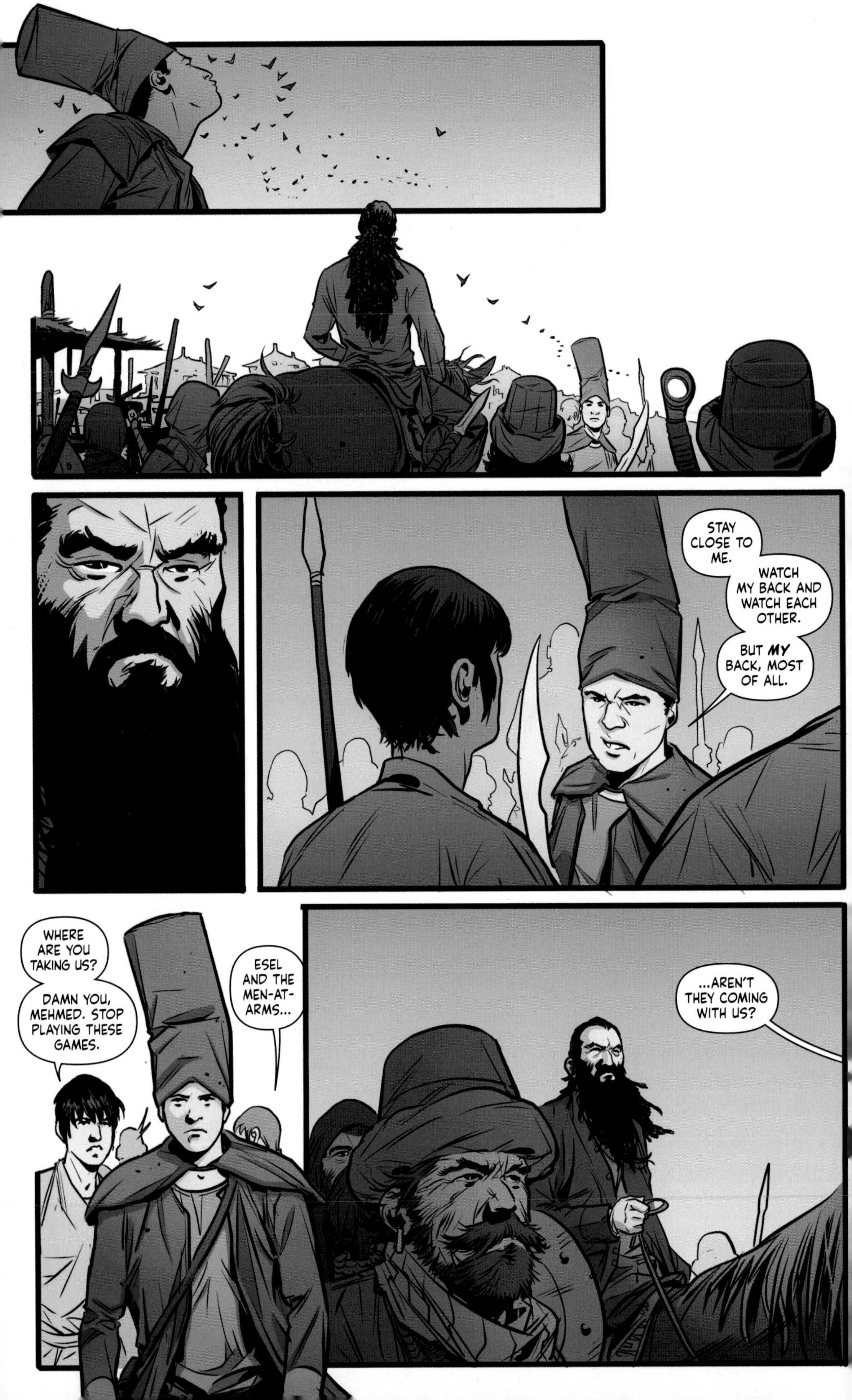
STAY CLOSE TO ME.
WATCH MY BACK AND WATCH EACH OTHER.
BUT MY BACK, MOST OF ALL.
WHERE ARE YOU TAKING US?
DAMN YOU, MEHMED. STOP PLAYING THESE GAMES.
ESEL AND THE MEN-AT-ARMS...
...AREN'T THEY COMING WITH US?

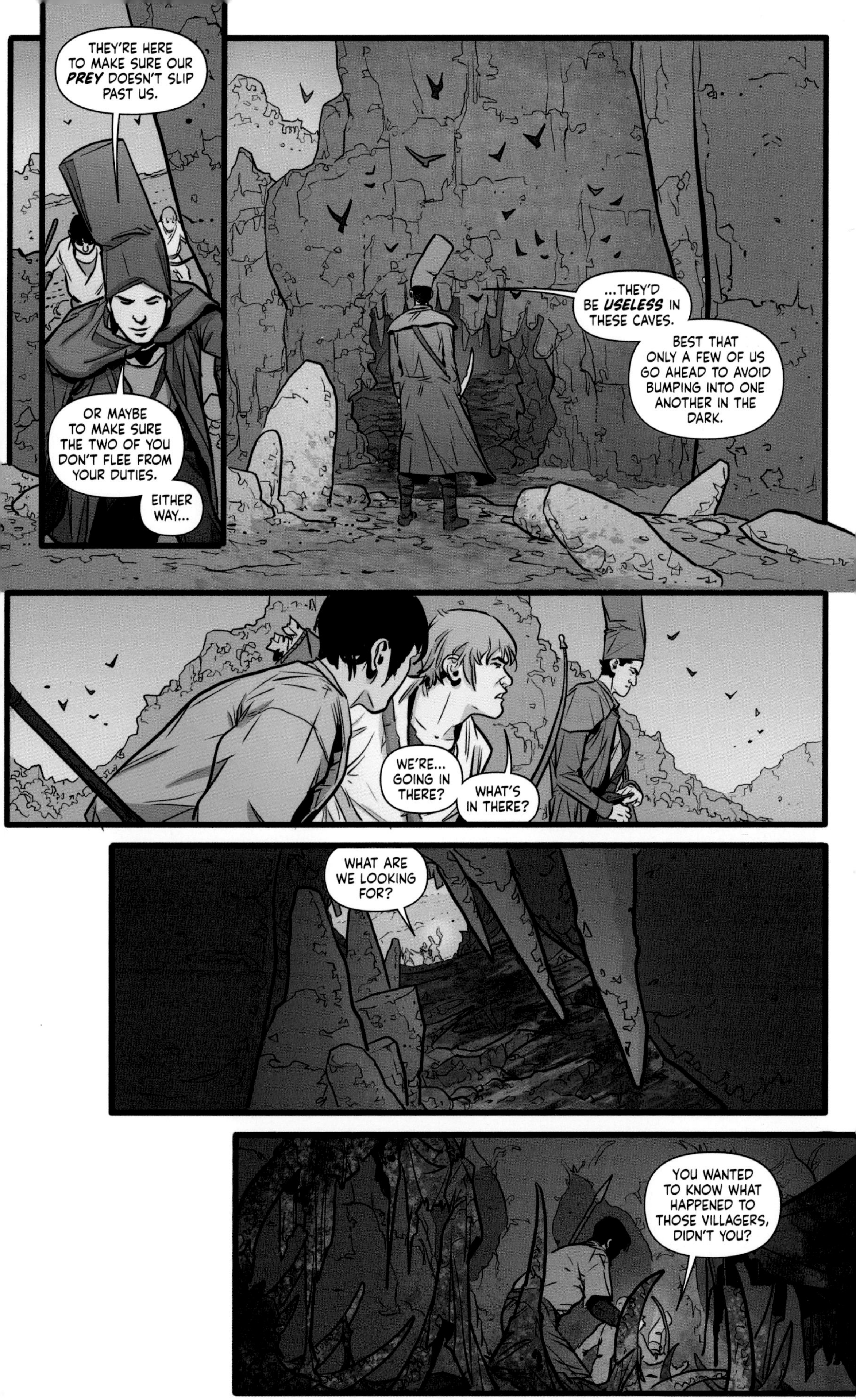
THEY'RE HERE TO MAKE SURE OUR PREY DOESN'T SLIP PAST US.
OR MAYBE TO MAKE SURE THE TWO OF YOU DON'T FLEE FROM YOUR DUTIES.
EITHER WAY...
...THEY'D BE USELESS IN THESE CAVES.
BEST THAT ONLY A FEW OF US GO AHEAD TO AVOID BUMPING INTO ONE ANOTHER IN THE DARK.
WE'RE... GOING IN THERE?
WHAT'S IN THERE?
WHAT ARE WE LOOKING FOR?
YOU WANTED TO KNOW WHAT HAPPENED TO THOSE VILLAGERS, DIDN'T YOU?

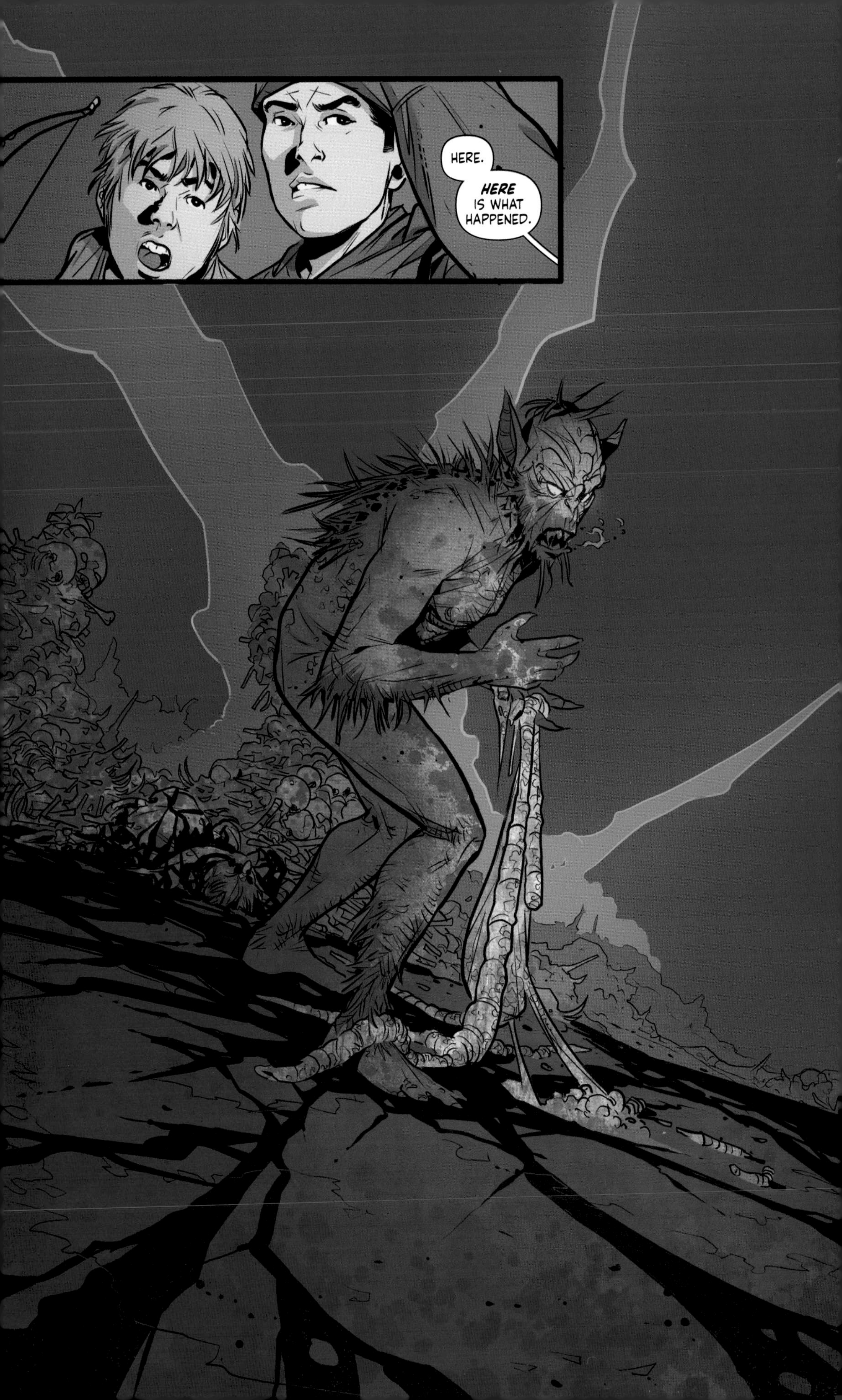
HERE.
HERE IS WHAT HAPPENED.

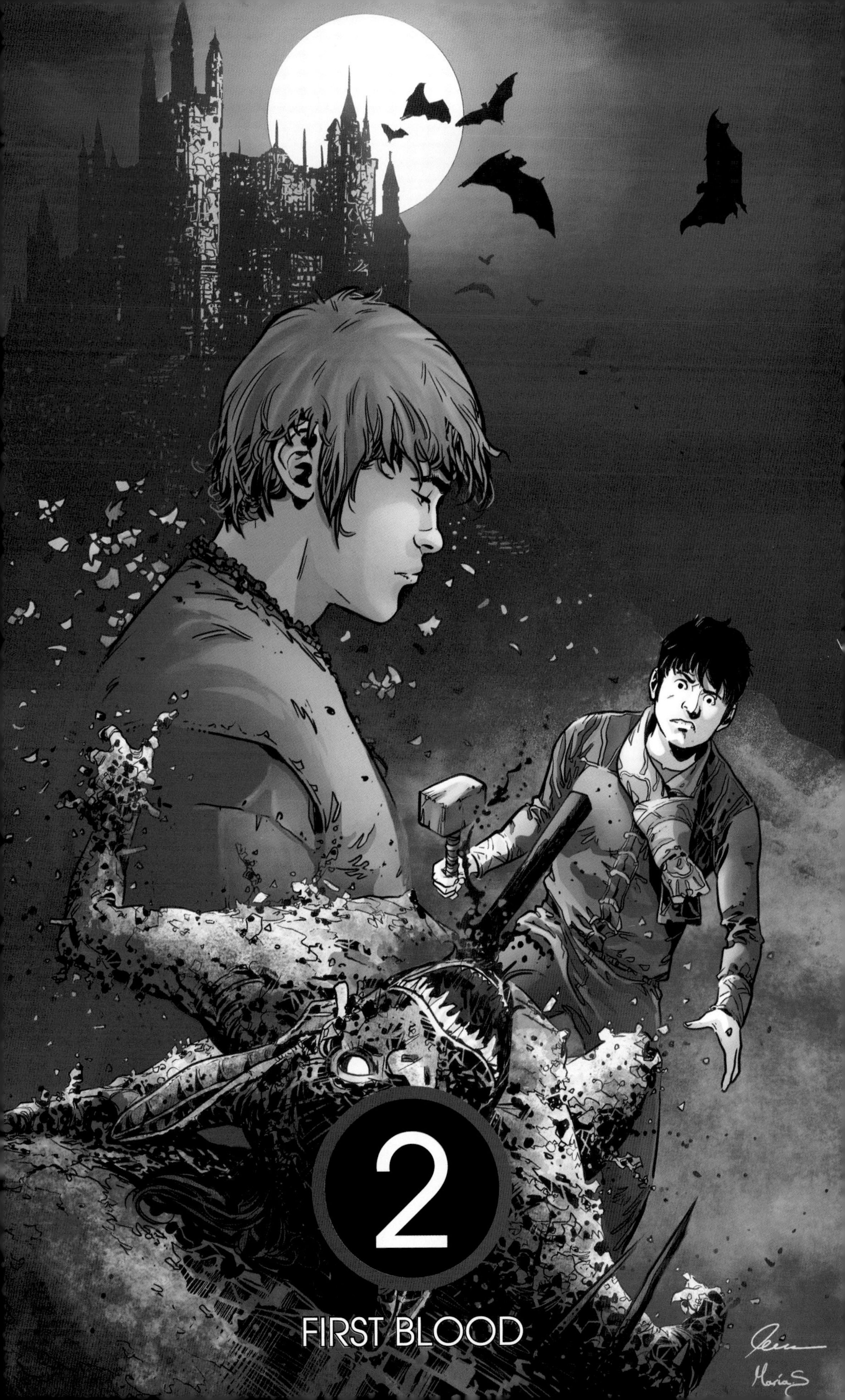
2
FIRST BLOOD

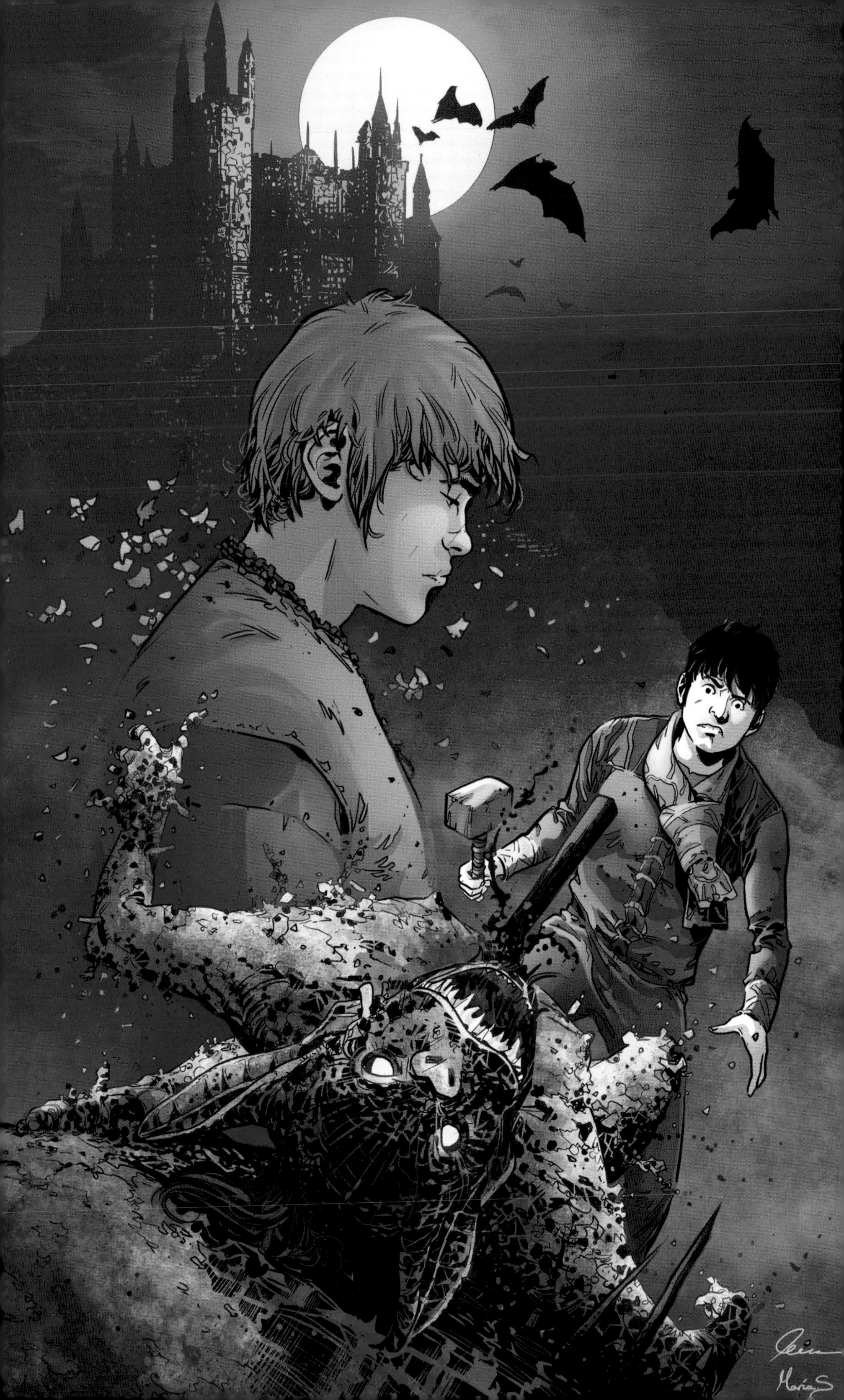

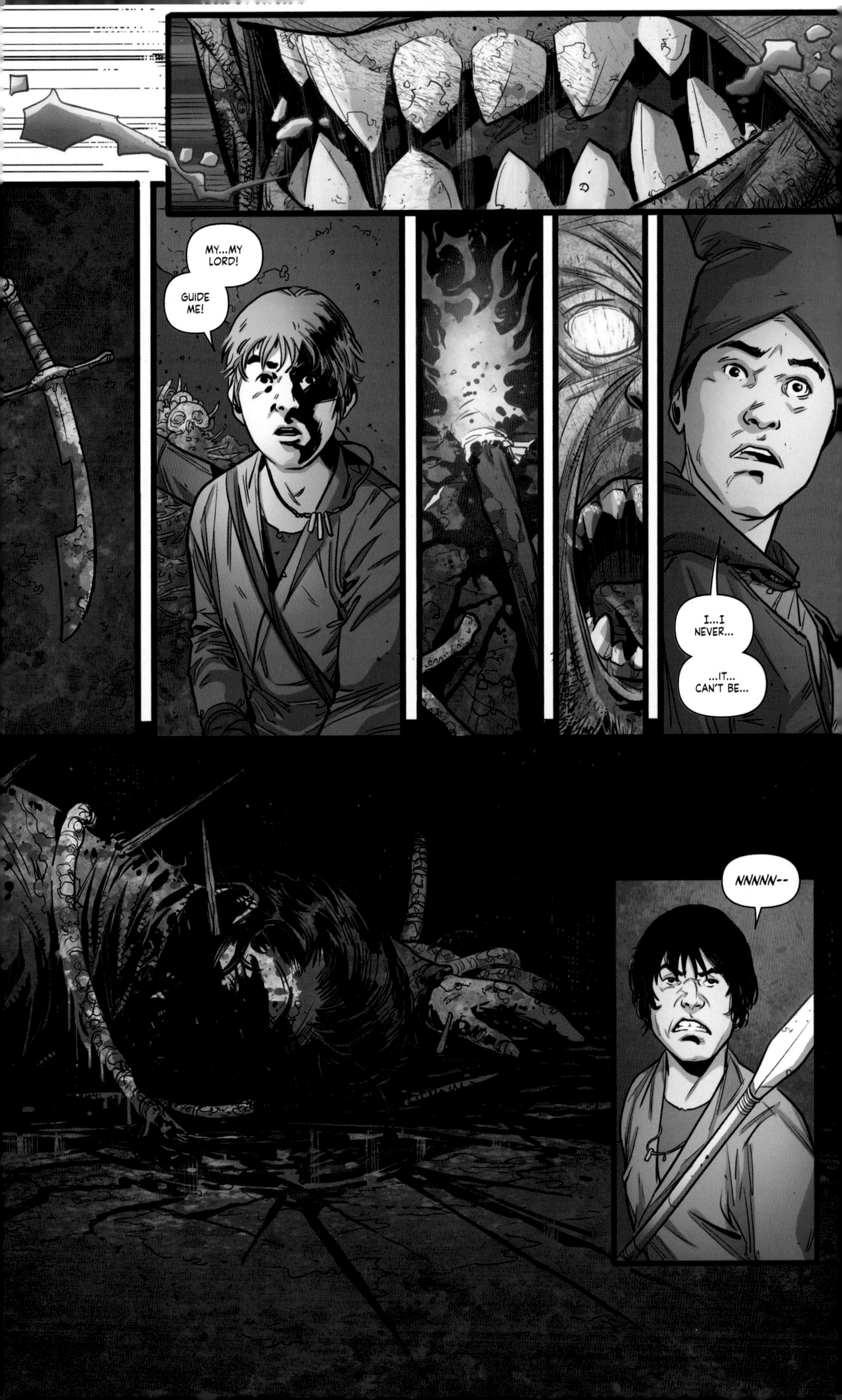
MY...MY LORD!
GUIDE ME!
I...I NEVER...
...IT... CAN'T BE...
NNNNN--

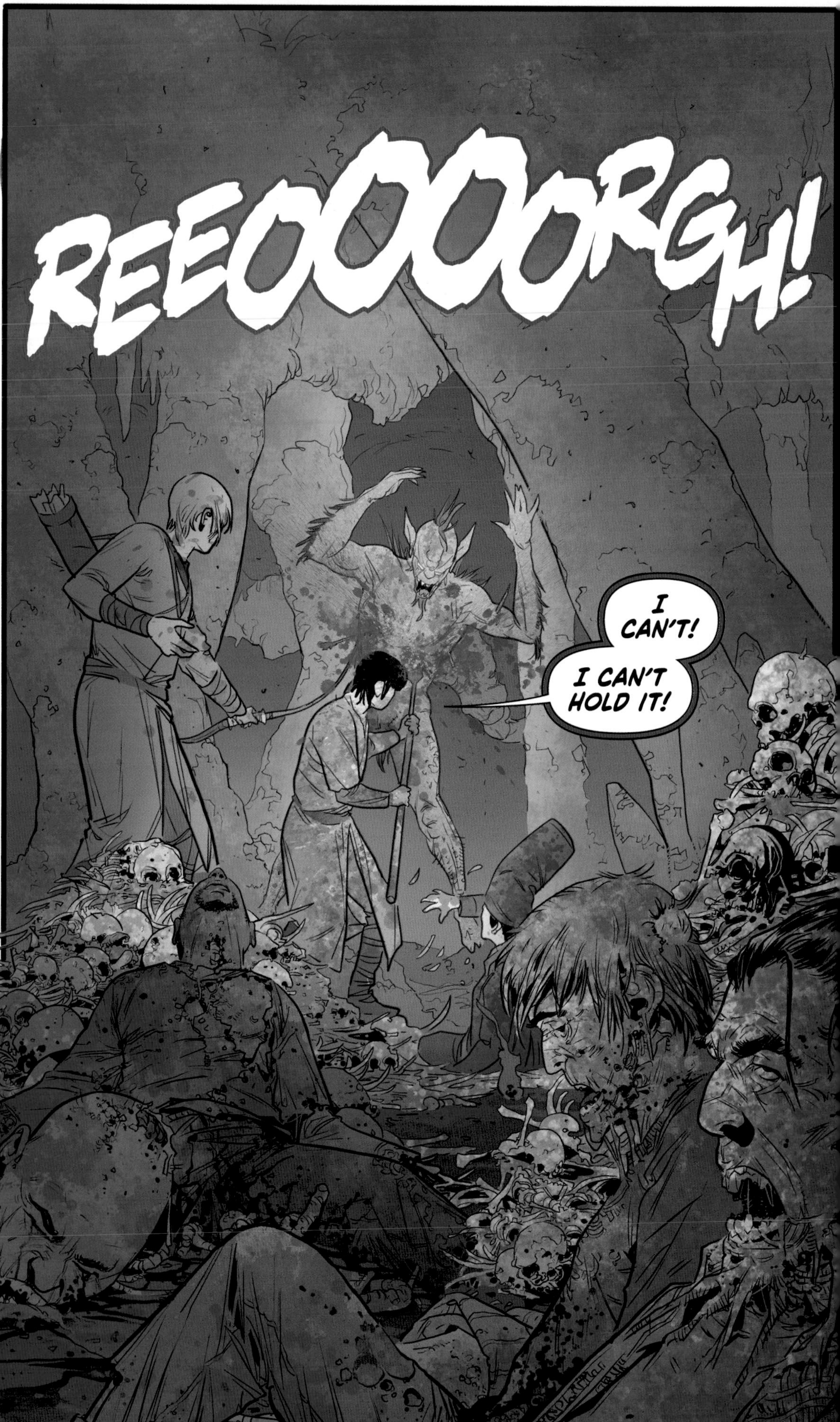
REEOOOOORGH!
I CAN'T!
I CAN'T HOLD IT!

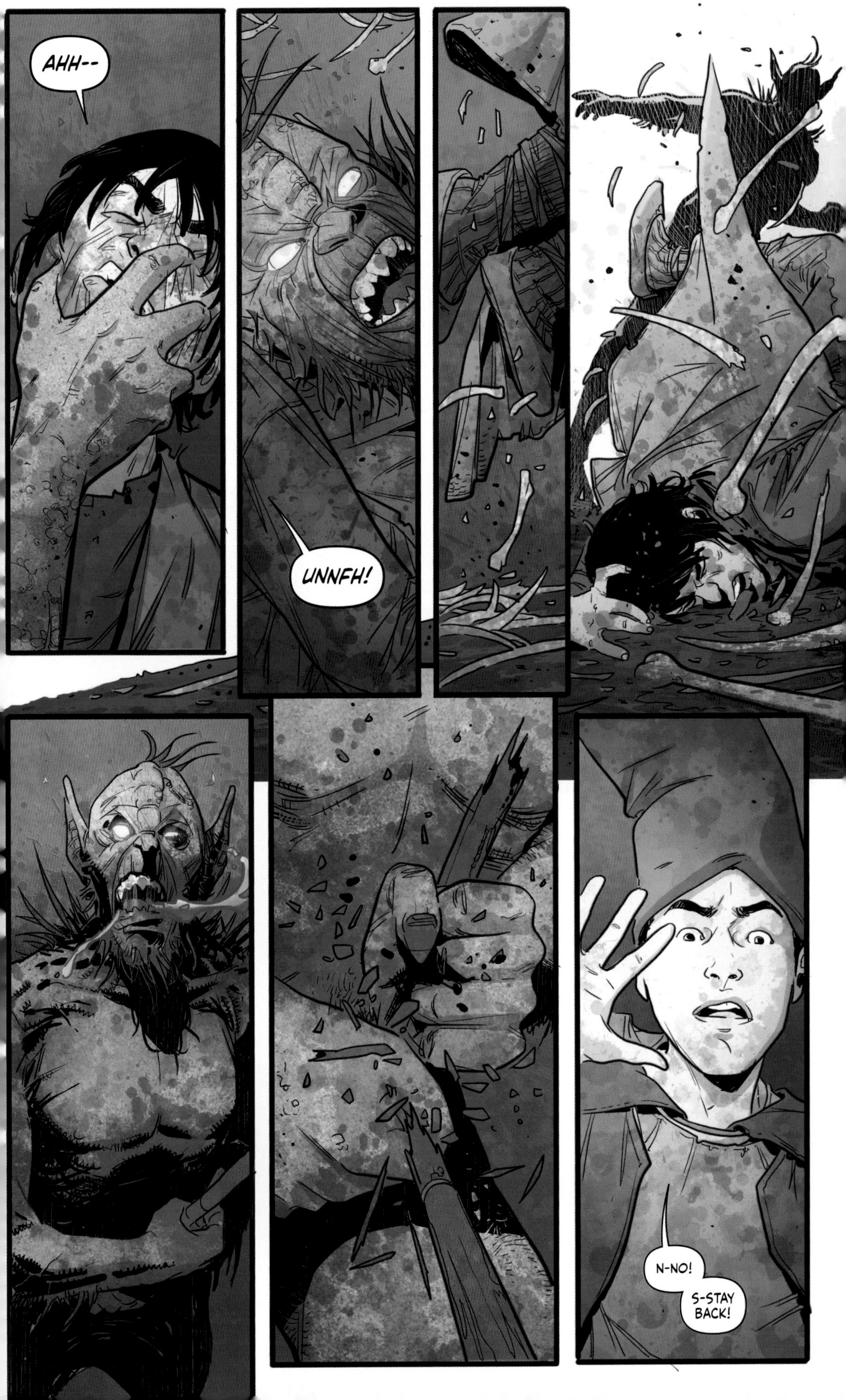
AHH--
UNNFH!
N-NO!
S-STAY BACK!

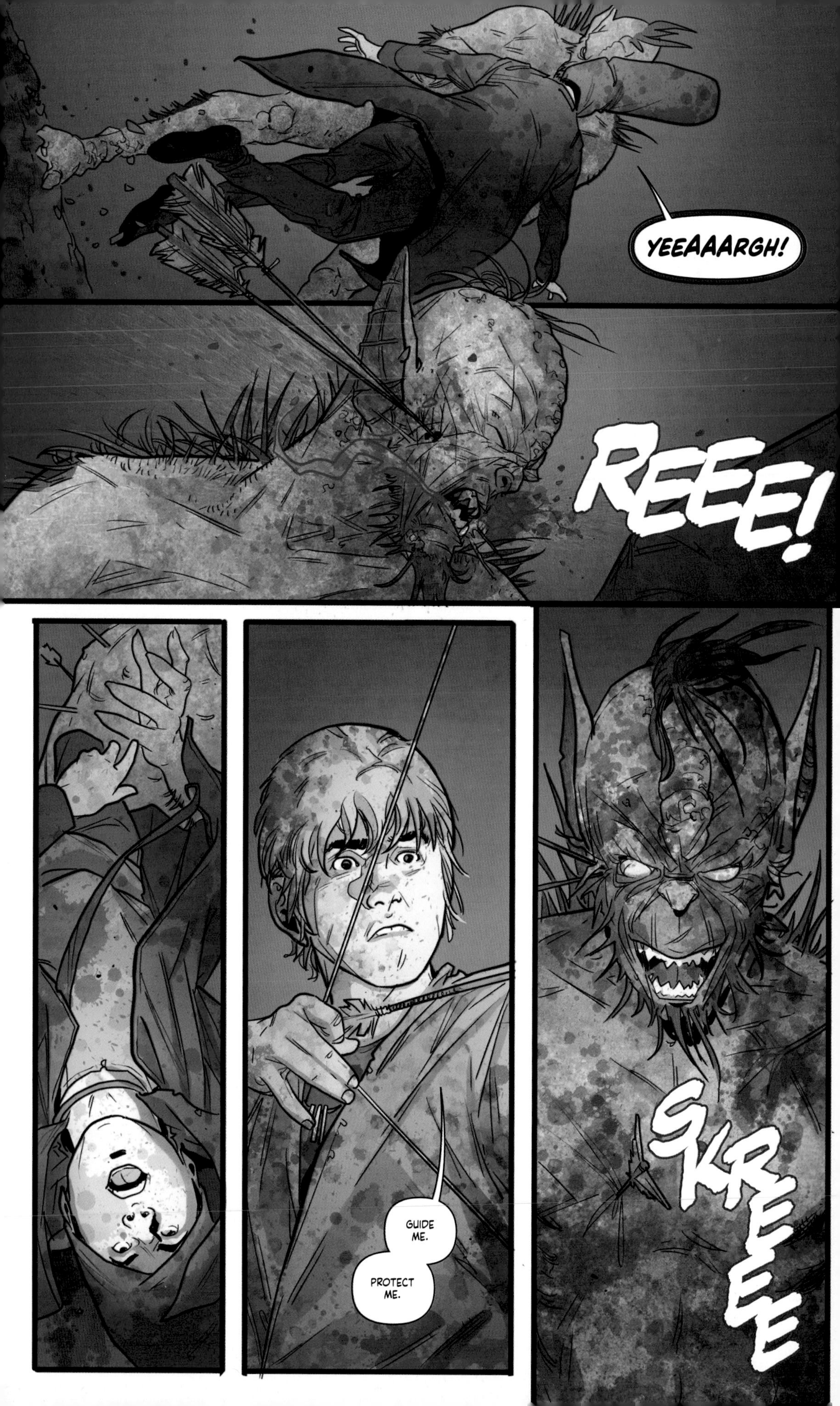

YEEAAARGH!
REEEE!
GUIDE ME.
PROTECT ME.
SKREEEE

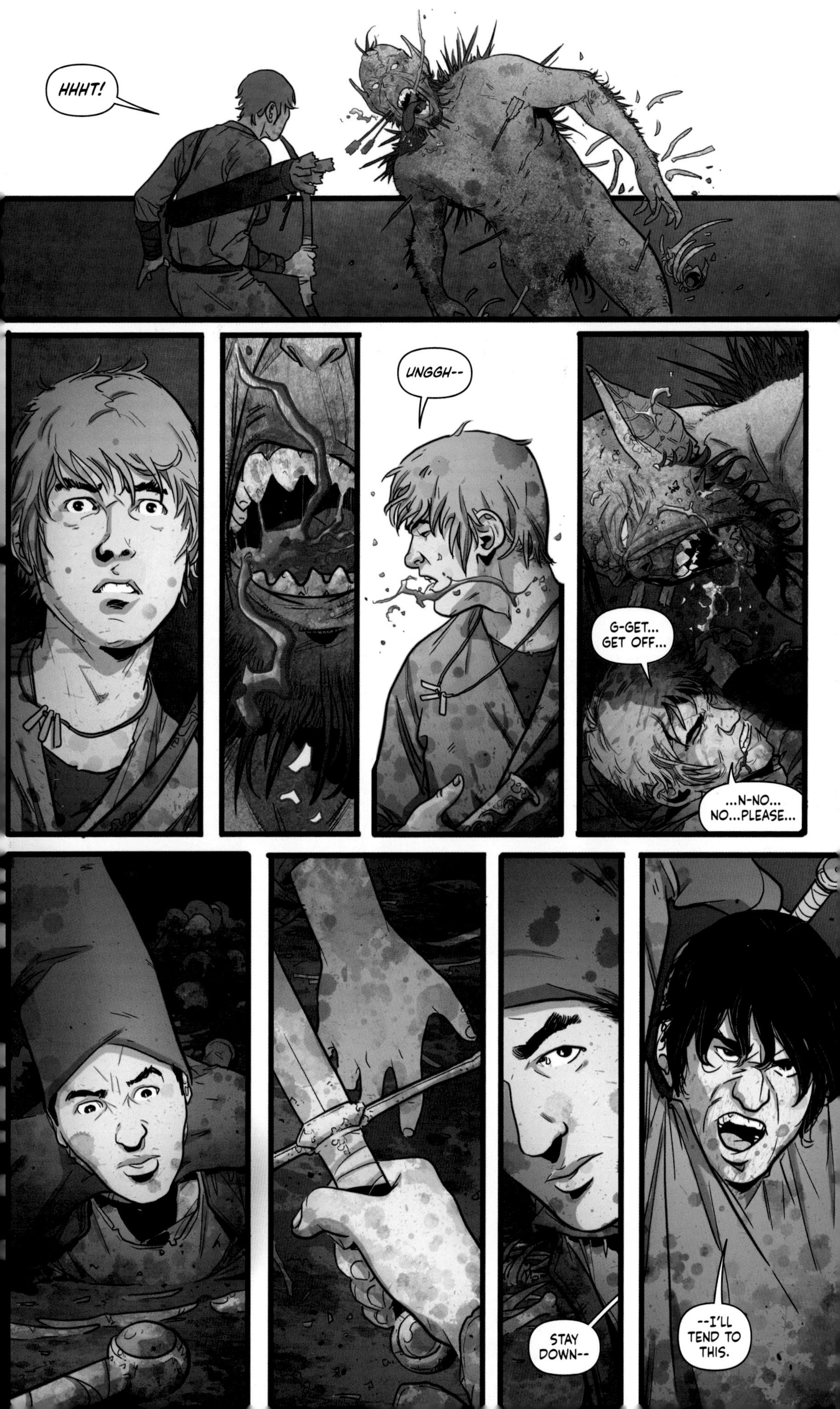
HHHT!
UNGGH--
G-GET... GET OFF...
...N-NO... NO...PLEASE...
STAY DOWN--
--I'LL TEND TO THIS.

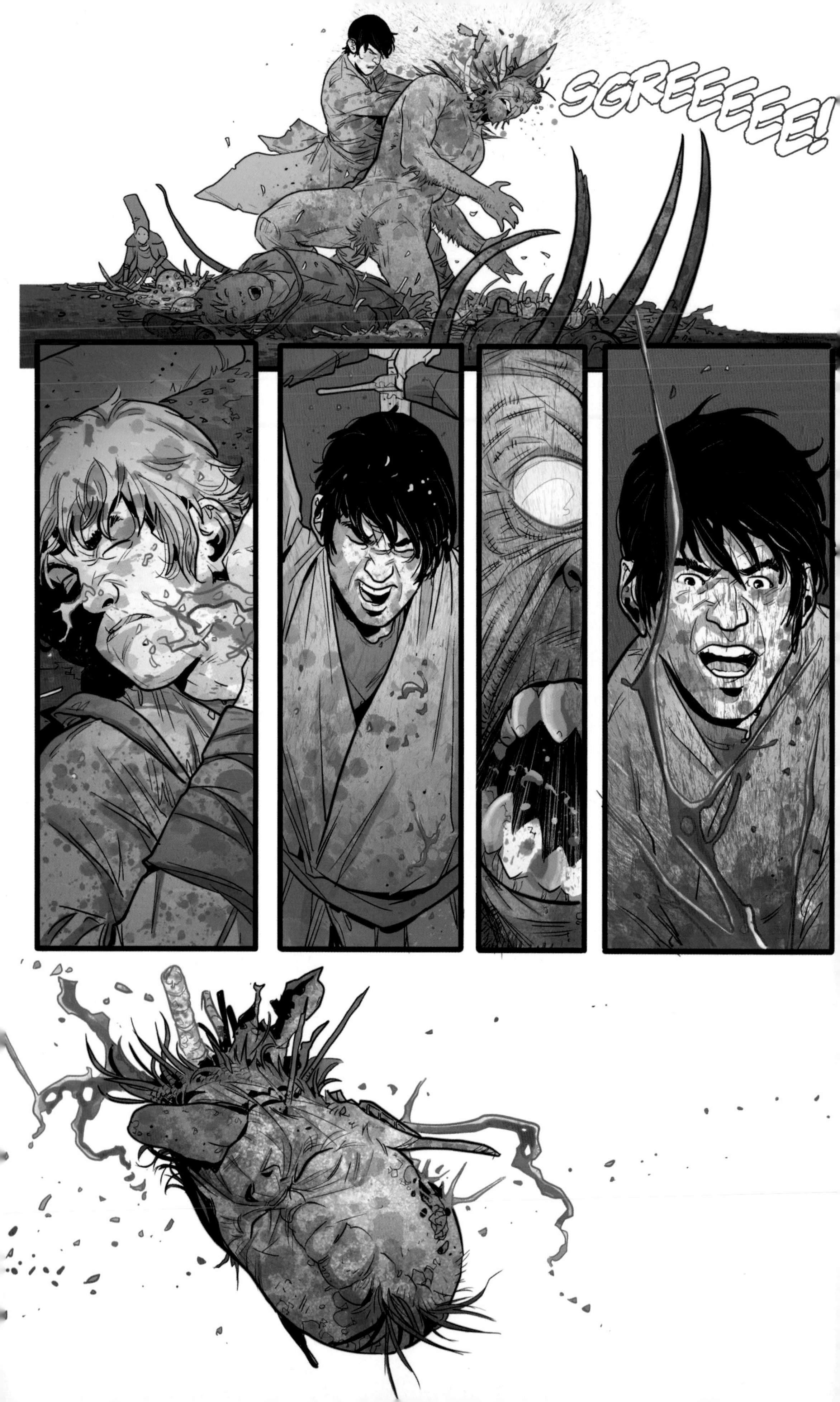
SCREEEEEE!

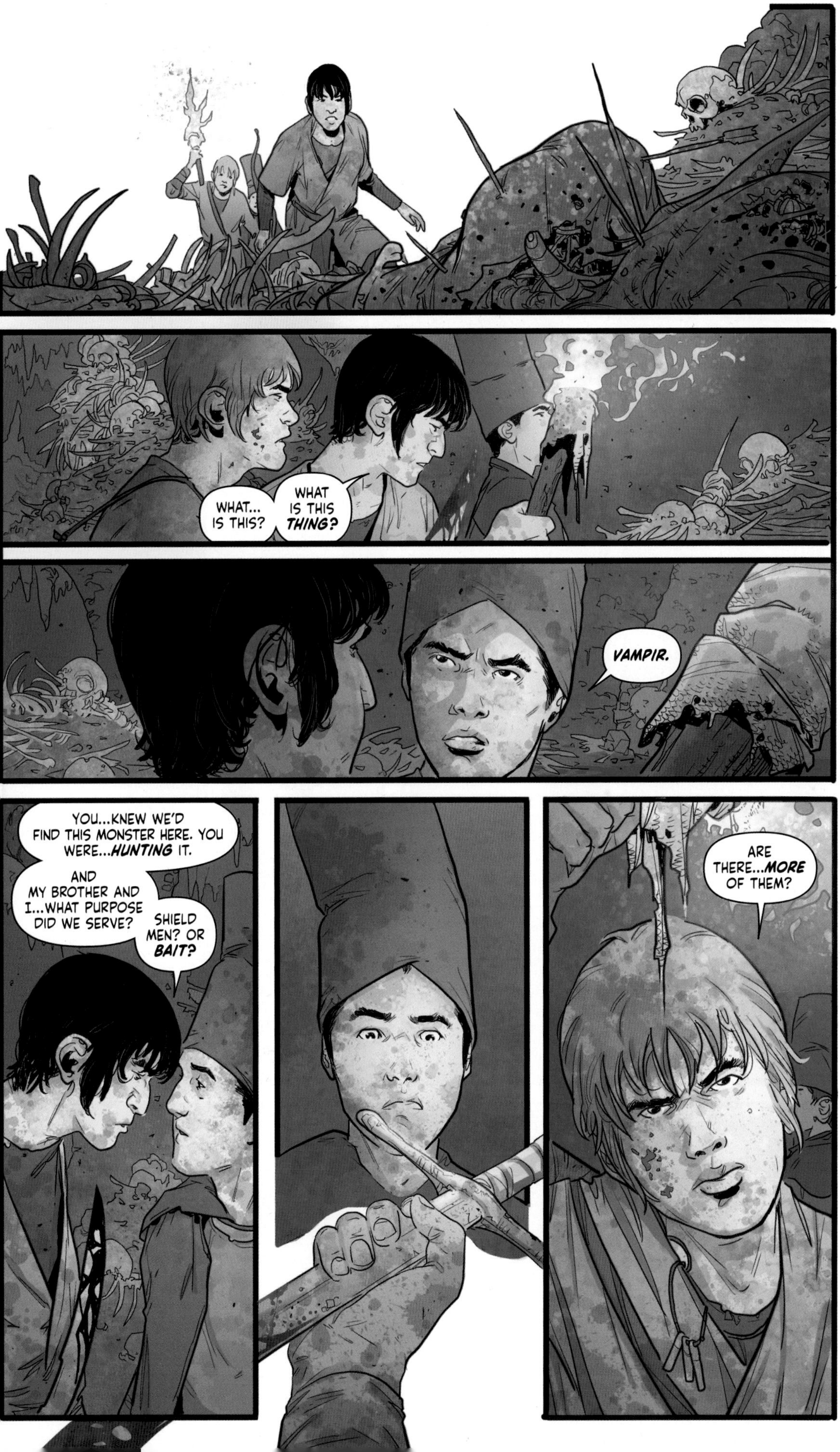
WHAT... IS THIS?
WHAT IS THIS *THING?*
VAMPIR.
YOU...KNEW WE'D FIND THIS MONSTER HERE. YOU WERE...*HUNTING* IT.
AND MY BROTHER AND I...WHAT PURPOSE DID WE SERVE?
SHIELD MEN? OR *BAIT?*
ARE THERE...*MORE* OF THEM?

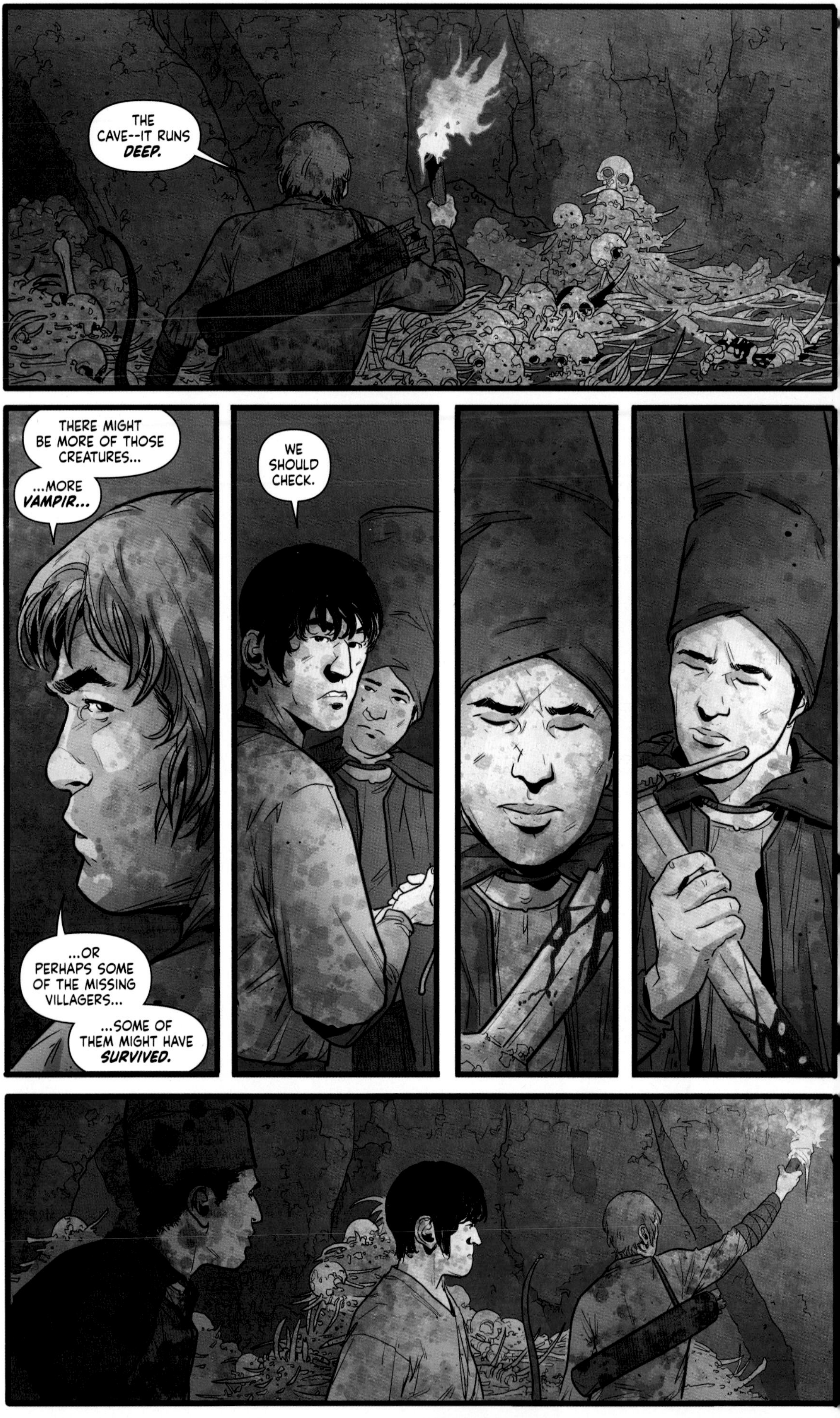

THE CAVE--IT RUNS DEEP.
THERE MIGHT BE MORE OF THOSE CREATURES...
...MORE VAMPIR...
...OR PERHAPS SOME OF THE MISSING VILLAGERS...
...SOME OF THEM MIGHT HAVE SURVIVED.
WE SHOULD CHECK.

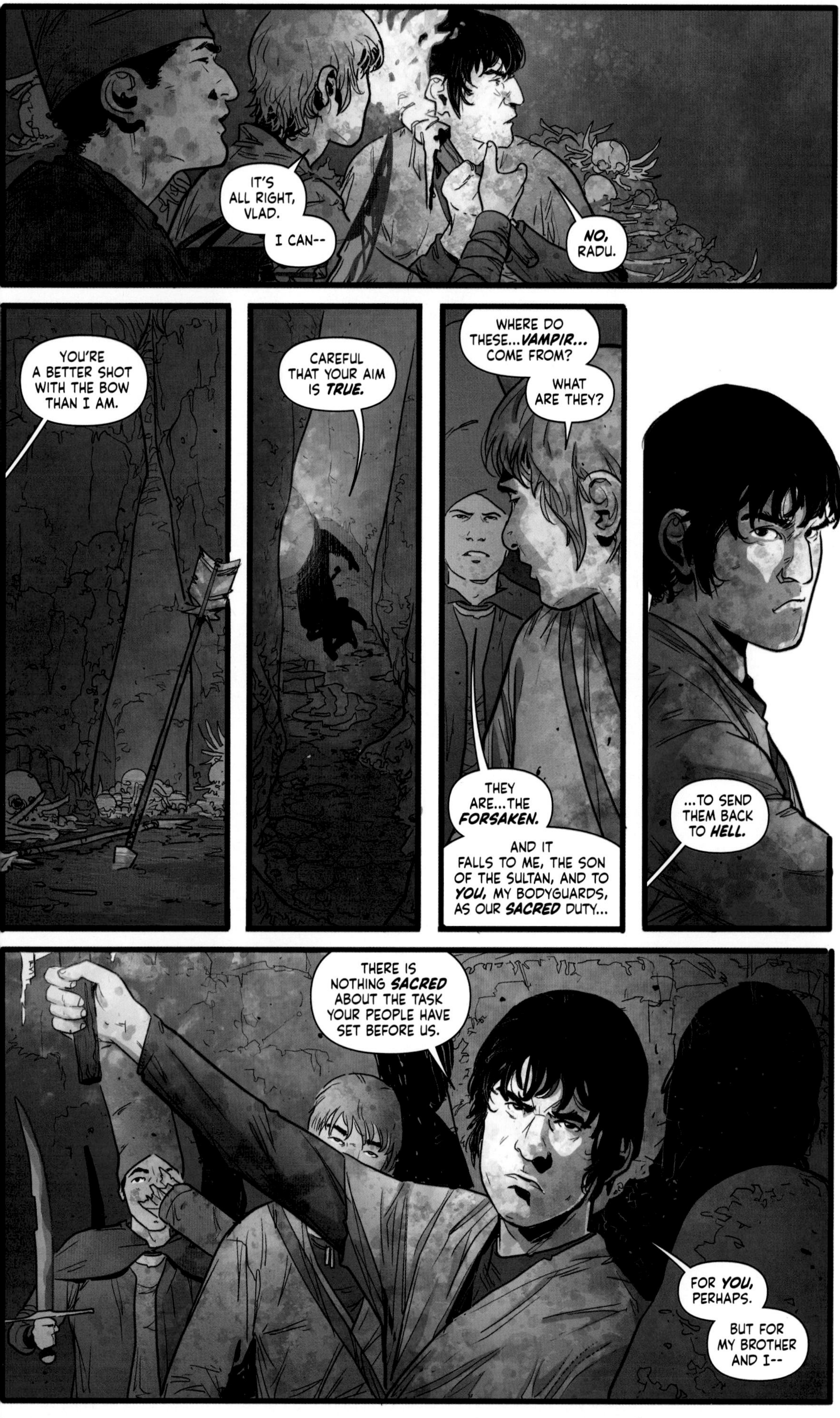
IT'S ALL RIGHT, VLAD.
I CAN--
NO, RADU.
YOU'RE A BETTER SHOT WITH THE BOW THAN I AM.
CAREFUL THAT YOUR AIM IS TRUE.
WHERE DO THESE...VAMPIR... COME FROM?
WHAT ARE THEY?
THEY ARE...THE FORSAKEN.
AND IT FALLS TO ME, THE SON OF THE SULTAN, AND TO YOU, MY BODYGUARDS, AS OUR SACRED DUTY...
...TO SEND THEM BACK TO HELL.
THERE IS NOTHING SACRED ABOUT THE TASK YOUR PEOPLE HAVE SET BEFORE US.
FOR YOU, PERHAPS.
BUT FOR MY BROTHER AND I--

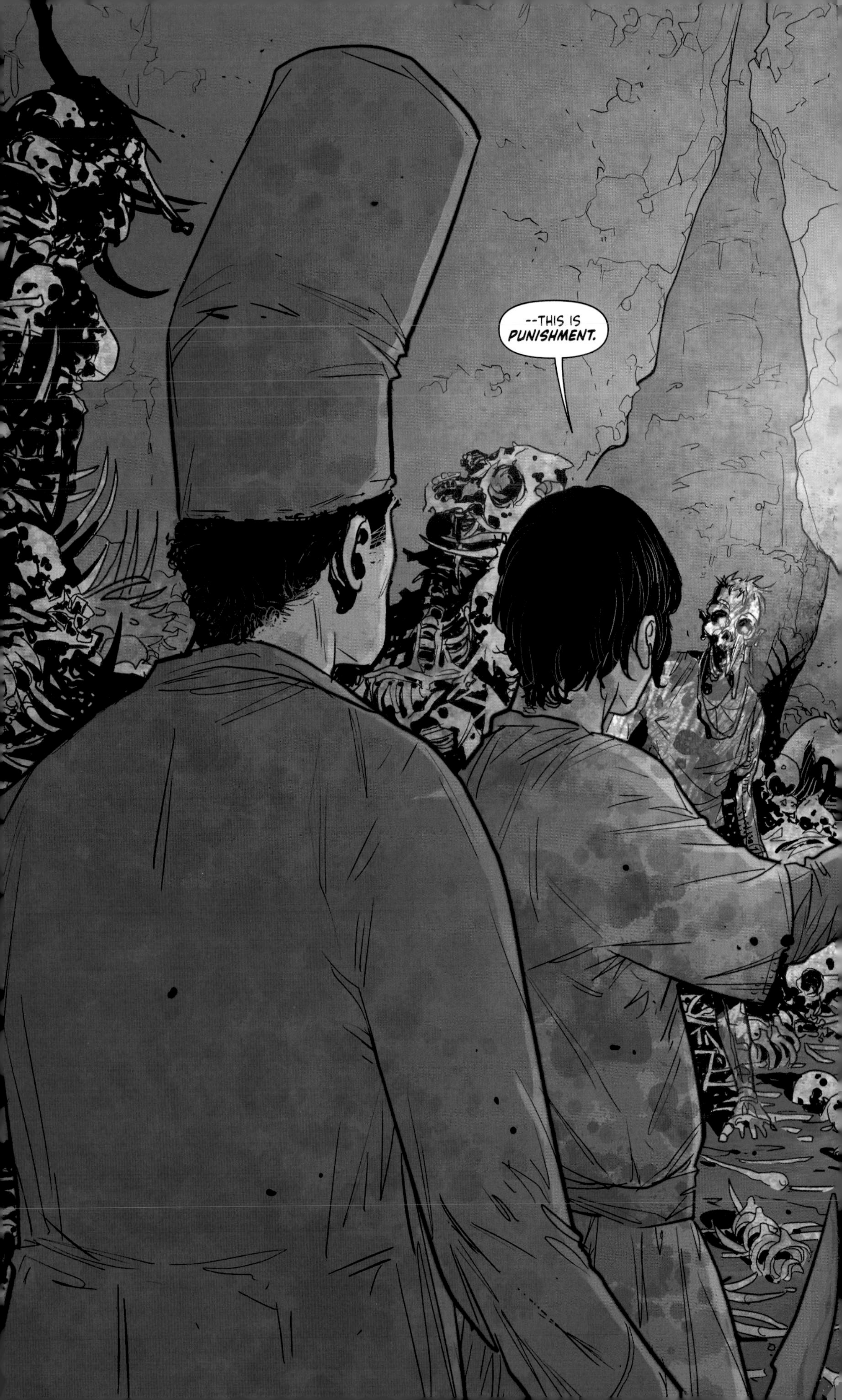
--THIS IS PUNISHMENT.

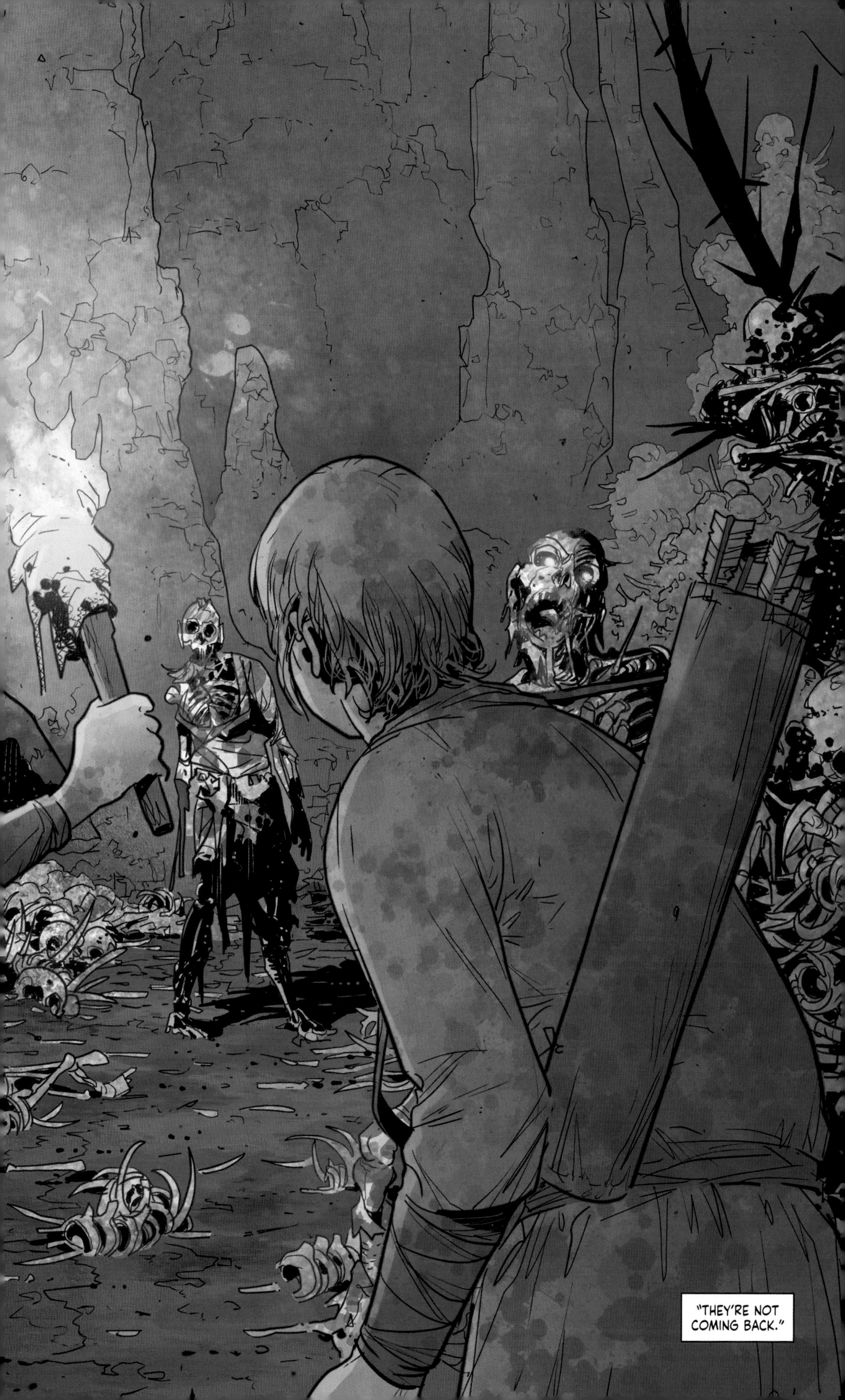
"THEY'RE NOT COMING BACK."

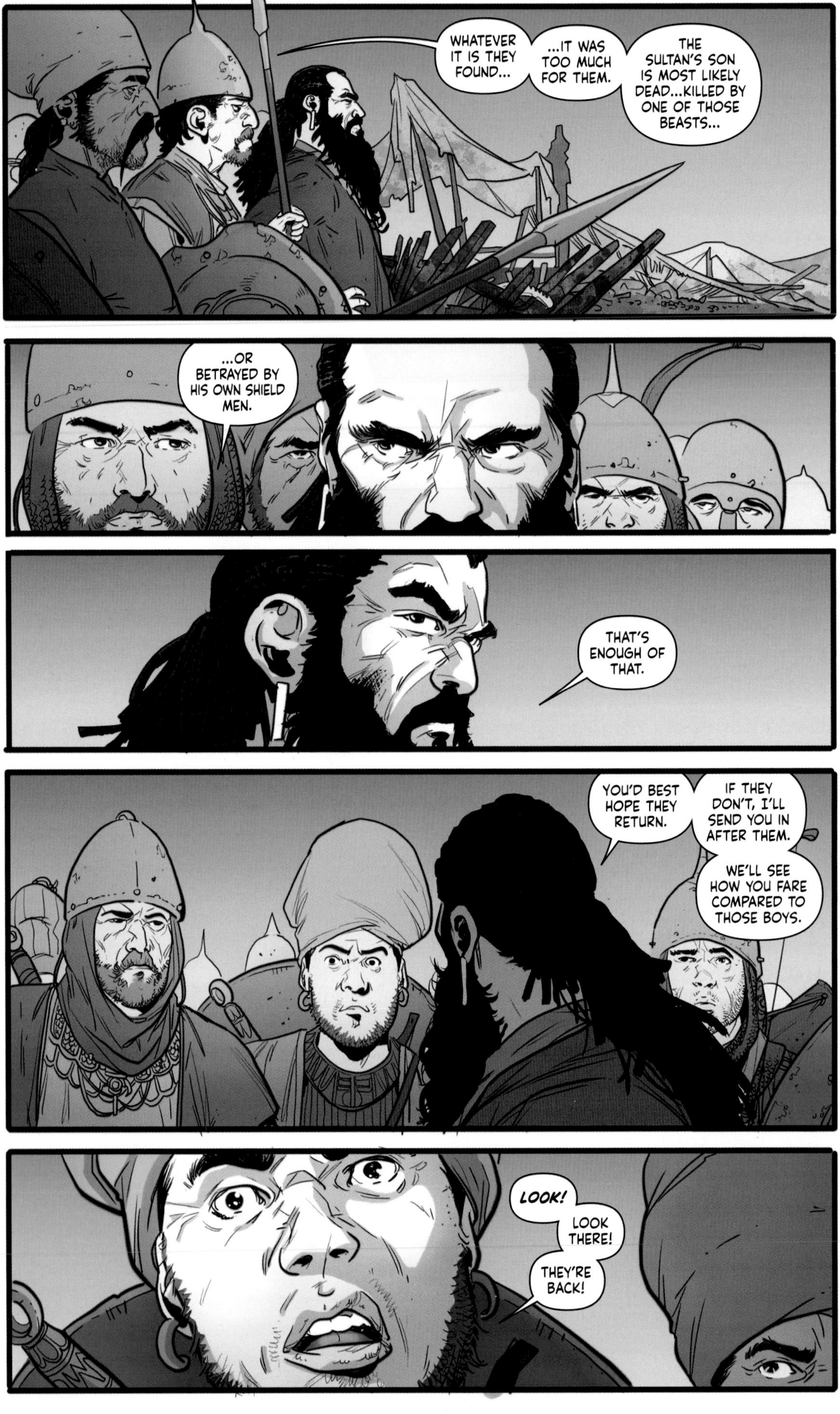
WHATEVER IT IS THEY FOUND...
...IT WAS TOO MUCH FOR THEM.
THE SULTAN'S SON IS MOST LIKELY DEAD...KILLED BY ONE OF THOSE BEASTS...
...OR BETRAYED BY HIS OWN SHIELD MEN.
THAT'S ENOUGH OF THAT.
YOU'D BEST HOPE THEY RETURN.
IF THEY DON'T, I'LL SEND YOU IN AFTER THEM.
WE'LL SEE HOW YOU FARE COMPARED TO THOSE BOYS.
LOOK!
LOOK THERE!
THEY'RE BACK!

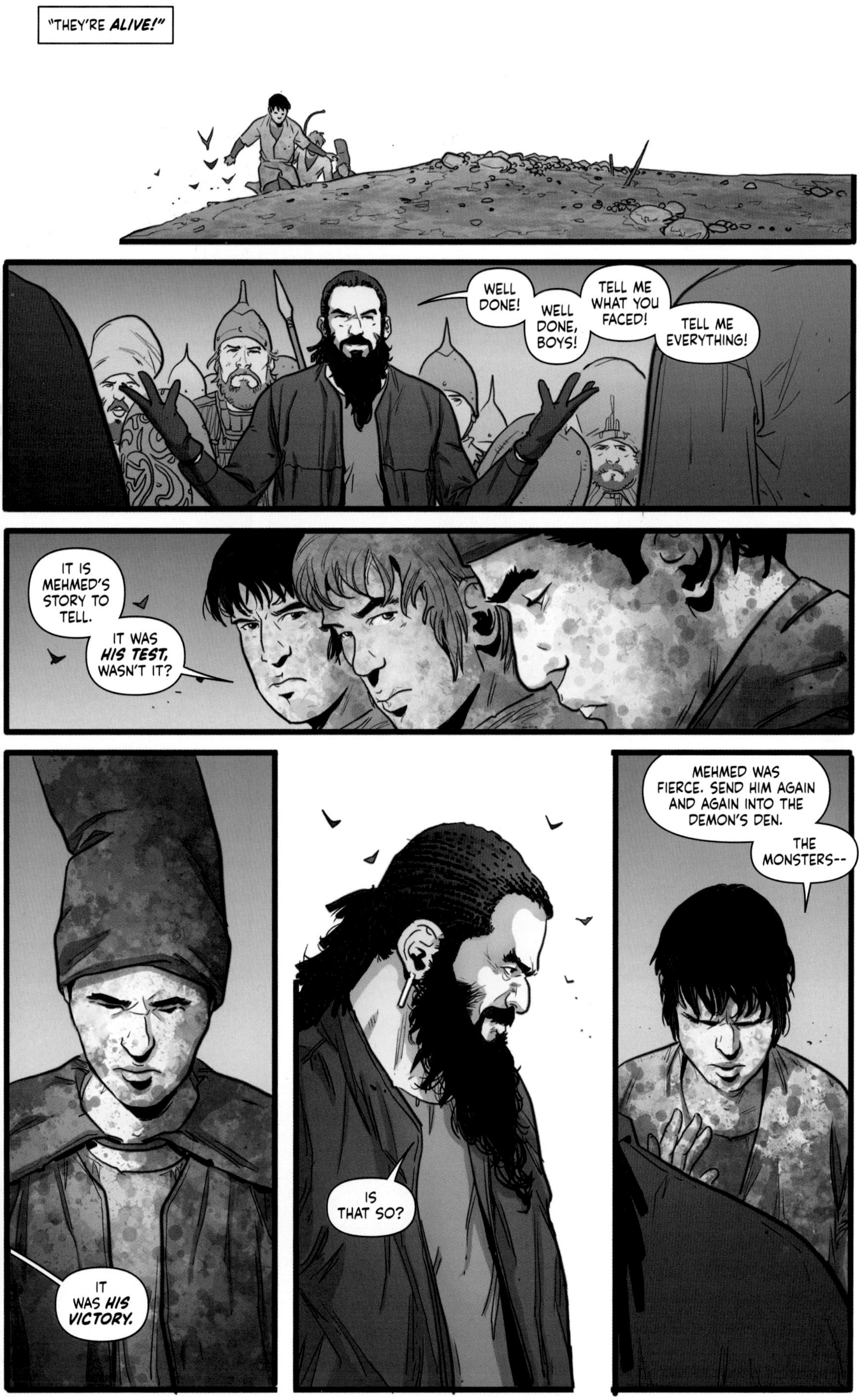
"THEY'RE ***ALIVE!***"
WELL DONE!
WELL DONE, BOYS!
TELL ME WHAT YOU FACED!
TELL ME EVERYTHING!
IT IS MEHMED'S STORY TO TELL.
IT WAS ***HIS TEST,*** WASN'T IT?
IT WAS ***HIS VICTORY.***
IS THAT SO?
MEHMED WAS FIERCE. SEND HIM AGAIN AND AGAIN INTO THE DEMON'S DEN.
THE MONSTERS--

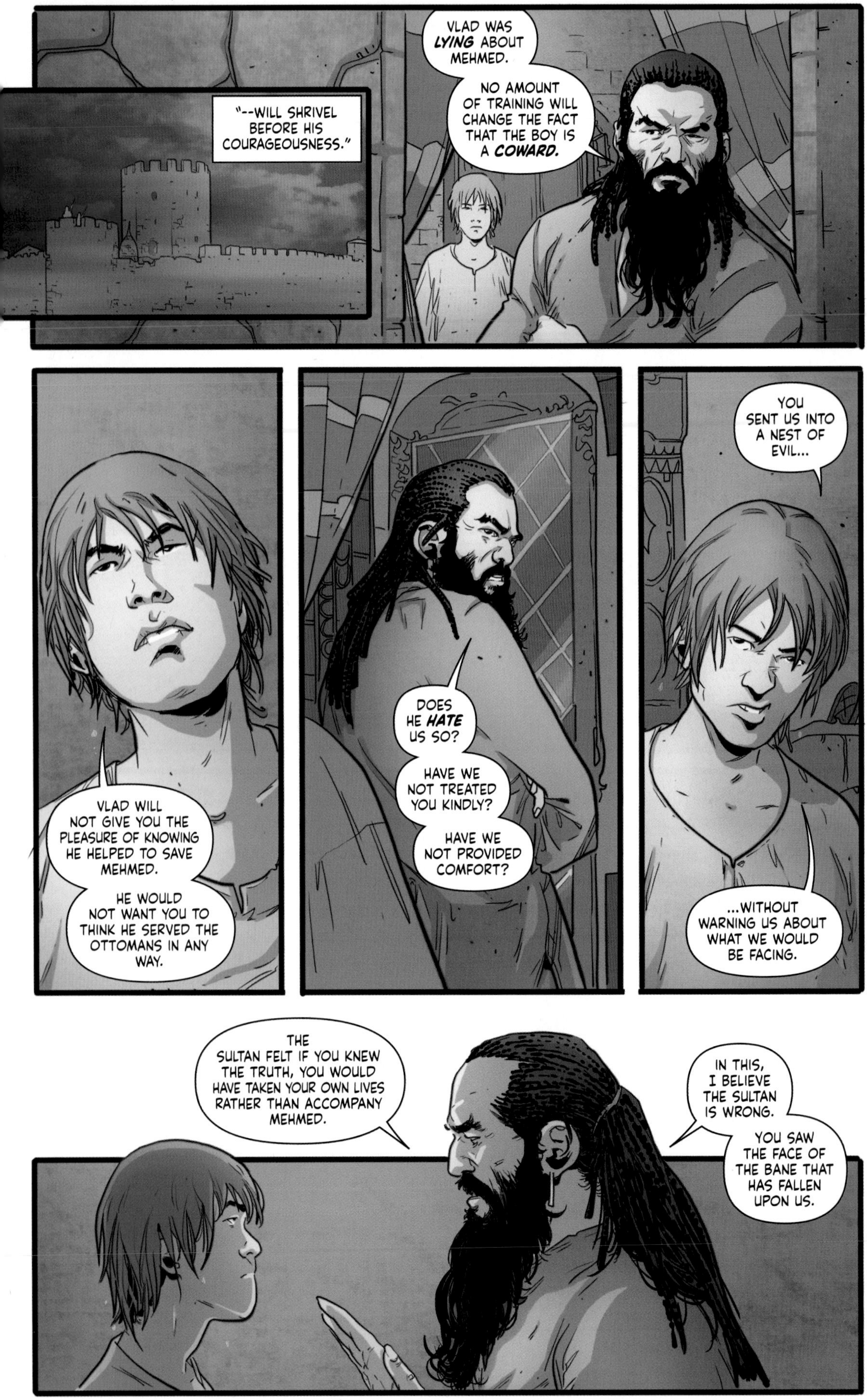
"--WILL SHRIVEL BEFORE HIS COURAGEOUSNESS."
VLAD WAS *LYING* ABOUT MEHMED.
NO AMOUNT OF TRAINING WILL CHANGE THE FACT THAT THE BOY IS A *COWARD.*
VLAD WILL NOT GIVE YOU THE PLEASURE OF KNOWING HE HELPED TO SAVE MEHMED.
HE WOULD NOT WANT YOU TO THINK HE SERVED THE OTTOMANS IN ANY WAY.
DOES HE *HATE* US SO?
HAVE WE NOT TREATED YOU KINDLY?
HAVE WE NOT PROVIDED COMFORT?
YOU SENT US INTO A NEST OF EVIL...
...WITHOUT WARNING US ABOUT WHAT WE WOULD BE FACING.
THE SULTAN FELT IF YOU KNEW THE TRUTH, YOU WOULD HAVE TAKEN YOUR OWN LIVES RATHER THAN ACCOMPANY MEHMED.
IN THIS, I BELIEVE THE SULTAN IS WRONG.
YOU SAW THE FACE OF THE BANE THAT HAS FALLEN UPON US.

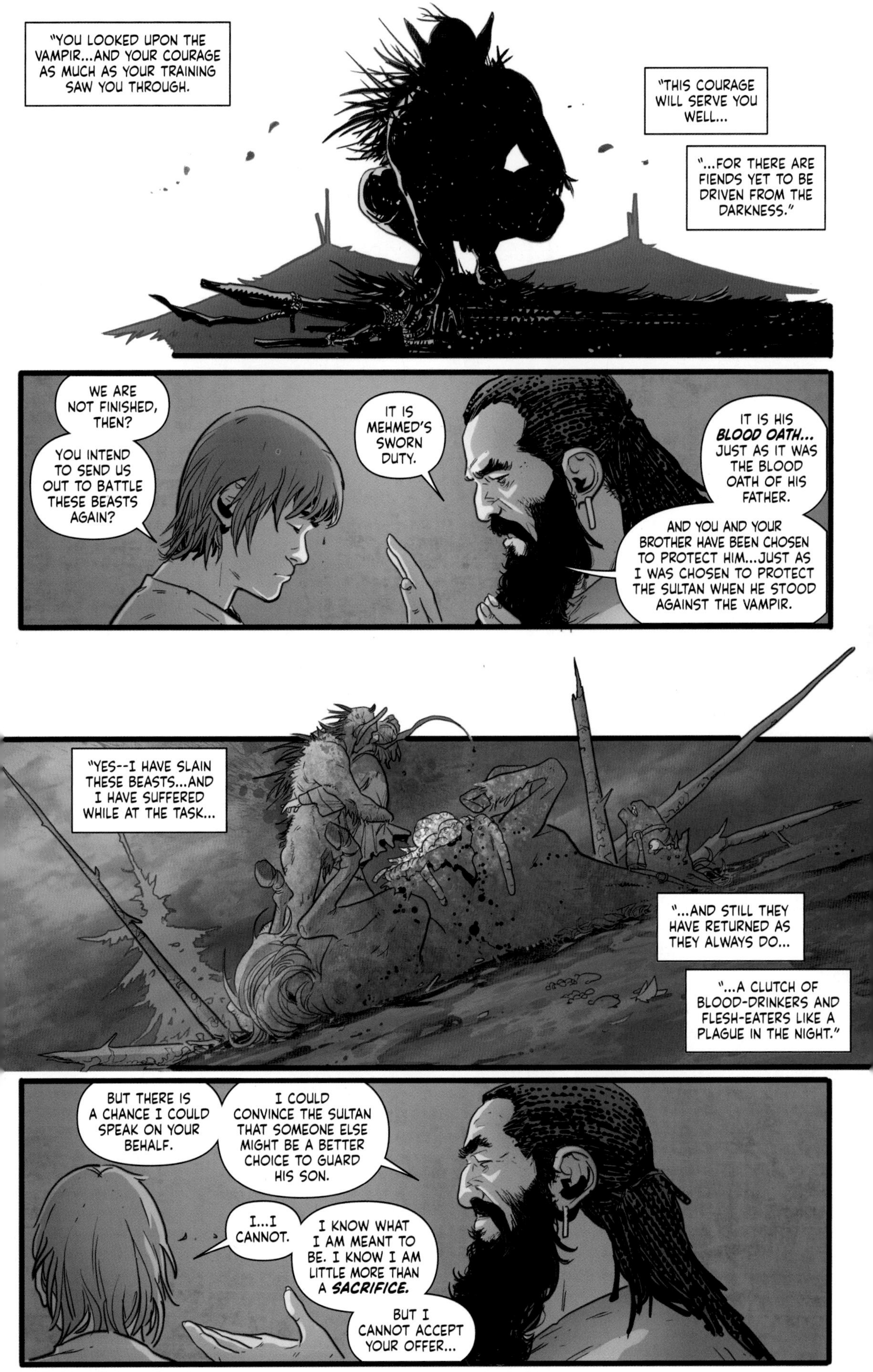
"YOU LOOKED UPON THE VAMPIR...AND YOUR COURAGE AS MUCH AS YOUR TRAINING SAW YOU THROUGH.
"THIS COURAGE WILL SERVE YOU WELL...
"...FOR THERE ARE FIENDS YET TO BE DRIVEN FROM THE DARKNESS."
WE ARE NOT FINISHED, THEN?
YOU INTEND TO SEND US OUT TO BATTLE THESE BEASTS AGAIN?
IT IS MEHMED'S SWORN DUTY.
IT IS HIS ***BLOOD OATH...*** JUST AS IT WAS THE BLOOD OATH OF HIS FATHER.
AND YOU AND YOUR BROTHER HAVE BEEN CHOSEN TO PROTECT HIM...JUST AS I WAS CHOSEN TO PROTECT THE SULTAN WHEN HE STOOD AGAINST THE VAMPIR.
"YES--I HAVE SLAIN THESE BEASTS...AND I HAVE SUFFERED WHILE AT THE TASK...
"...AND STILL THEY HAVE RETURNED AS THEY ALWAYS DO...
"...A CLUTCH OF BLOOD-DRINKERS AND FLESH-EATERS LIKE A PLAGUE IN THE NIGHT."
BUT THERE IS A CHANCE I COULD SPEAK ON YOUR BEHALF.
I COULD CONVINCE THE SULTAN THAT SOMEONE ELSE MIGHT BE A BETTER CHOICE TO GUARD HIS SON.
I...I CANNOT.
I KNOW WHAT I AM MEANT TO BE. I KNOW I AM LITTLE MORE THAN A ***SACRIFICE.***
BUT I CANNOT ACCEPT YOUR OFFER...

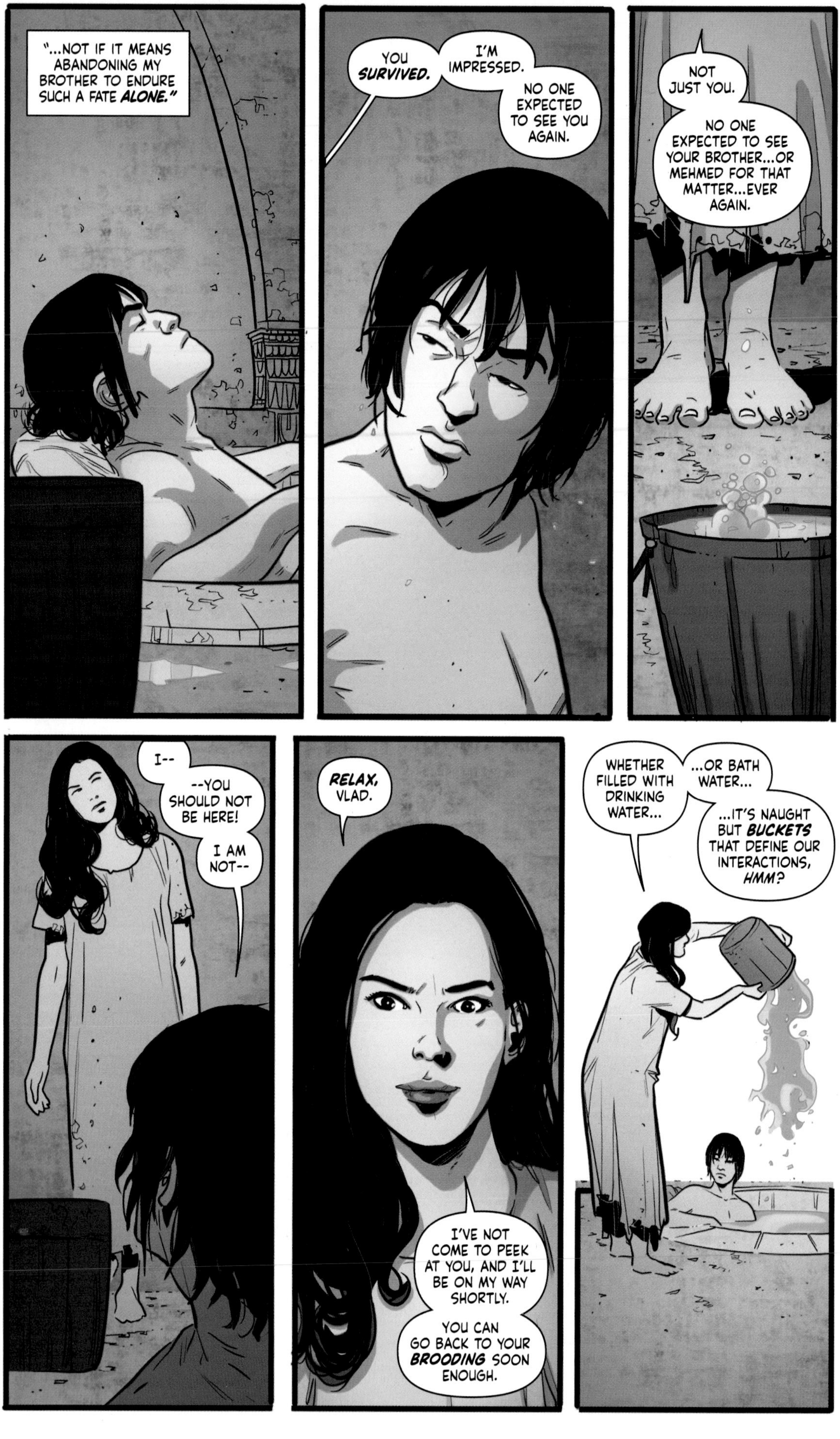
"...NOT IF IT MEANS ABANDONING MY BROTHER TO ENDURE SUCH A FATE ALONE."
YOU SURVIVED.
I'M IMPRESSED.
NO ONE EXPECTED TO SEE YOU AGAIN.
NOT JUST YOU.
NO ONE EXPECTED TO SEE YOUR BROTHER...OR MEHMED FOR THAT MATTER...EVER AGAIN.
I--
--YOU SHOULD NOT BE HERE!
I AM NOT--
RELAX, VLAD.
I'VE NOT COME TO PEEK AT YOU, AND I'LL BE ON MY WAY SHORTLY.
YOU CAN GO BACK TO YOUR BROODING SOON ENOUGH.
WHETHER FILLED WITH DRINKING WATER...
...OR BATH WATER...
...IT'S NAUGHT BUT BUCKETS THAT DEFINE OUR INTERACTIONS, HMM?

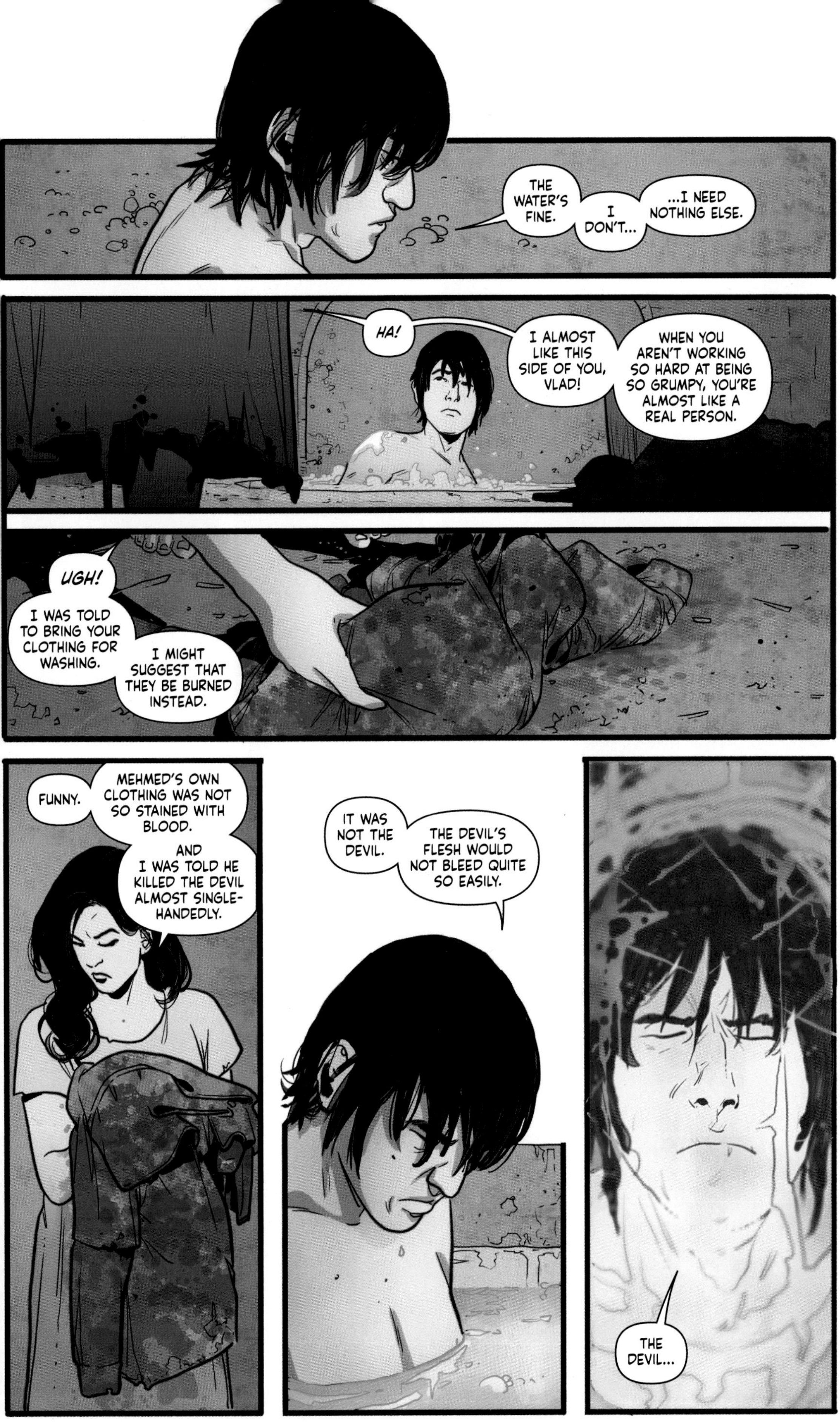
THE WATER'S FINE.
I DON'T...
...I NEED NOTHING ELSE.
HA!
I ALMOST LIKE THIS SIDE OF YOU, VLAD!
WHEN YOU AREN'T WORKING SO HARD AT BEING SO GRUMPY, YOU'RE ALMOST LIKE A REAL PERSON.
UGH!
I WAS TOLD TO BRING YOUR CLOTHING FOR WASHING.
I MIGHT SUGGEST THAT THEY BE BURNED INSTEAD.
FUNNY.
MEHMED'S OWN CLOTHING WAS NOT SO STAINED WITH BLOOD.
AND I WAS TOLD HE KILLED THE DEVIL ALMOST SINGLE-HANDEDLY.
IT WAS NOT THE DEVIL.
THE DEVIL'S FLESH WOULD NOT BLEED QUITE SO EASILY.
THE DEVIL...

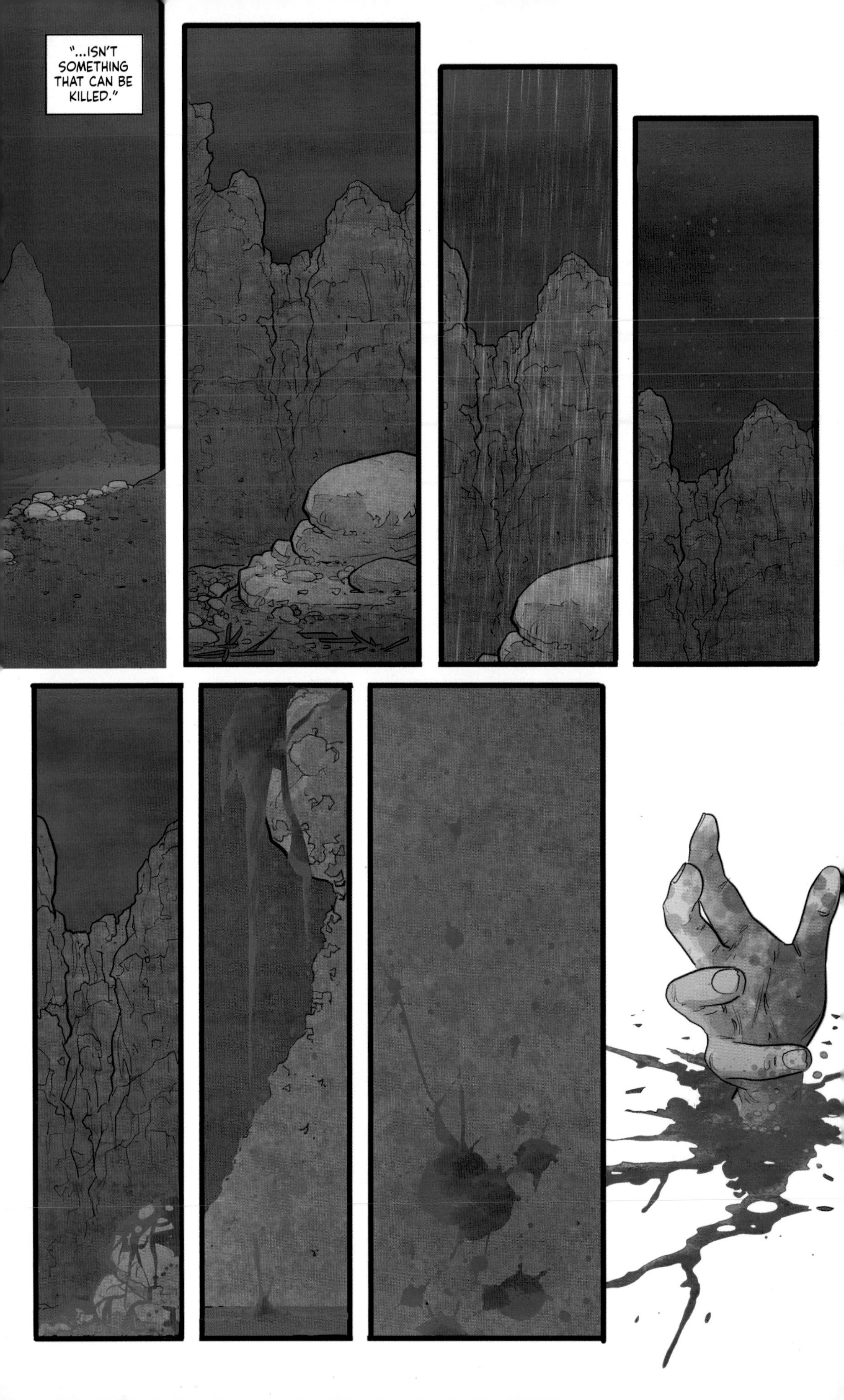
"...ISN'T SOMETHING THAT CAN BE KILLED."

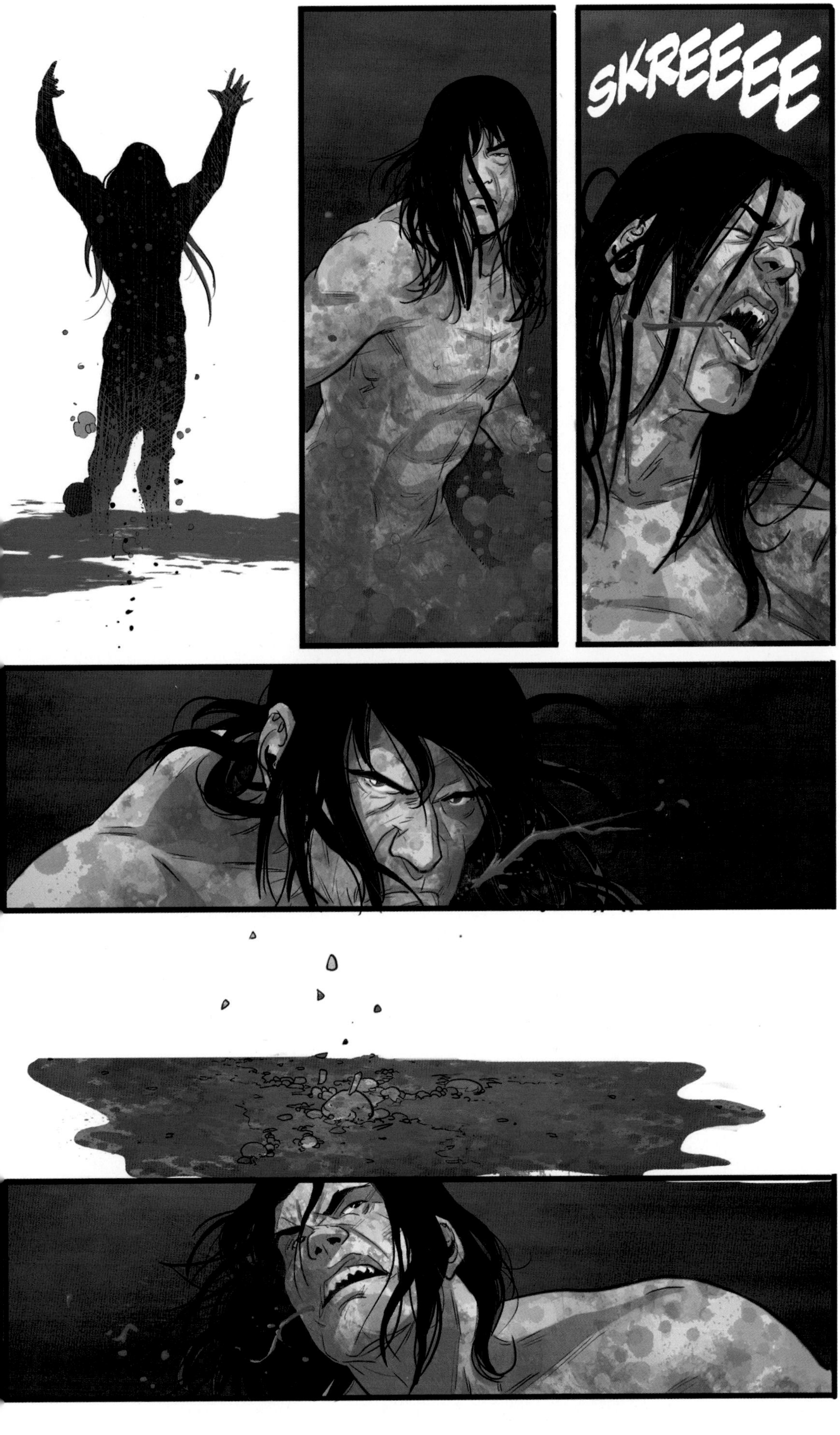
SKREEEEE

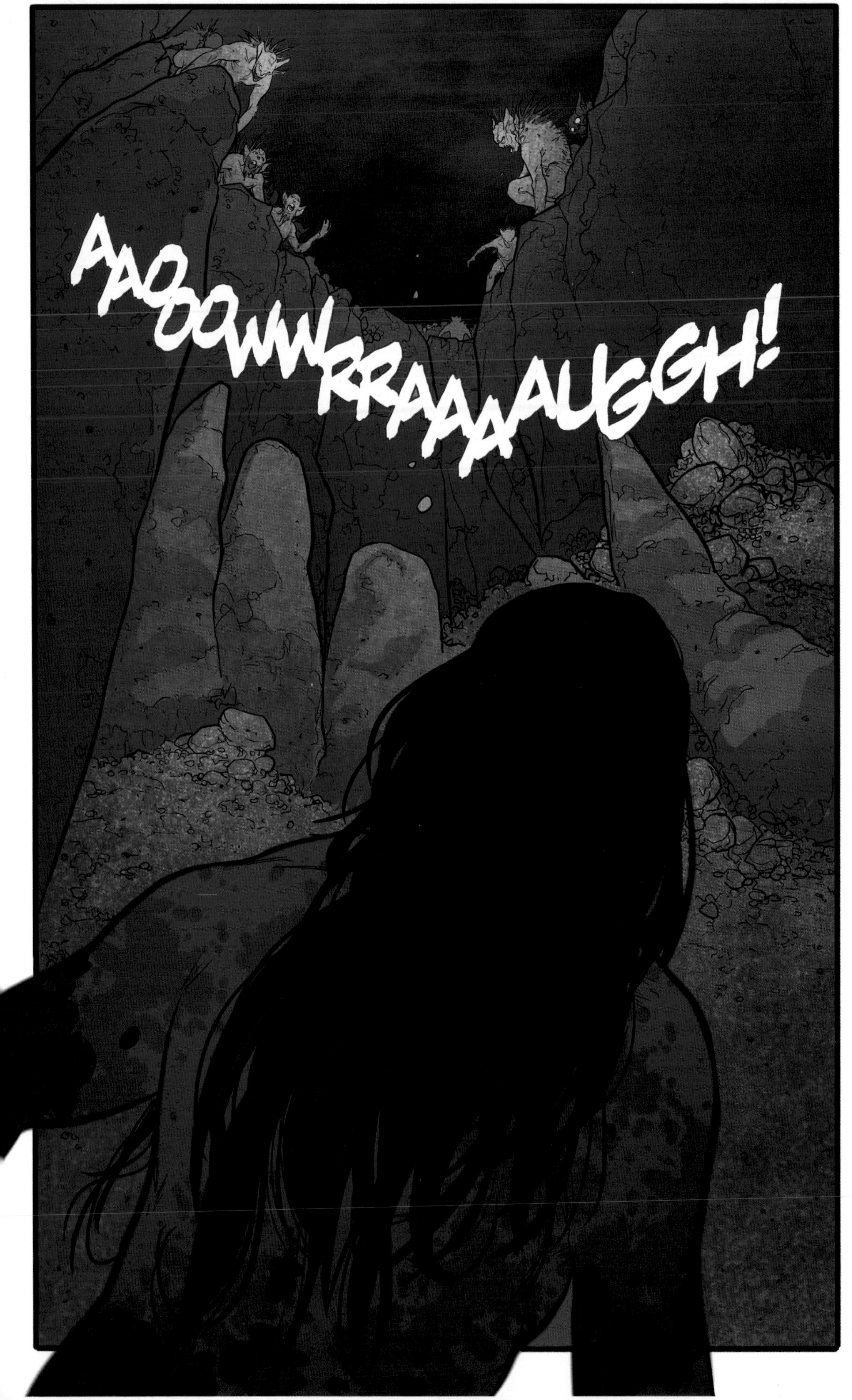
AAOOOWWRRAAAAUGGH!

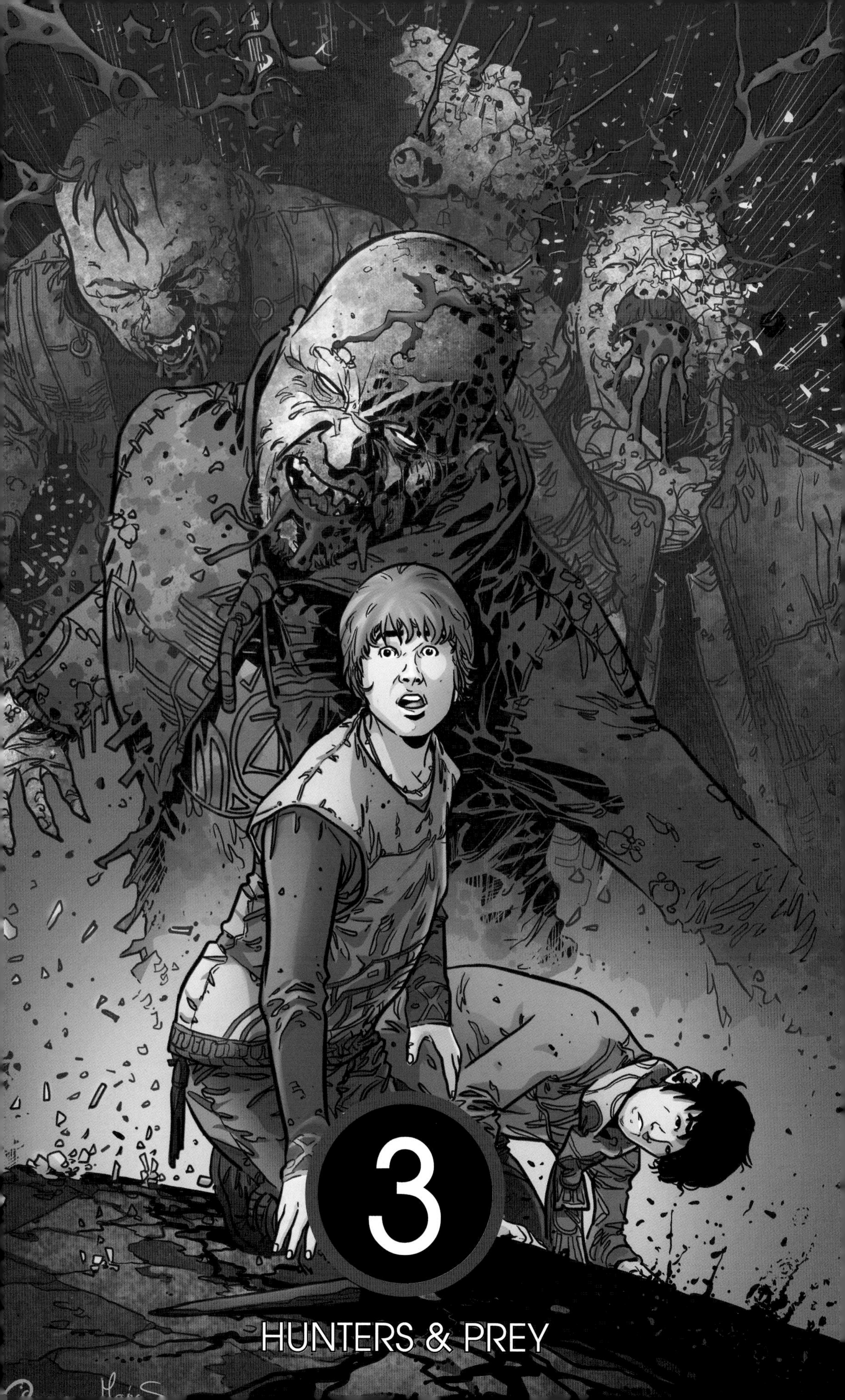

3

HUNTERS & PREY

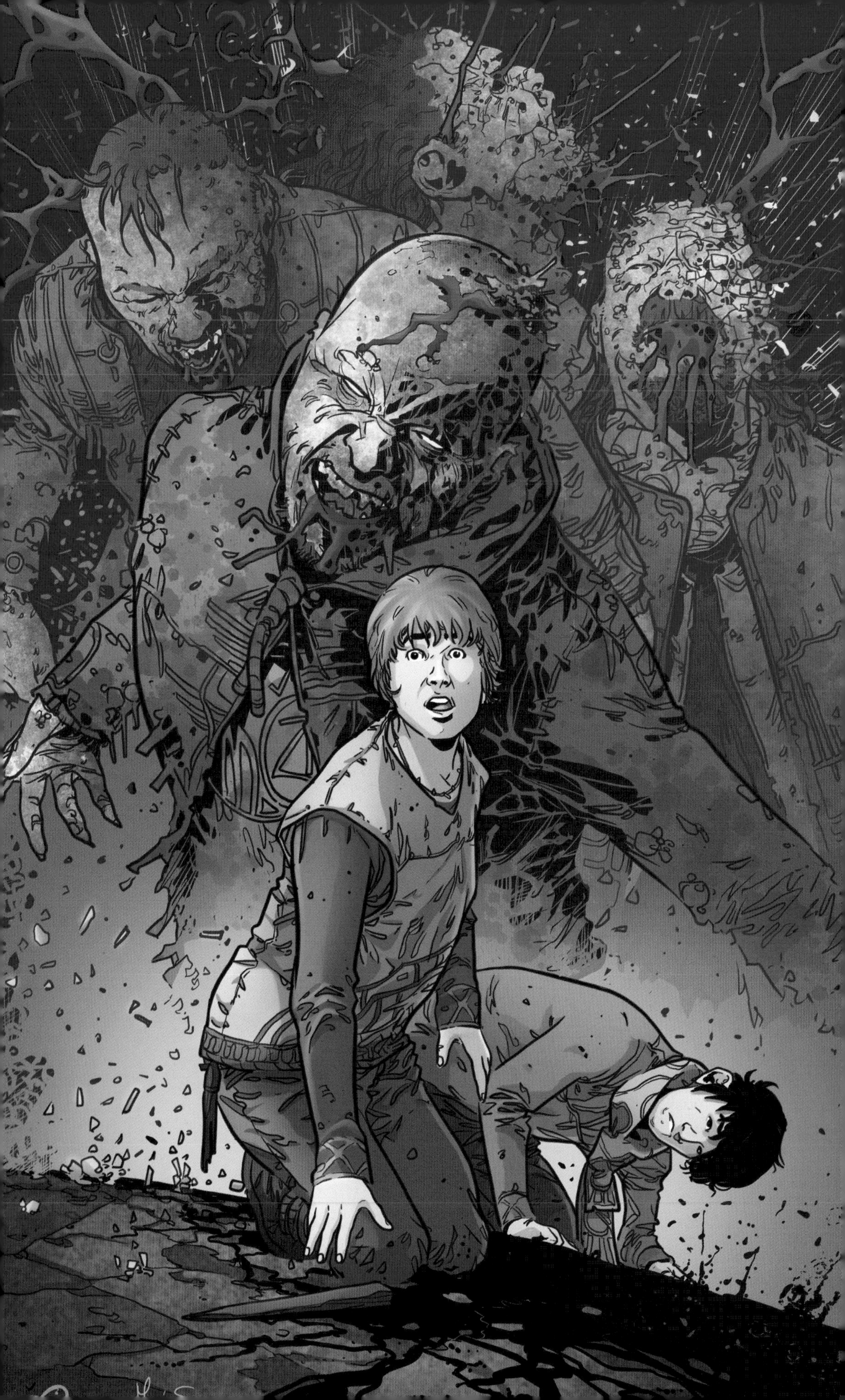

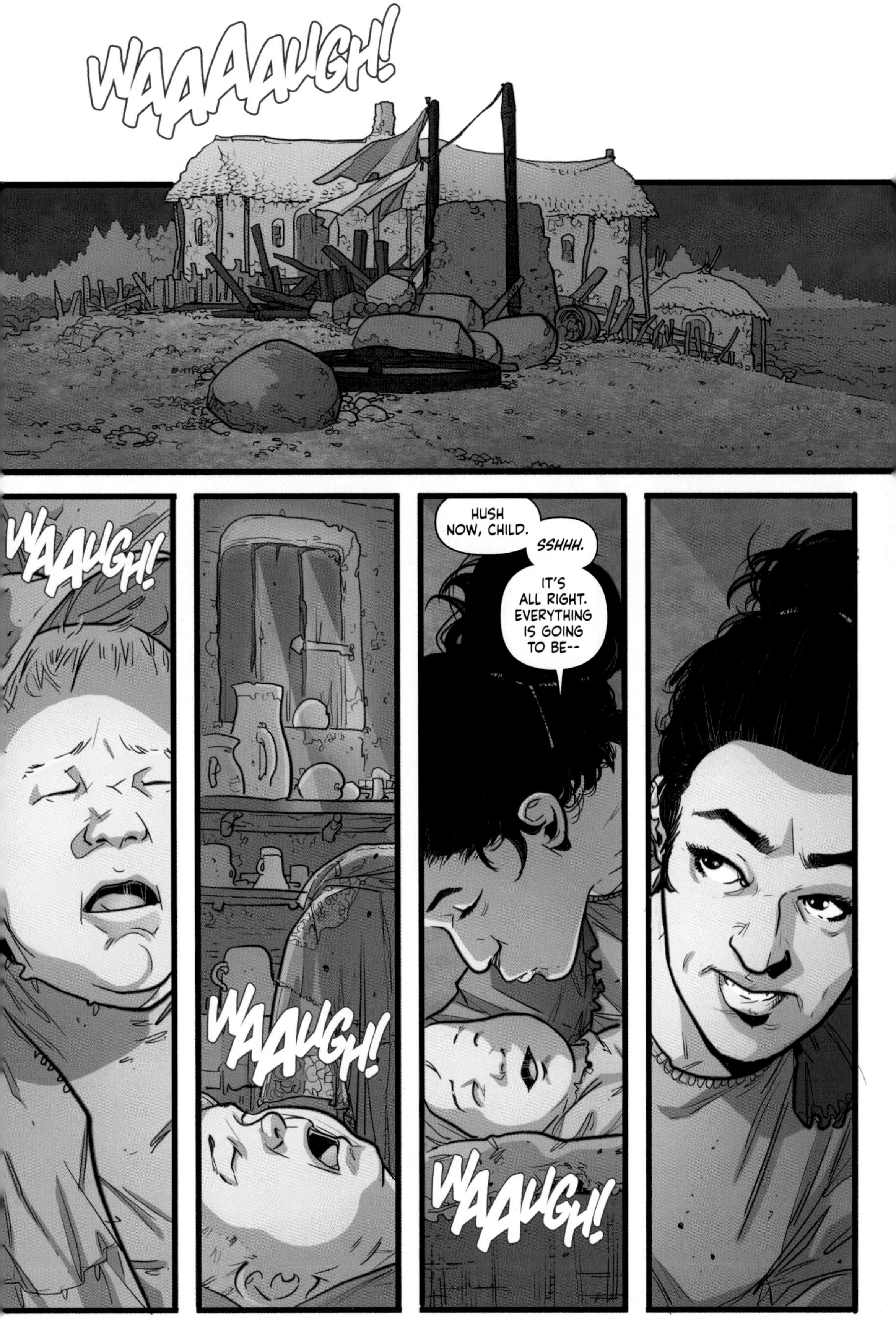
WAAAAAUGH!
WAAUGH!
WAAUGH!
HUSH NOW, CHILD.
SSHHH.
IT'S ALL RIGHT. EVERYTHING IS GOING TO BE--
WAAUGH!

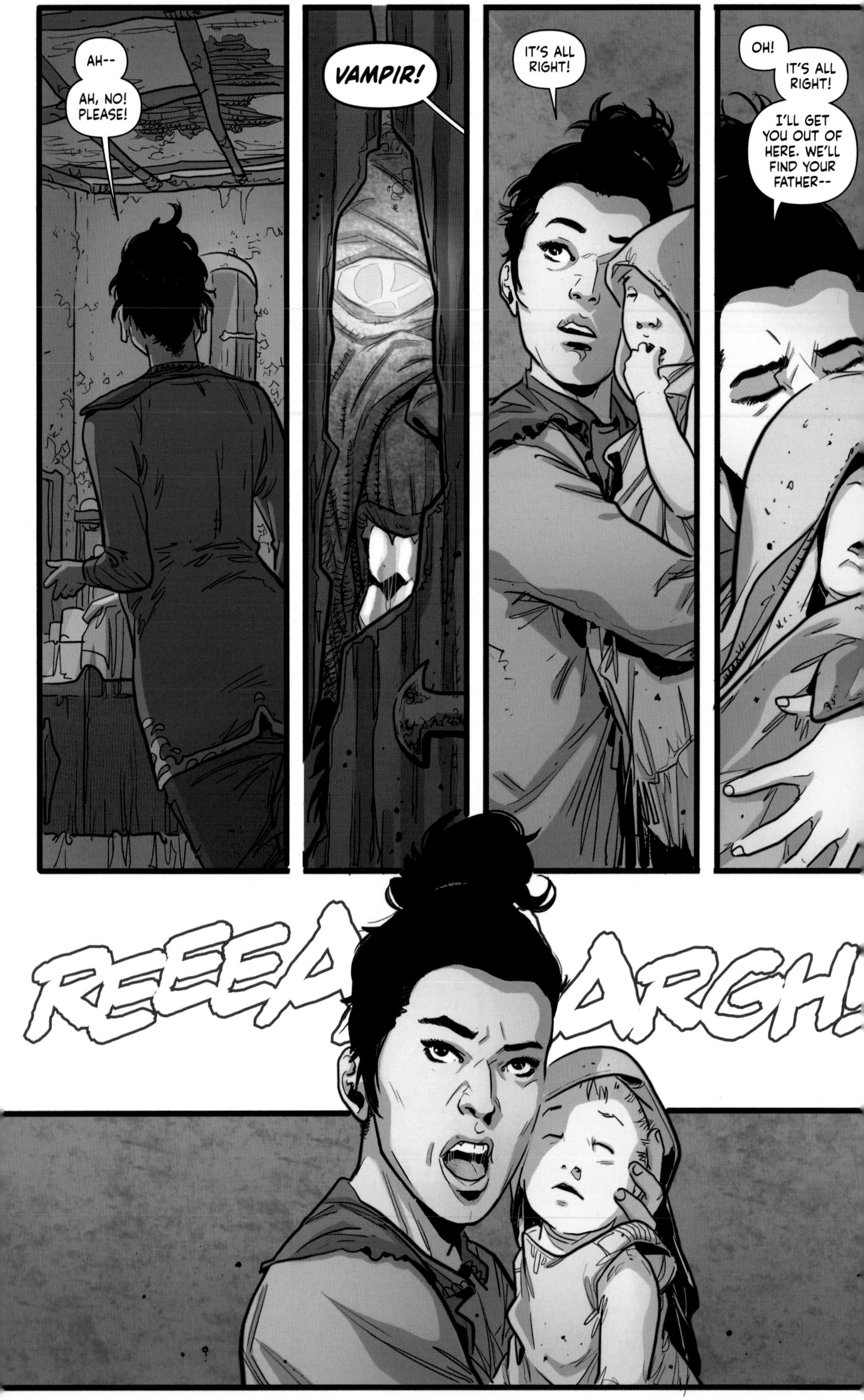
AH--
AH, NO! PLEASE!
VAMPIR!
IT'S ALL RIGHT!
OH!
IT'S ALL RIGHT!
I'LL GET YOU OUT OF HERE. WE'LL FIND YOUR FATHER--
REEEA ARGH!

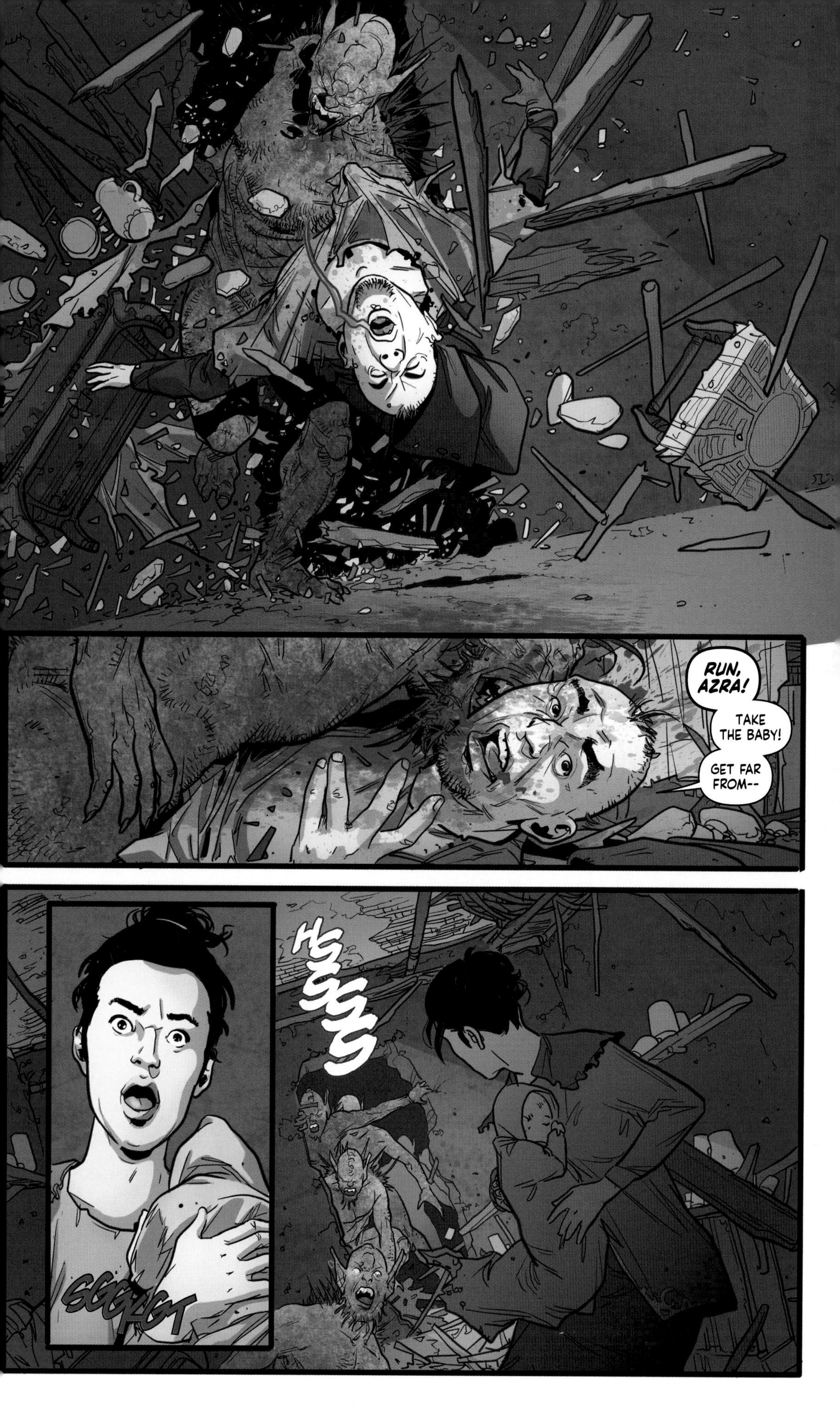
RUN, AZRA!
TAKE THE BABY!
GET FAR FROM--
HSSSS

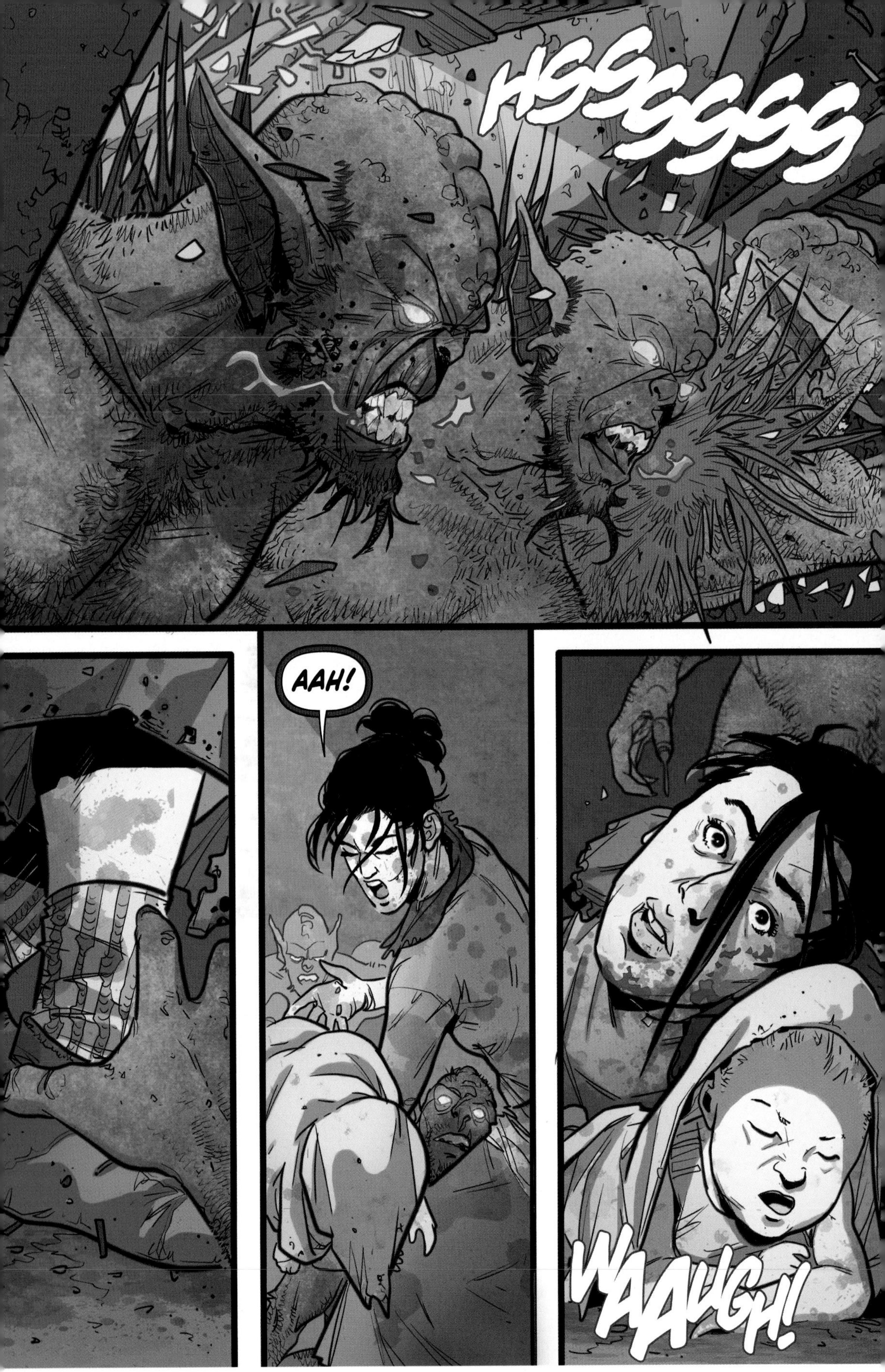
HSSSSSSS
AAH!
WAAUGH!

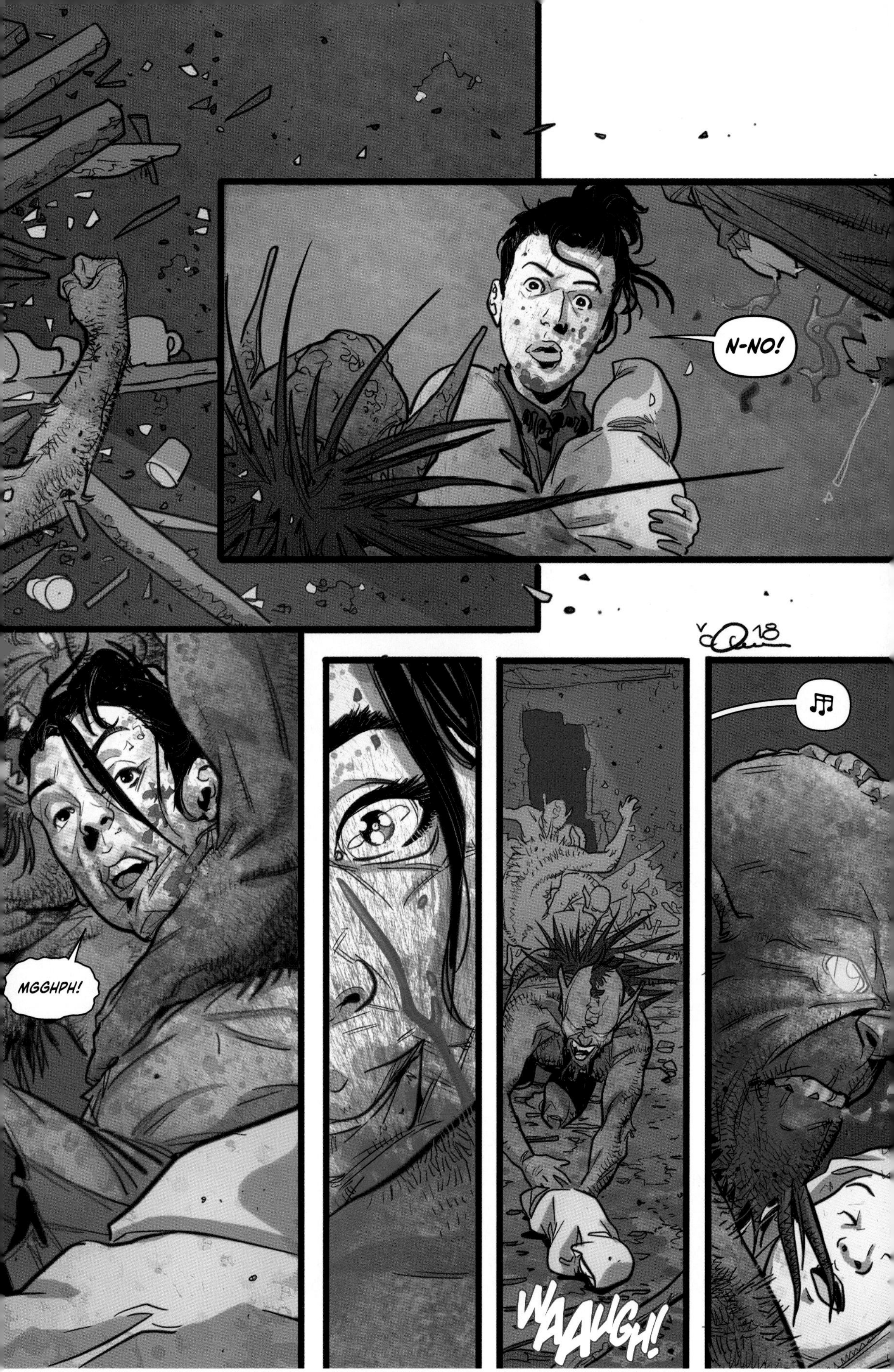
N-NO!
MGGHPH!
♬
WAAUGH!

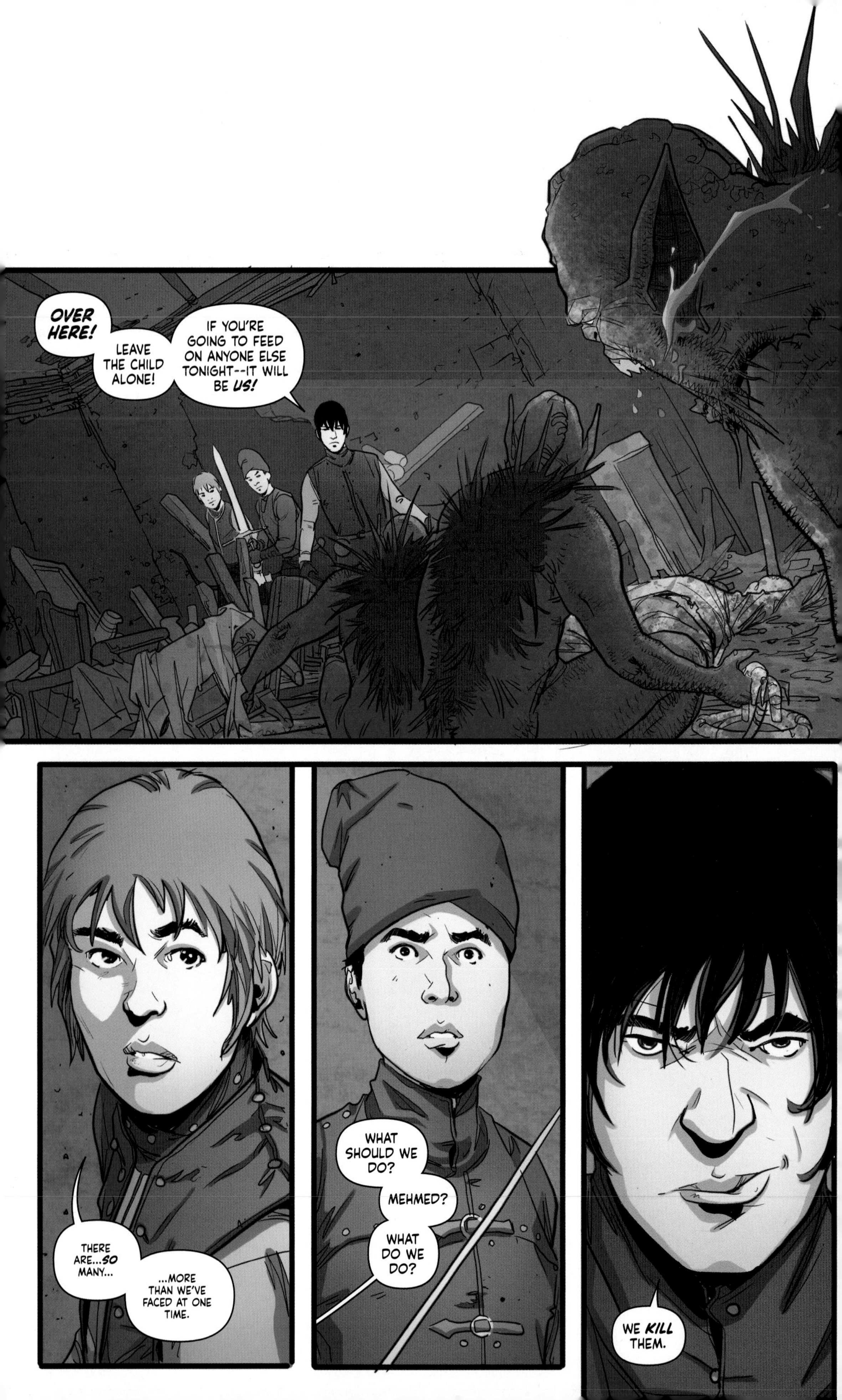
OVER HERE!
LEAVE THE CHILD ALONE!
IF YOU'RE GOING TO FEED ON ANYONE ELSE TONIGHT--IT WILL BE US!
THERE ARE...SO MANY...
...MORE THAN WE'VE FACED AT ONE TIME.
WHAT SHOULD WE DO?
MEHMED?
WHAT DO WE DO?
WE KILL THEM.

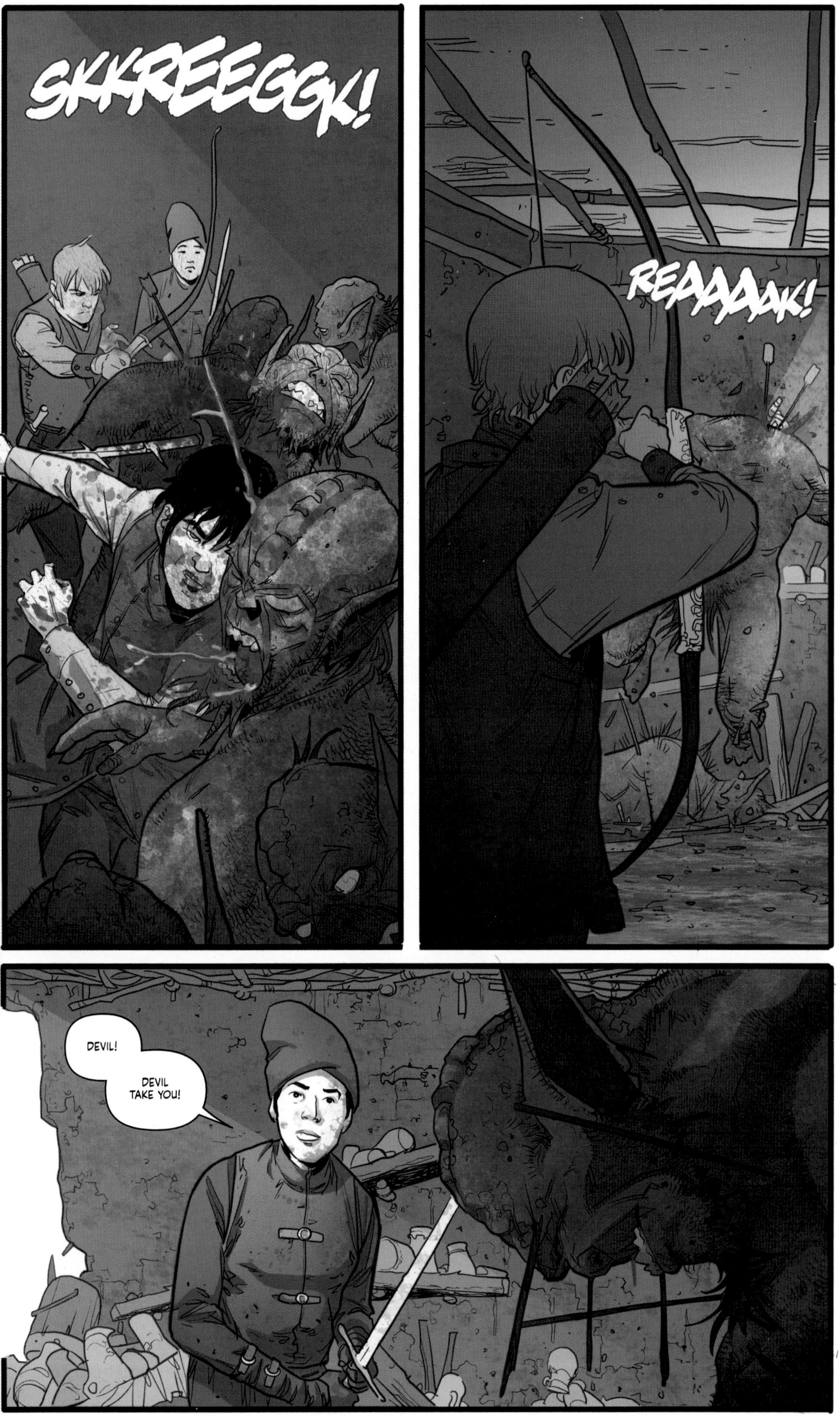
SKKREEGGK!
REAAAAK!
DEVIL!
DEVIL TAKE YOU!

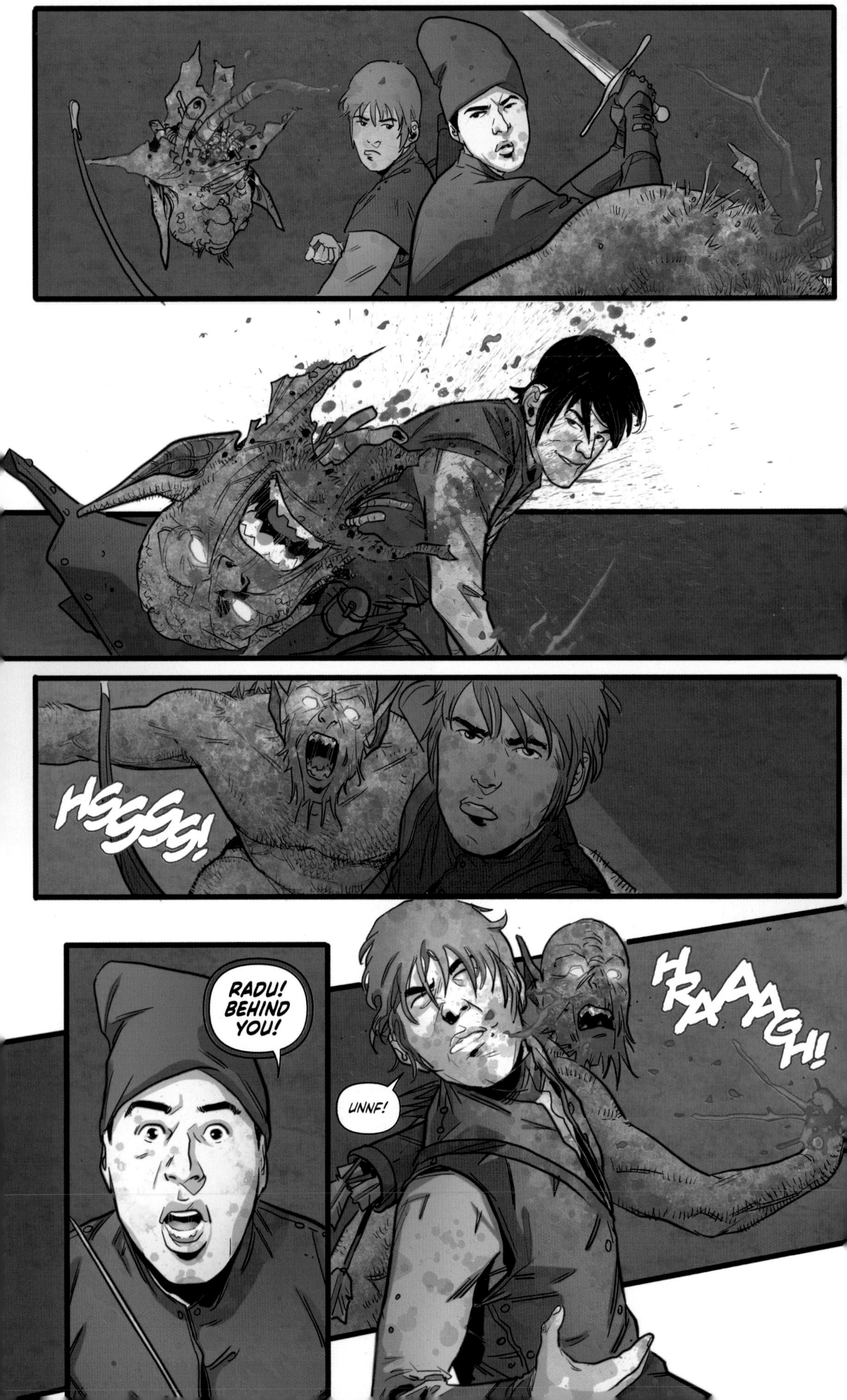
HSSSS!
RADU! BEHIND YOU!
UNNF!
HRAAAGH!

NNN--

NO!

RADU!

NO!

MEHMED!

HELP HIM!

HELP MY BROTHER!

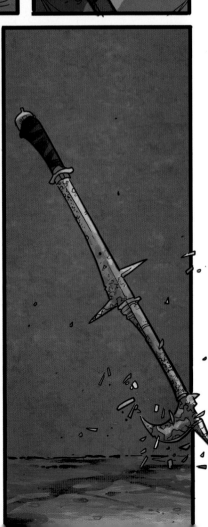

SKREEEOORGH!

REEEEE--

YAAAGH!

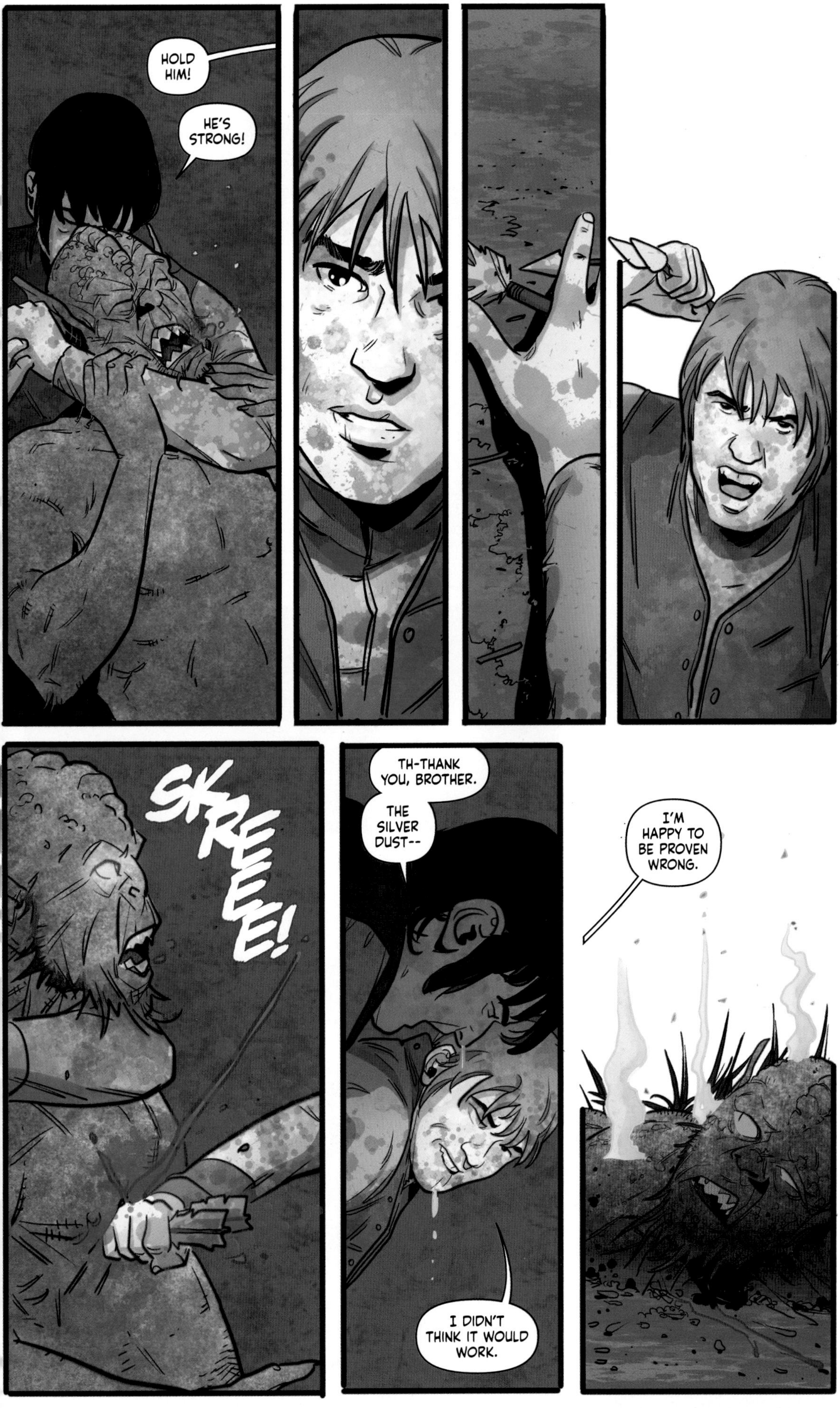
HOLD HIM!
HE'S STRONG!
SKREEEE!
TH-THANK YOU, BROTHER.
THE SILVER DUST--
I DIDN'T THINK IT WOULD WORK.
I'M HAPPY TO BE PROVEN WRONG.

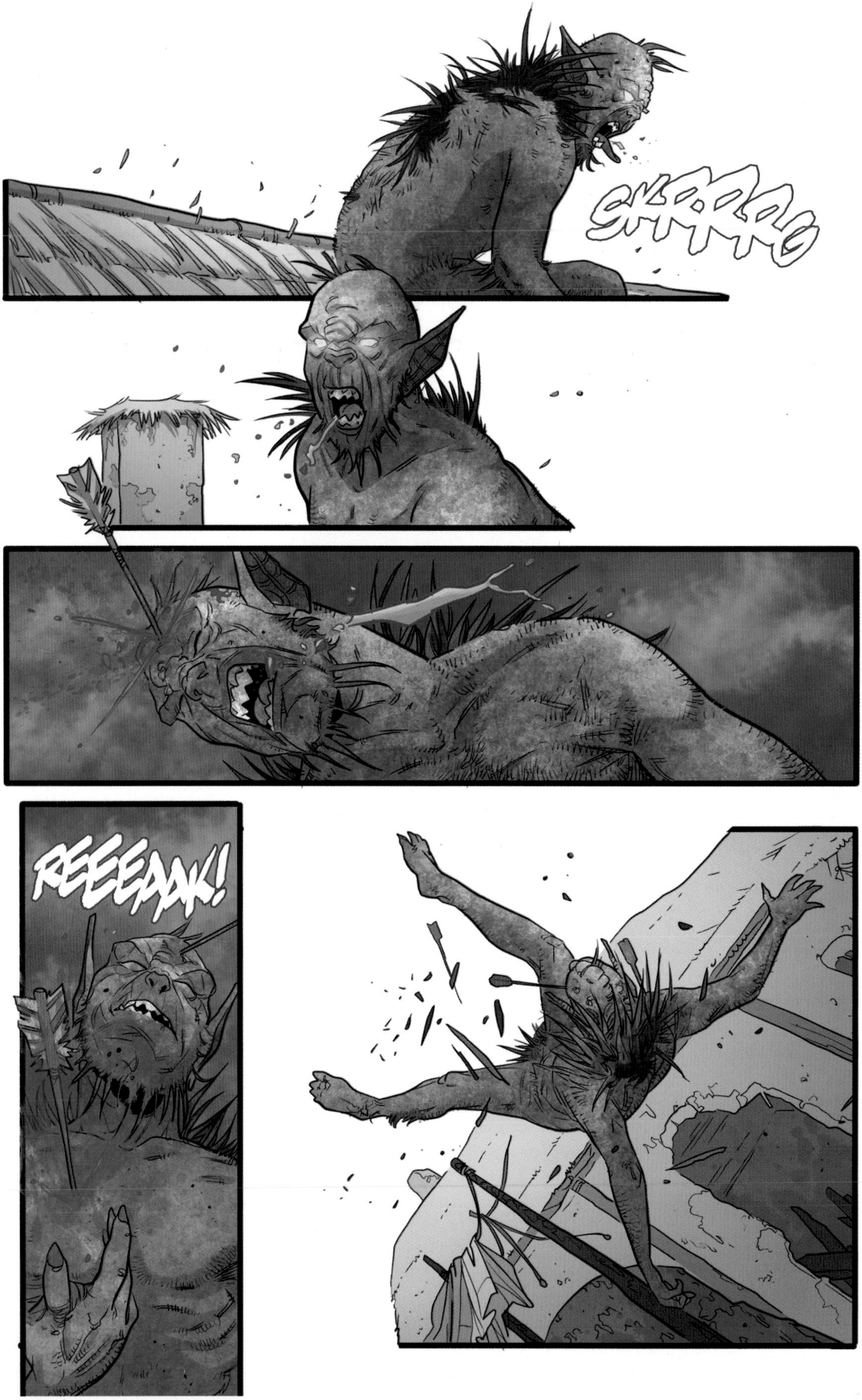
SKRRRG
REEEAAK!

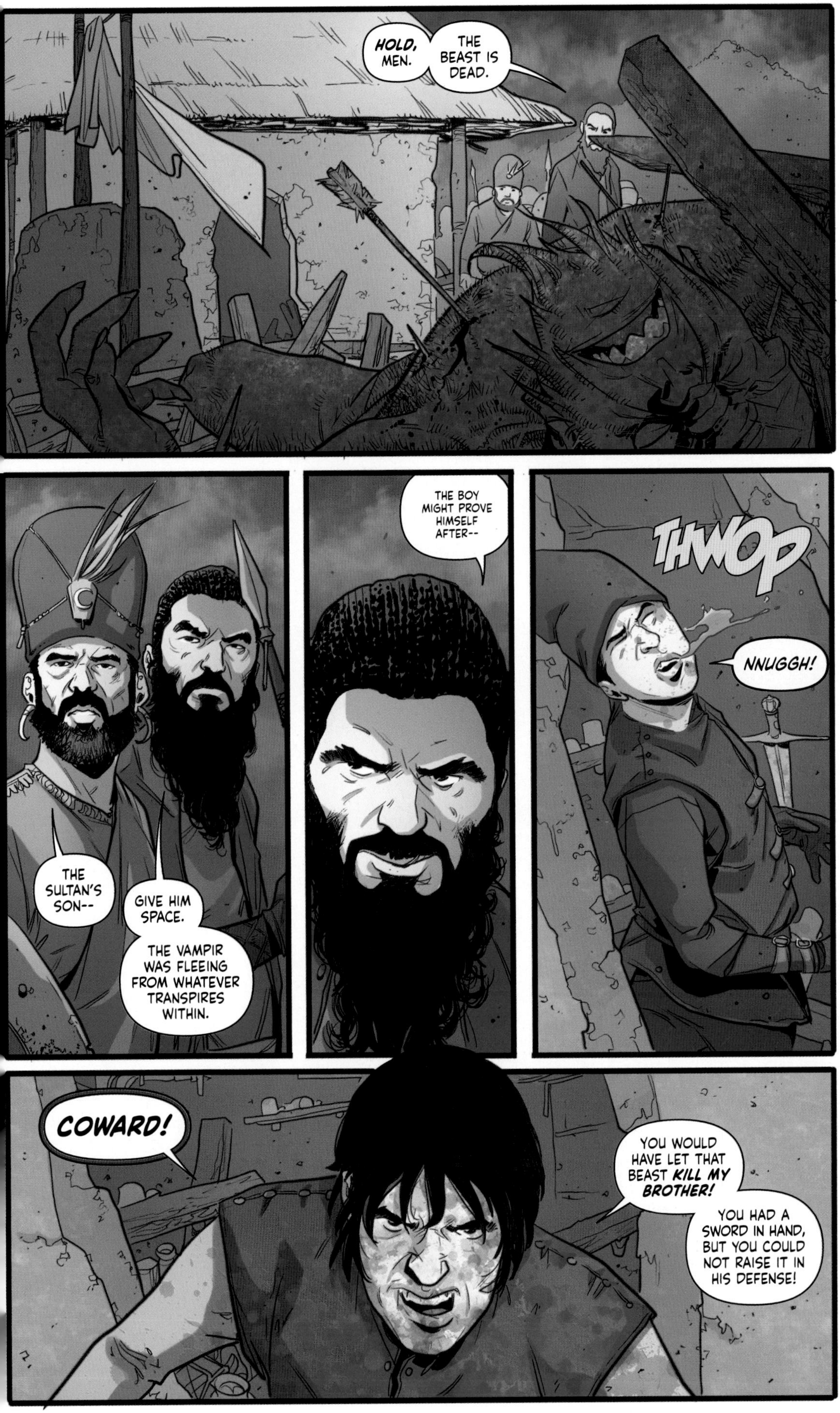

HOLD, MEN.
THE BEAST IS DEAD.
THE SULTAN'S SON--
GIVE HIM SPACE.
THE VAMPIR WAS FLEEING FROM WHATEVER TRANSPIRES WITHIN.
THE BOY MIGHT PROVE HIMSELF AFTER--
THWOP
NNUGGH!
COWARD!
YOU WOULD HAVE LET THAT BEAST KILL MY BROTHER!
YOU HAD A SWORD IN HAND, BUT YOU COULD NOT RAISE IT IN HIS DEFENSE!

YOU AND YOUR BROTHER ARE MY SHIELD MEN.

YOU PROTECT *ME*.

IT'S NOT THE OTHER WAY AROUND.

I'LL FEED YOU TO THOSE THINGS BEFORE I--

STAND DOWN, VLAD.

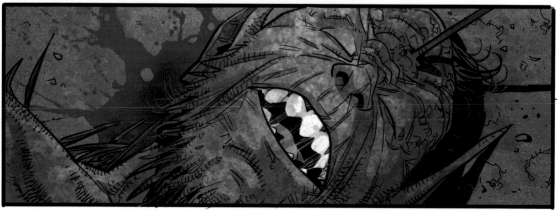

I COULD HAVE YOU THROWN BACK INTO A CELL, VLAD.

YOU AND YOUR BROTHER BOTH.

DO THAT--AND WHO WILL WATCH YOUR BACK WHILE YOU'RE PISSING YOURSELF?

A SURVIVOR!

BEST TO LEAVE THE CHILD, RADU.

WE HAVE A LONG TREK BACK TO EGRIGÖZ.

AND, BESIDES, WHO WILL CARE FOR THE CHILD ONCE WE GET THERE?

I'LL NOT--

--YOU CAN'T JUST LEAVE A *BABY* HERE TO *DIE!*

THERE ARE WOMEN BACK AT THE FORTRESS WHO WILL LOOK AFTER HIM...AND IF NOT THEM--

EVEN IF SOMEONE DOES CARE FOR THE BABY, HE'LL PROBABLY GROW UP TO BE USED AS FODDER FOR THE VAMPIR.

THE MERCIFUL THING TO DO WOULD BE TO DASH ITS HEAD AGAINST A ROCK.

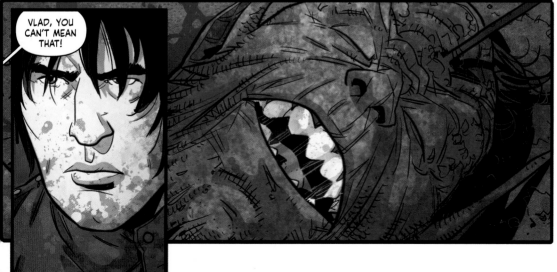

VLAD, YOU CAN'T MEAN THAT!

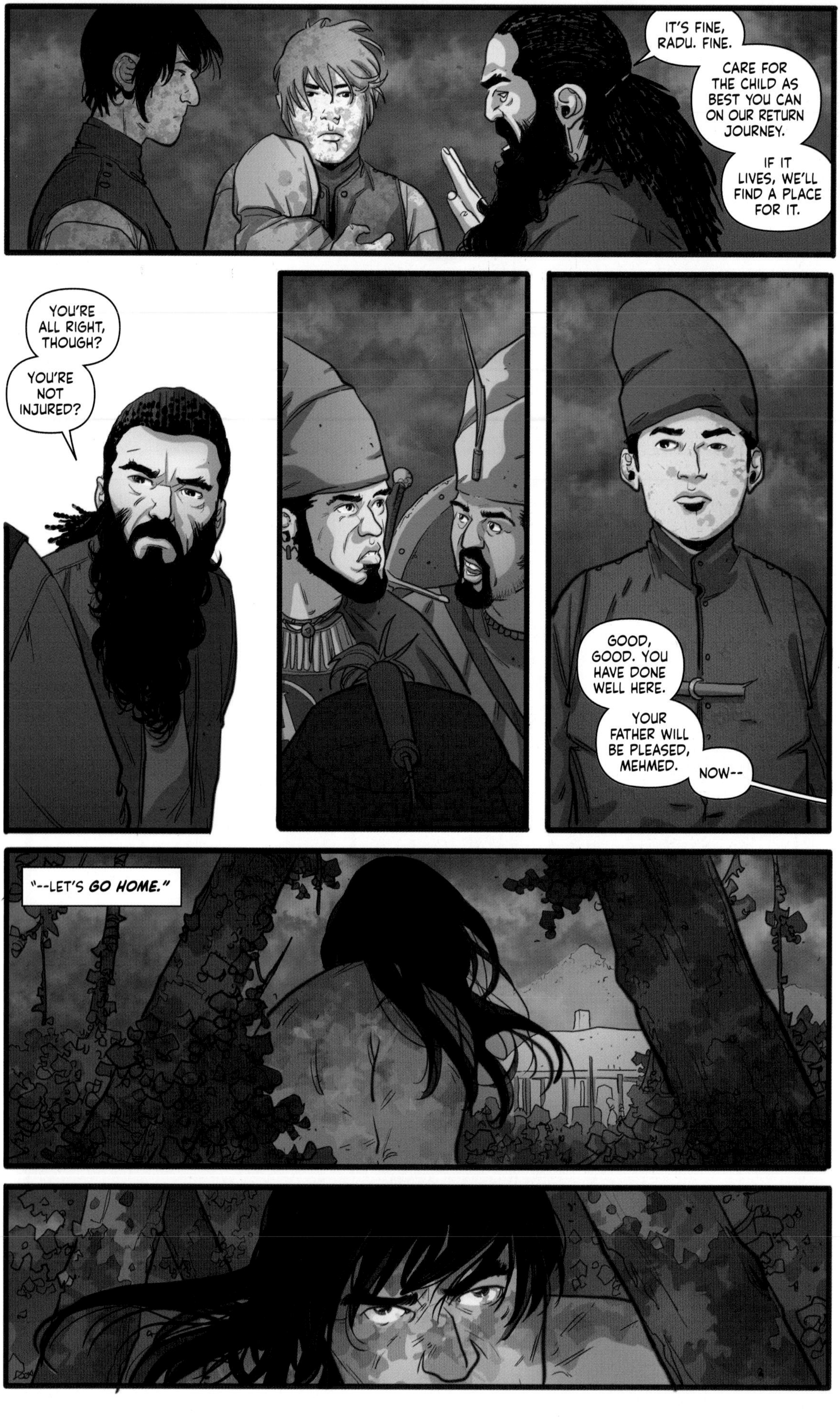
IT'S FINE, RADU. FINE.
CARE FOR THE CHILD AS BEST YOU CAN ON OUR RETURN JOURNEY.
IF IT LIVES, WE'LL FIND A PLACE FOR IT.
YOU'RE ALL RIGHT, THOUGH?
YOU'RE NOT INJURED?
GOOD, GOOD. YOU HAVE DONE WELL HERE.
YOUR FATHER WILL BE PLEASED, MEHMED.
NOW--
"--LET'S GO HOME."

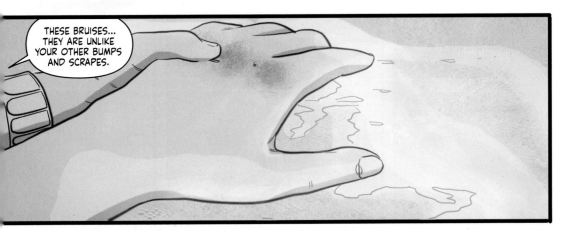

THESE BRUISES... THEY ARE UNLIKE YOUR OTHER BUMPS AND SCRAPES.

WERE YOU PUNCHING VAMPIR?

IT IS ALL A BLUR.

IT IS DIFFICULT TO RECALL.

I'D BET MEHMED RECALLS QUITE CLEARLY.

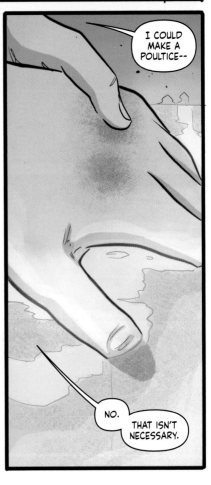

I COULD MAKE A POULTICE--

NO.

THAT ISN'T NECESSARY.

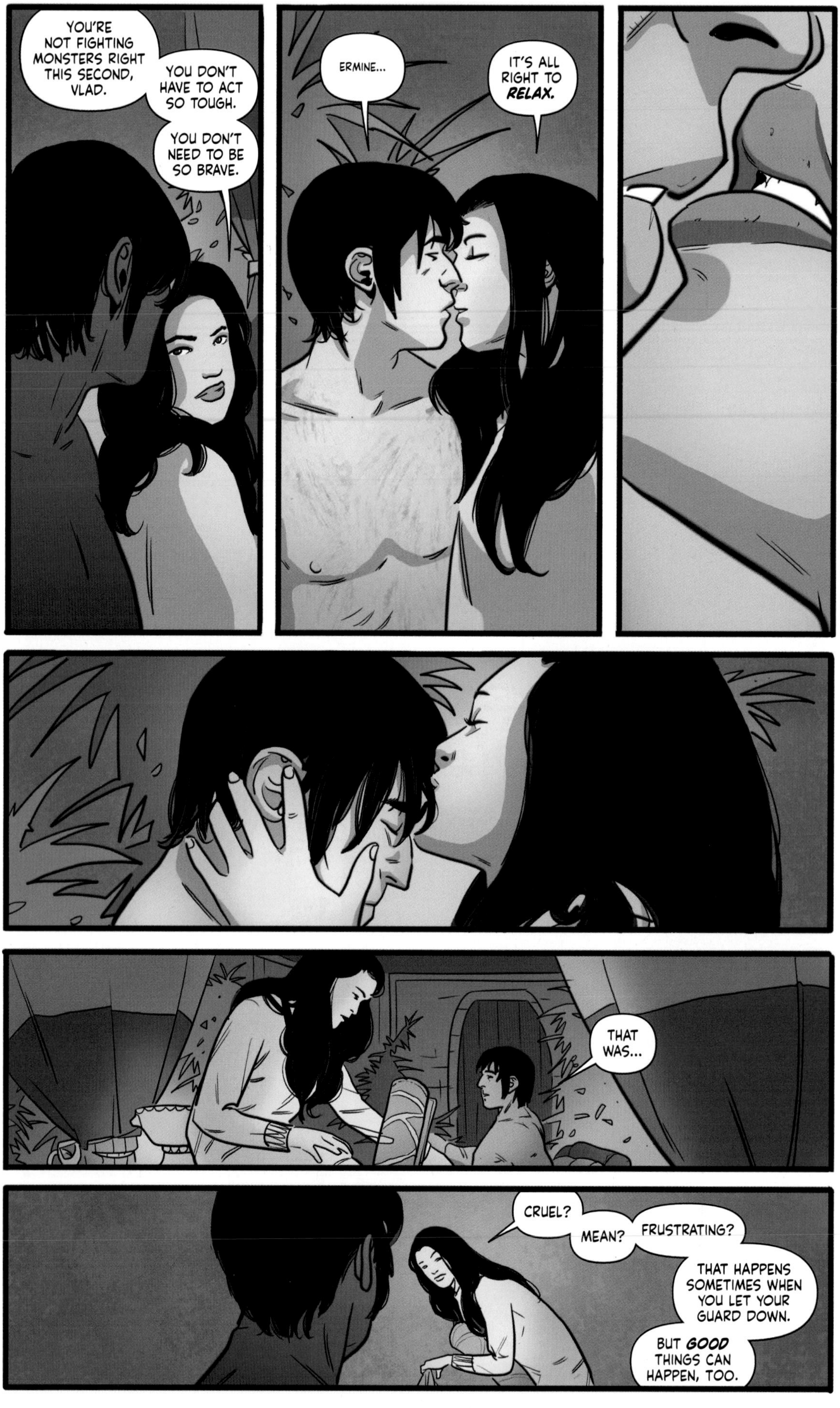
YOU'RE NOT FIGHTING MONSTERS RIGHT THIS SECOND, VLAD.
YOU DON'T HAVE TO ACT SO TOUGH.
YOU DON'T NEED TO BE SO BRAVE.
ERMINE...
IT'S ALL RIGHT TO RELAX.
THAT WAS...
CRUEL?
MEAN?
FRUSTRATING?
THAT HAPPENS SOMETIMES WHEN YOU LET YOUR GUARD DOWN.
BUT GOOD THINGS CAN HAPPEN, TOO.

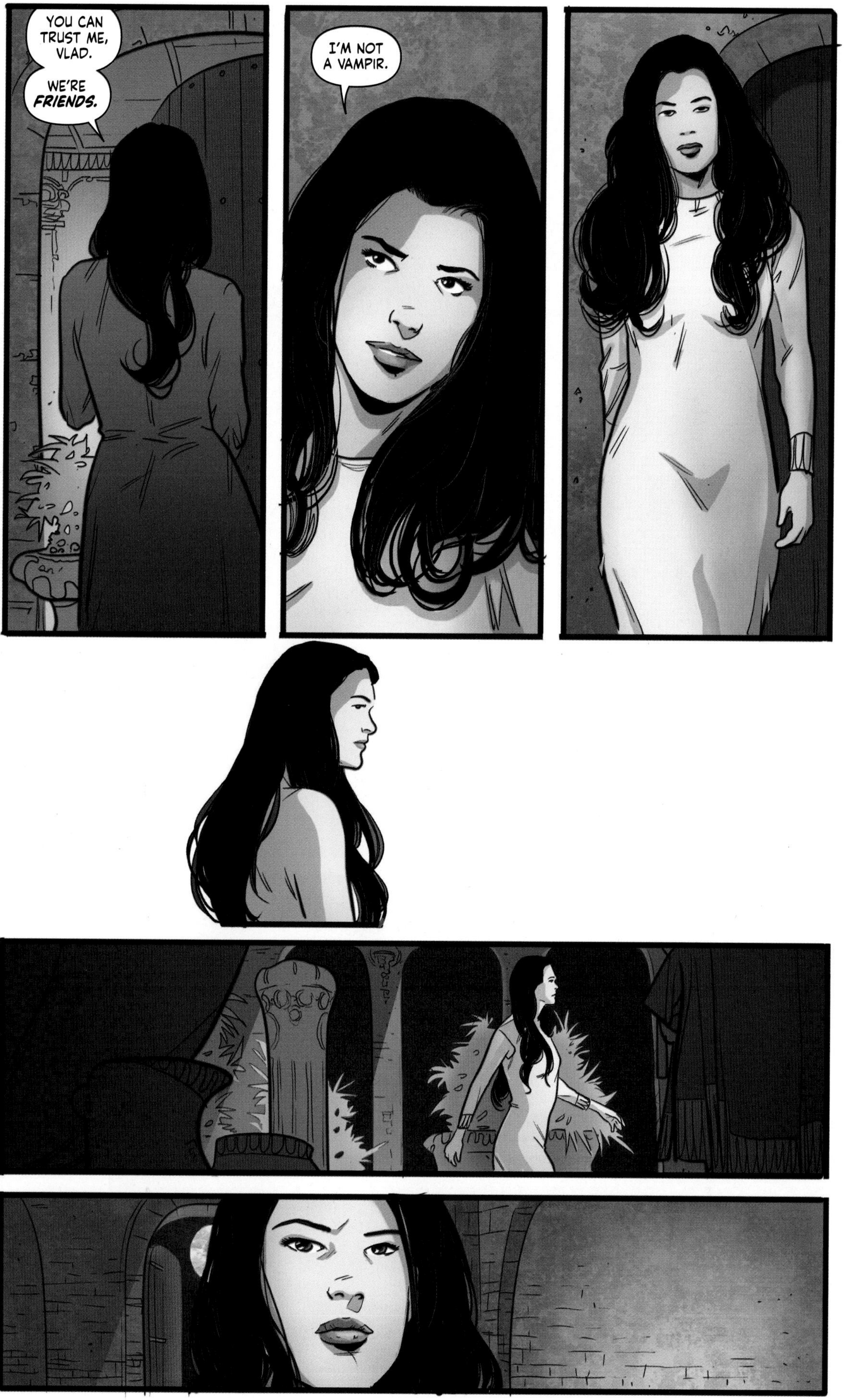
YOU CAN TRUST ME, VLAD.
WE'RE FRIENDS.
I'M NOT A VAMPIR.

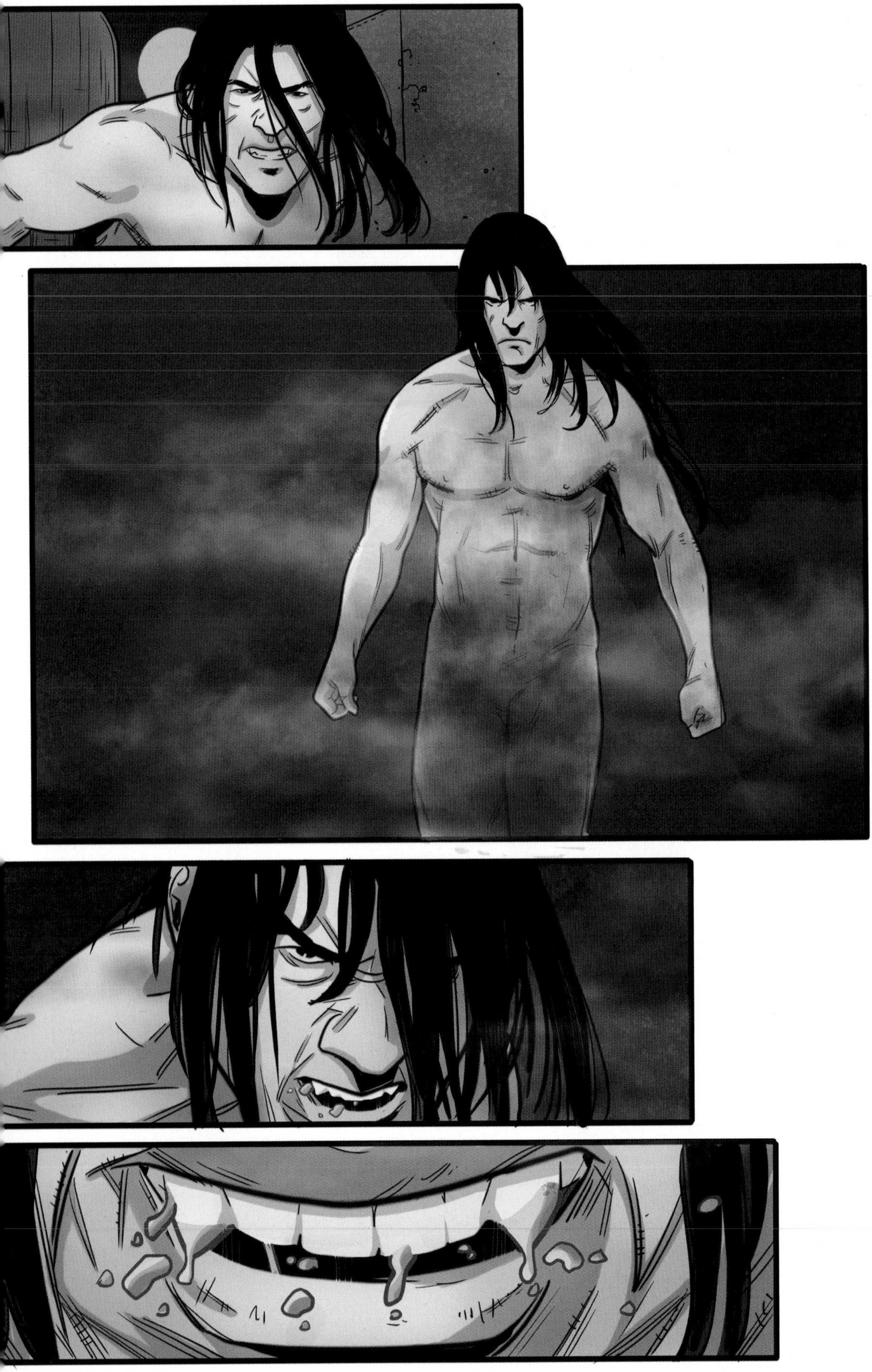

4

THE MISSING

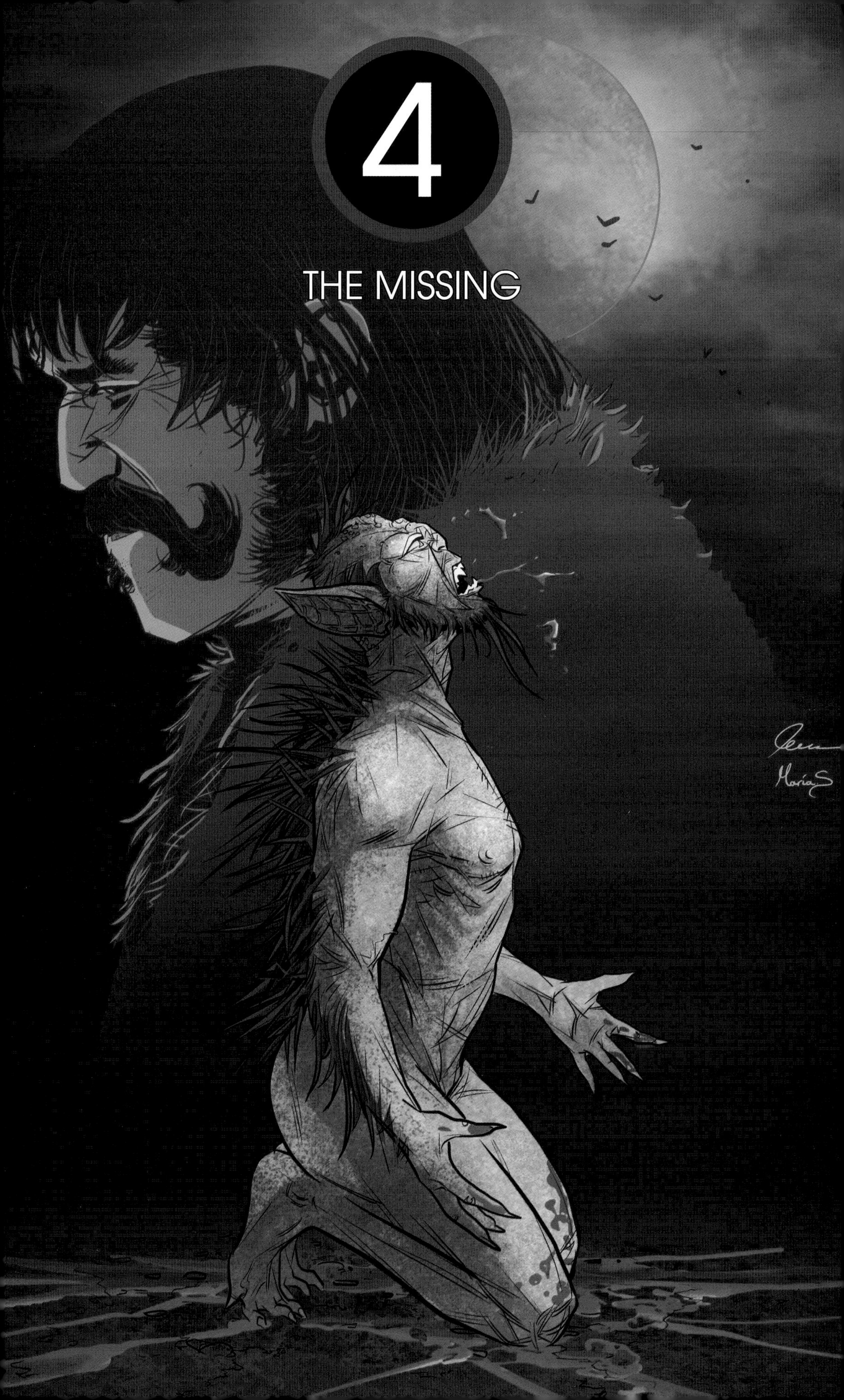

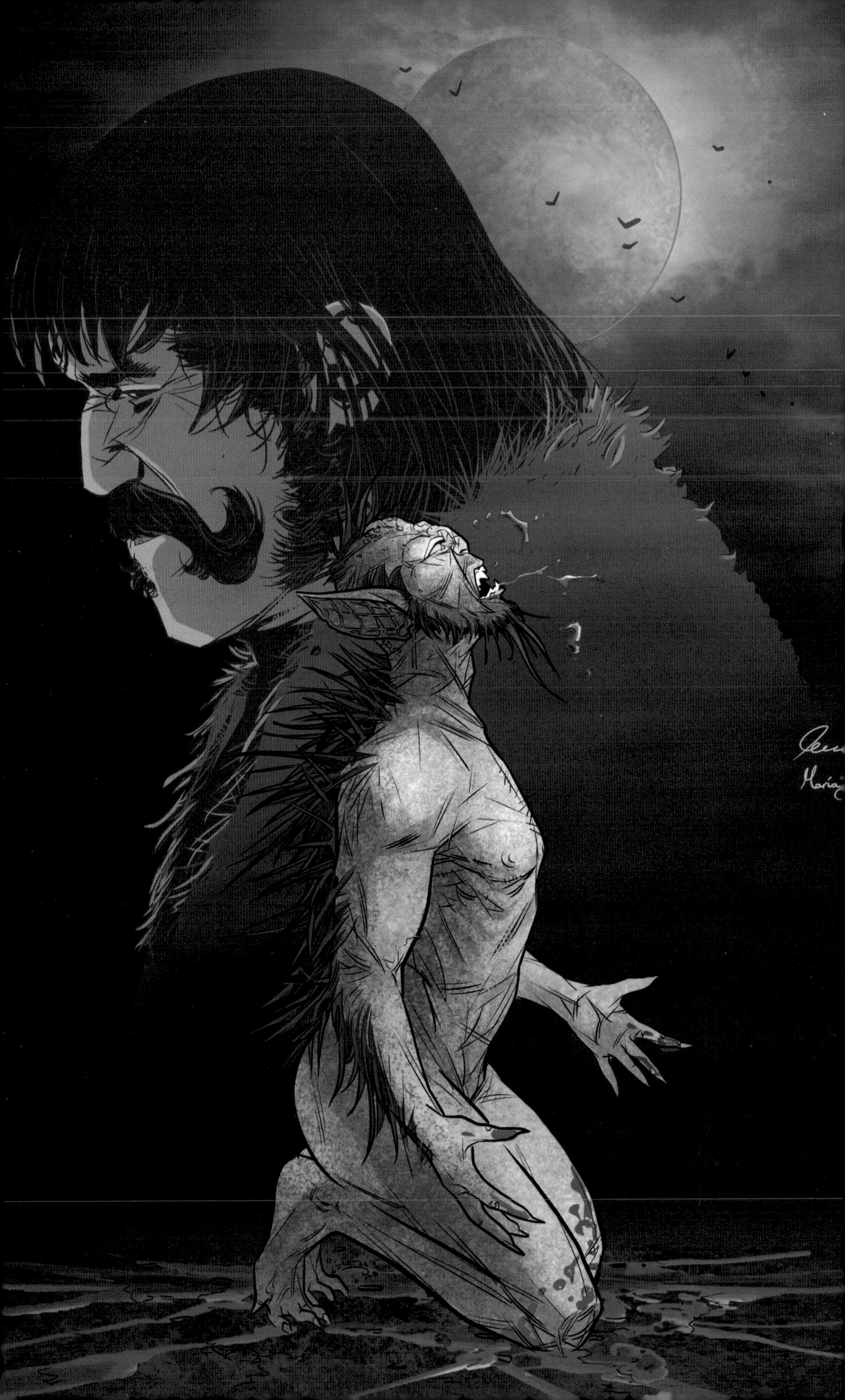

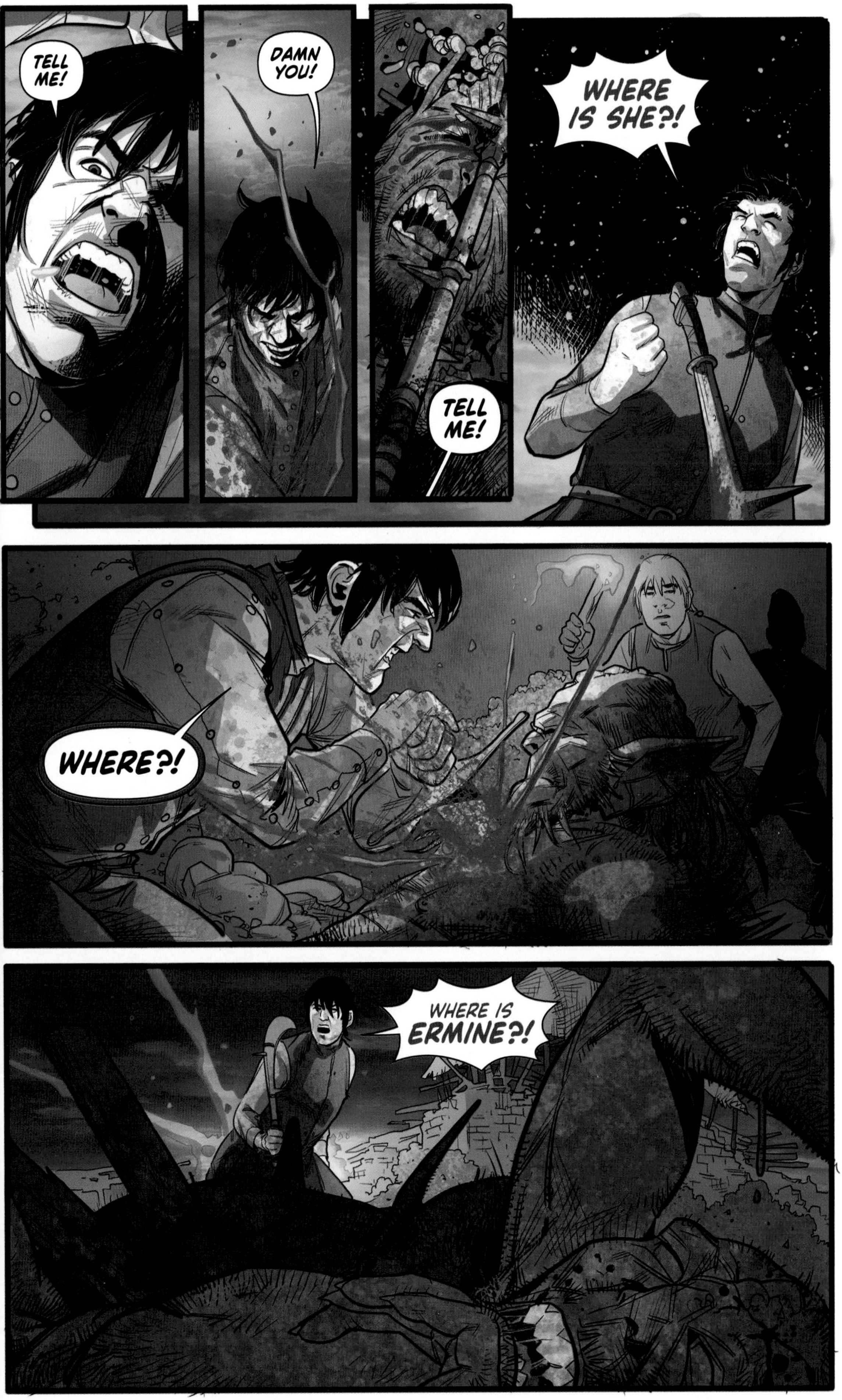
TELL ME!
DAMN YOU!
TELL ME!
WHERE IS SHE?!
WHERE?!
WHERE IS ERMINE?!

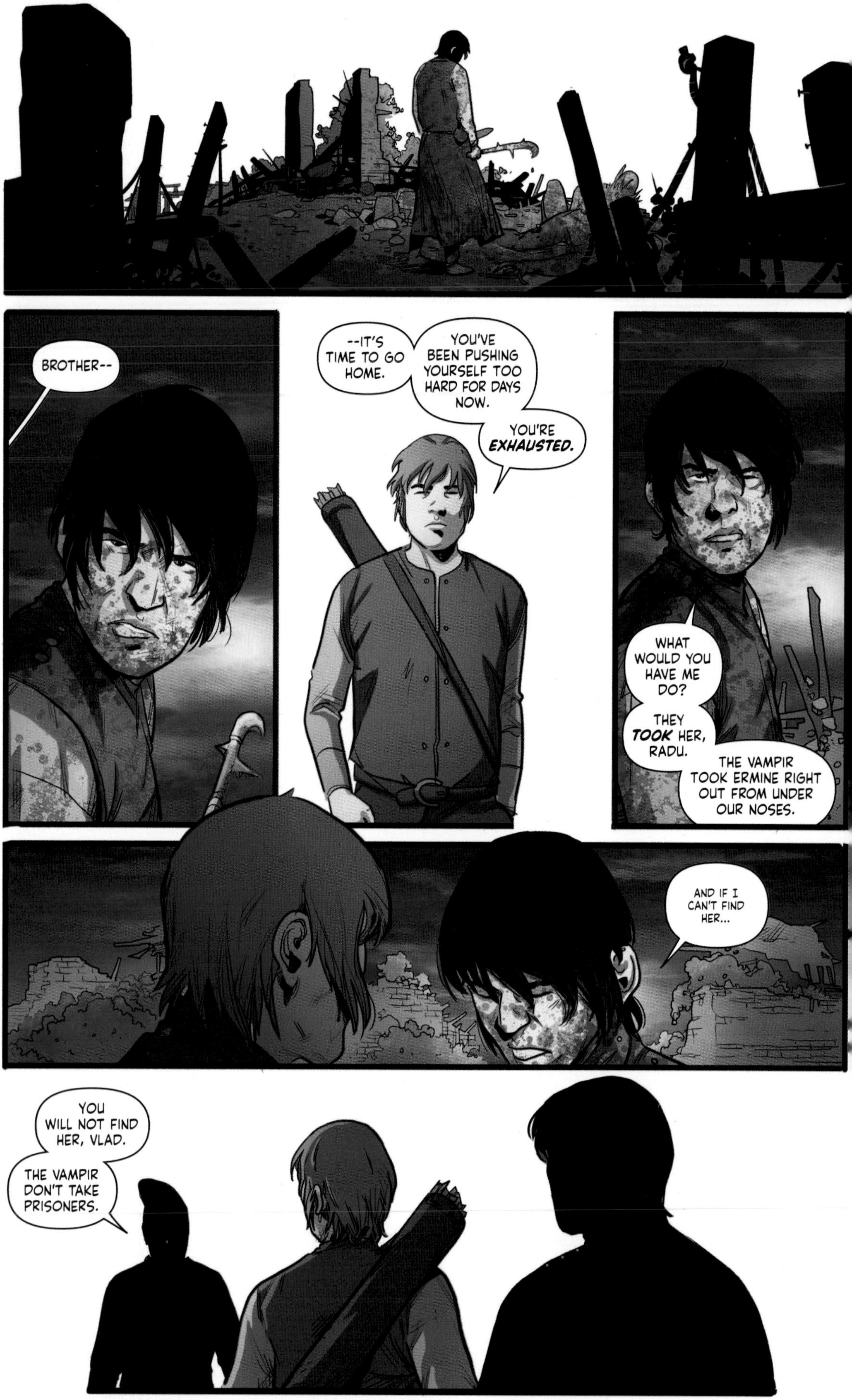
BROTHER--
--IT'S TIME TO GO HOME.
YOU'VE BEEN PUSHING YOURSELF TOO HARD FOR DAYS NOW.
YOU'RE *EXHAUSTED.*
WHAT WOULD YOU HAVE ME DO?
THEY *TOOK* HER, RADU.
THE VAMPIR TOOK ERMINE RIGHT OUT FROM UNDER OUR NOSES.
AND IF I CAN'T FIND HER...
YOU WILL NOT FIND HER, VLAD.
THE VAMPIR DON'T TAKE PRISONERS.

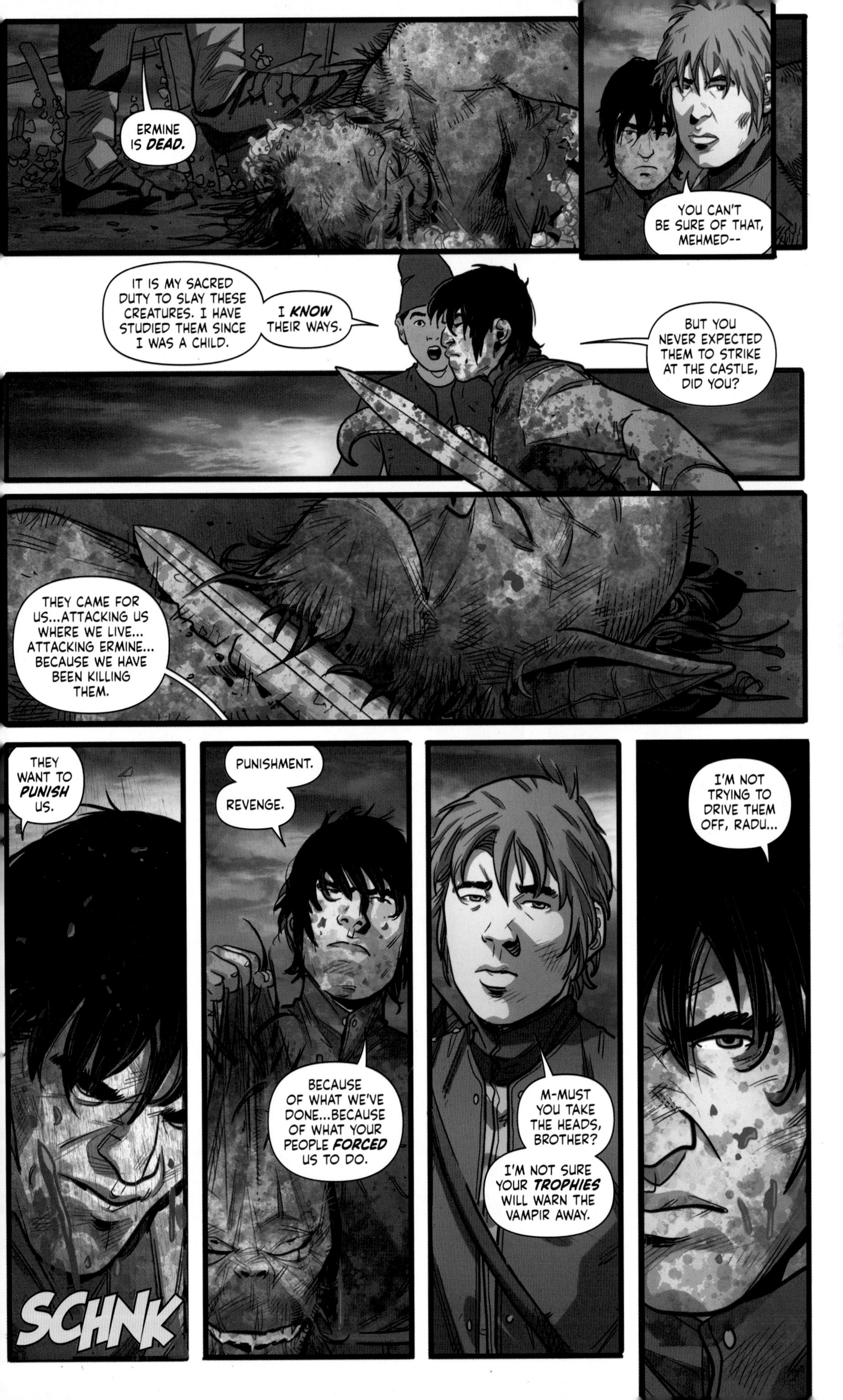

ERMINE IS *DEAD.*
YOU CAN'T BE SURE OF THAT, MEHMED--
IT IS MY SACRED DUTY TO SLAY THESE CREATURES. I HAVE STUDIED THEM SINCE I WAS A CHILD.
I *KNOW* THEIR WAYS.
BUT YOU NEVER EXPECTED THEM TO STRIKE AT THE CASTLE, DID YOU?
THEY CAME FOR US...ATTACKING US WHERE WE LIVE... ATTACKING ERMINE... BECAUSE WE HAVE BEEN KILLING THEM.
THEY WANT TO *PUNISH* US.
SCHNK
PUNISHMENT.
REVENGE.
BECAUSE OF WHAT WE'VE DONE...BECAUSE OF WHAT YOUR PEOPLE *FORCED* US TO DO.
M-MUST YOU TAKE THE HEADS, BROTHER?
I'M NOT SURE YOUR *TROPHIES* WILL WARN THE VAMPIR AWAY.
I'M NOT TRYING TO DRIVE THEM OFF, RADU...

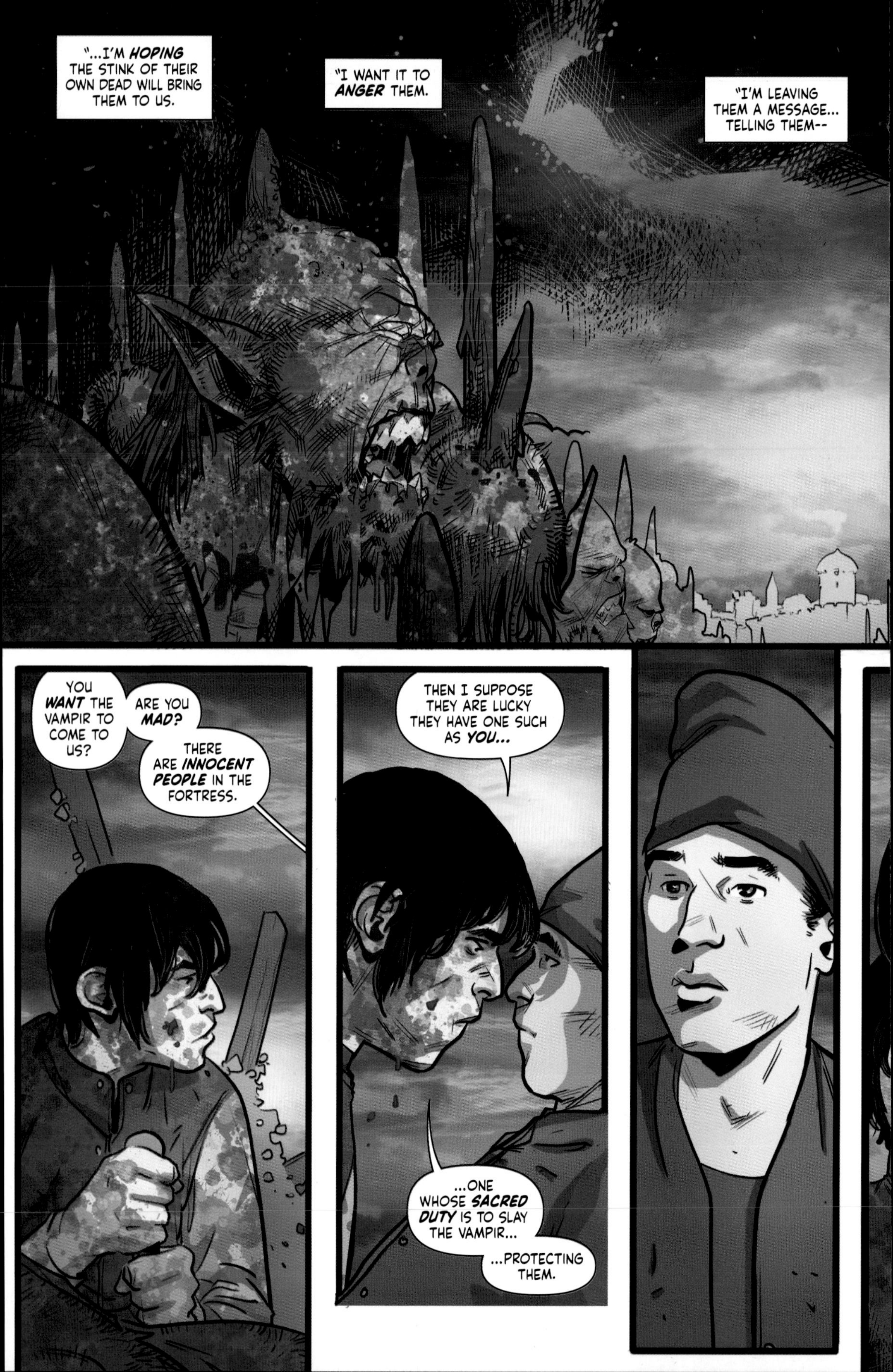
"...I'M HOPING THE STINK OF THEIR OWN DEAD WILL BRING THEM TO US.
"I WANT IT TO ANGER THEM.
"I'M LEAVING THEM A MESSAGE... TELLING THEM--
YOU WANT THE VAMPIR TO COME TO US?
ARE YOU MAD?
THERE ARE INNOCENT PEOPLE IN THE FORTRESS.
THEN I SUPPOSE THEY ARE LUCKY THEY HAVE ONE SUCH AS YOU...
...ONE WHOSE SACRED DUTY IS TO SLAY THE VAMPIR...
...PROTECTING THEM.

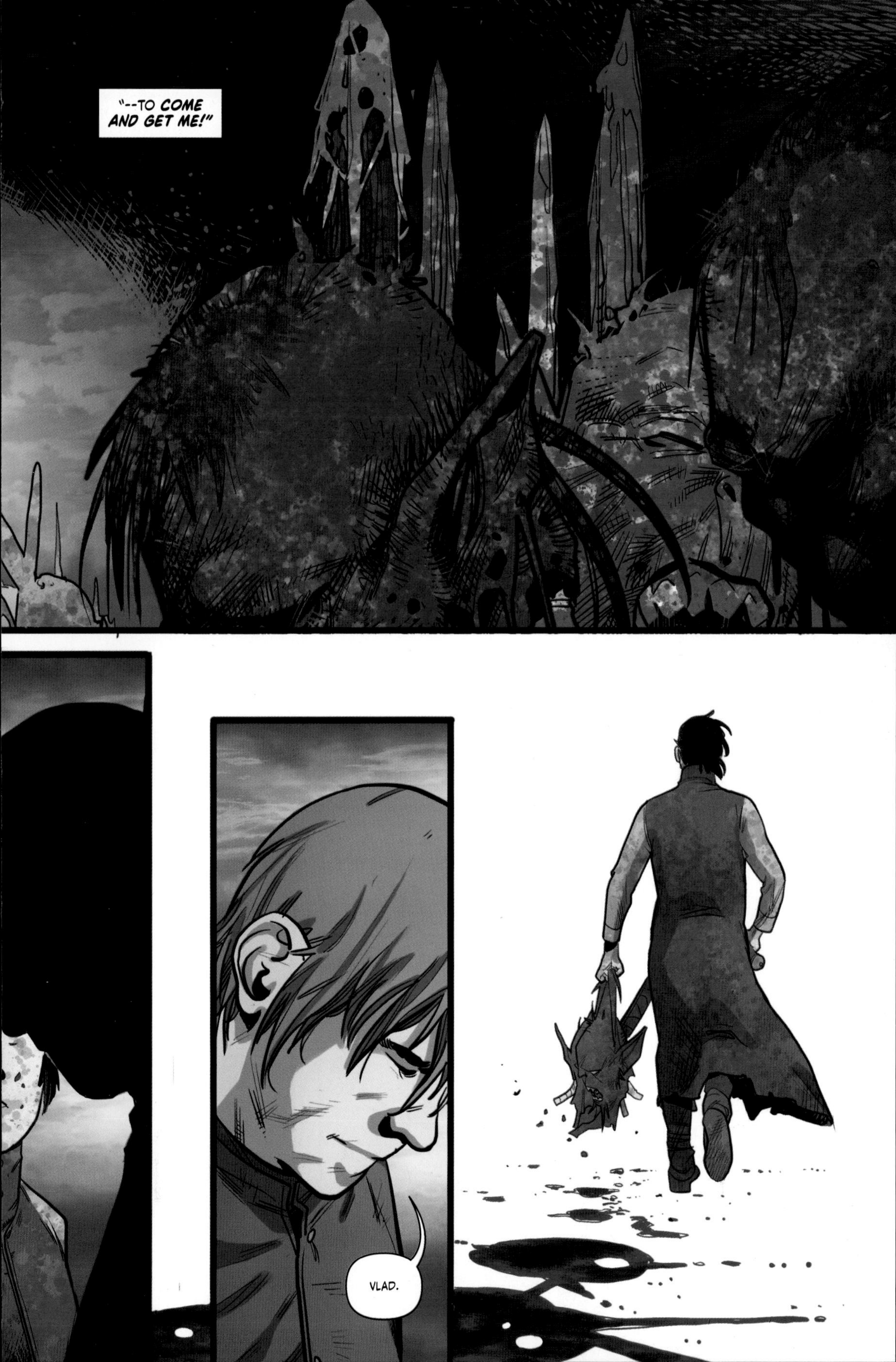
"--TO COME AND GET ME!"
VLAD.

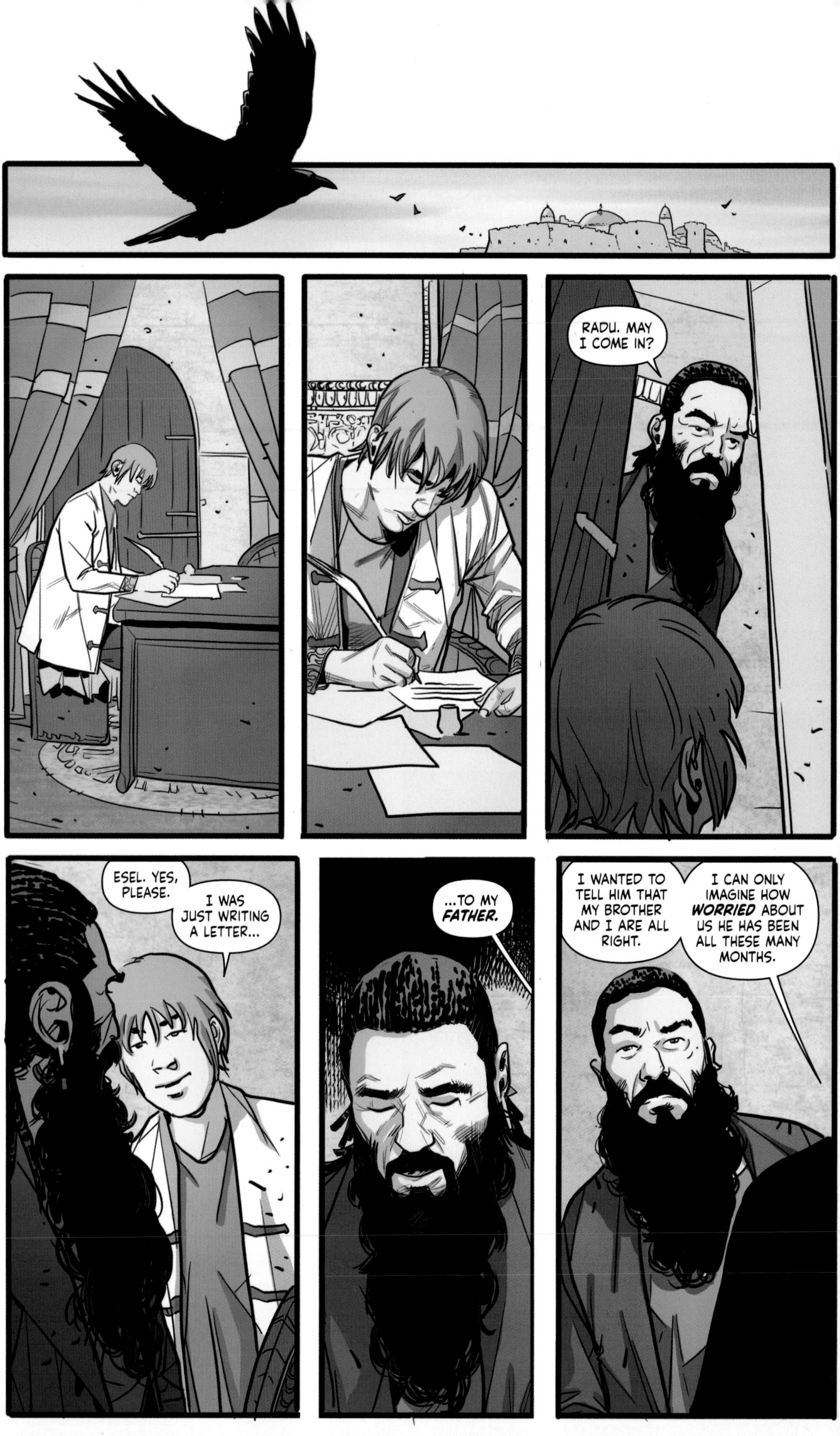
RADU. MAY I COME IN?
ESEL. YES, PLEASE.
I WAS JUST WRITING A LETTER...
...TO MY FATHER.
I WANTED TO TELL HIM THAT MY BROTHER AND I ARE ALL RIGHT.
I CAN ONLY IMAGINE HOW WORRIED ABOUT US HE HAS BEEN ALL THESE MANY MONTHS.

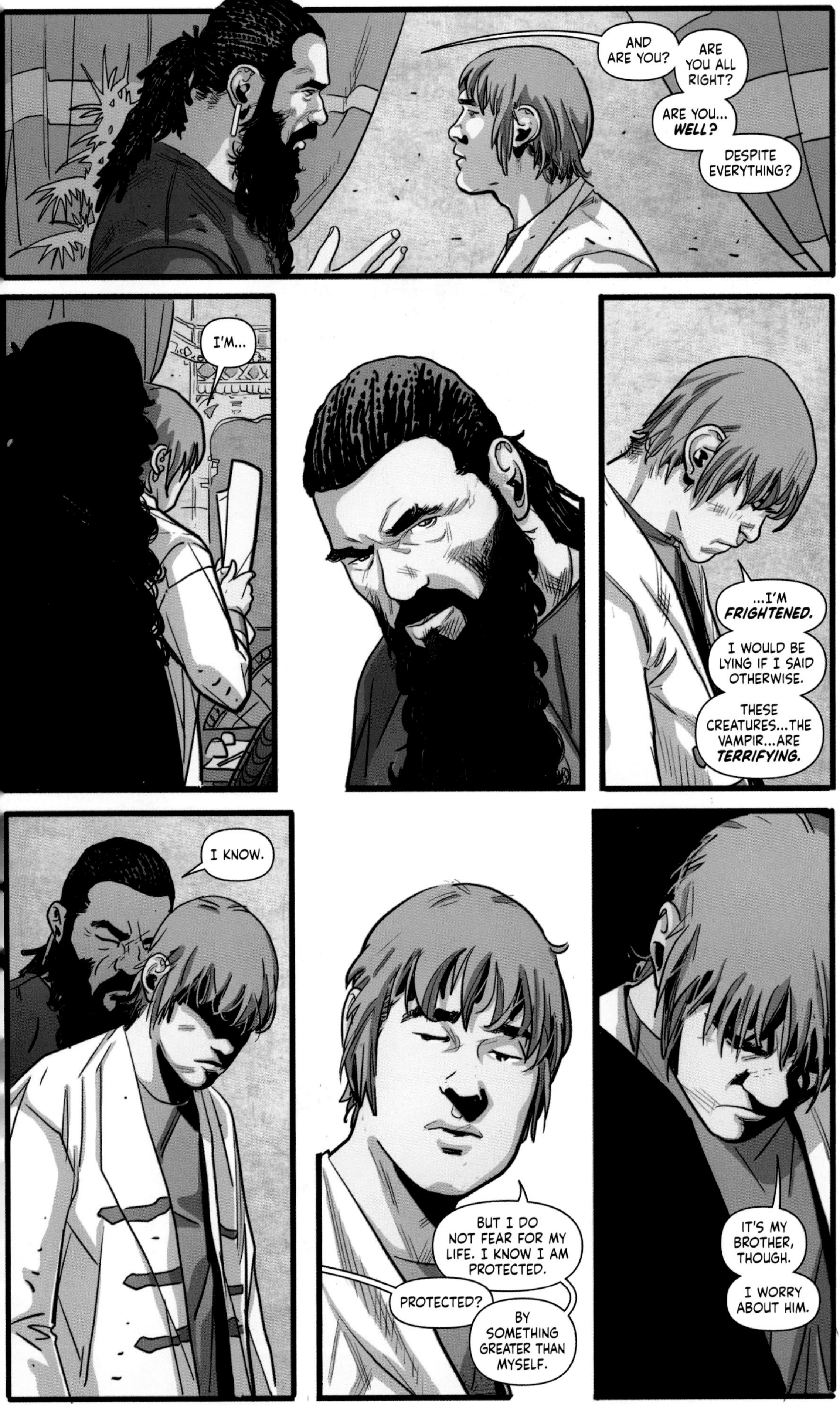
AND ARE YOU?
ARE YOU ALL RIGHT?
ARE YOU... WELL?
DESPITE EVERYTHING?
I'M...
...I'M FRIGHTENED.
I WOULD BE LYING IF I SAID OTHERWISE.
THESE CREATURES...THE VAMPIR...ARE TERRIFYING.
I KNOW.
BUT I DO NOT FEAR FOR MY LIFE. I KNOW I AM PROTECTED.
PROTECTED?
BY SOMETHING GREATER THAN MYSELF.
IT'S MY BROTHER, THOUGH.
I WORRY ABOUT HIM.

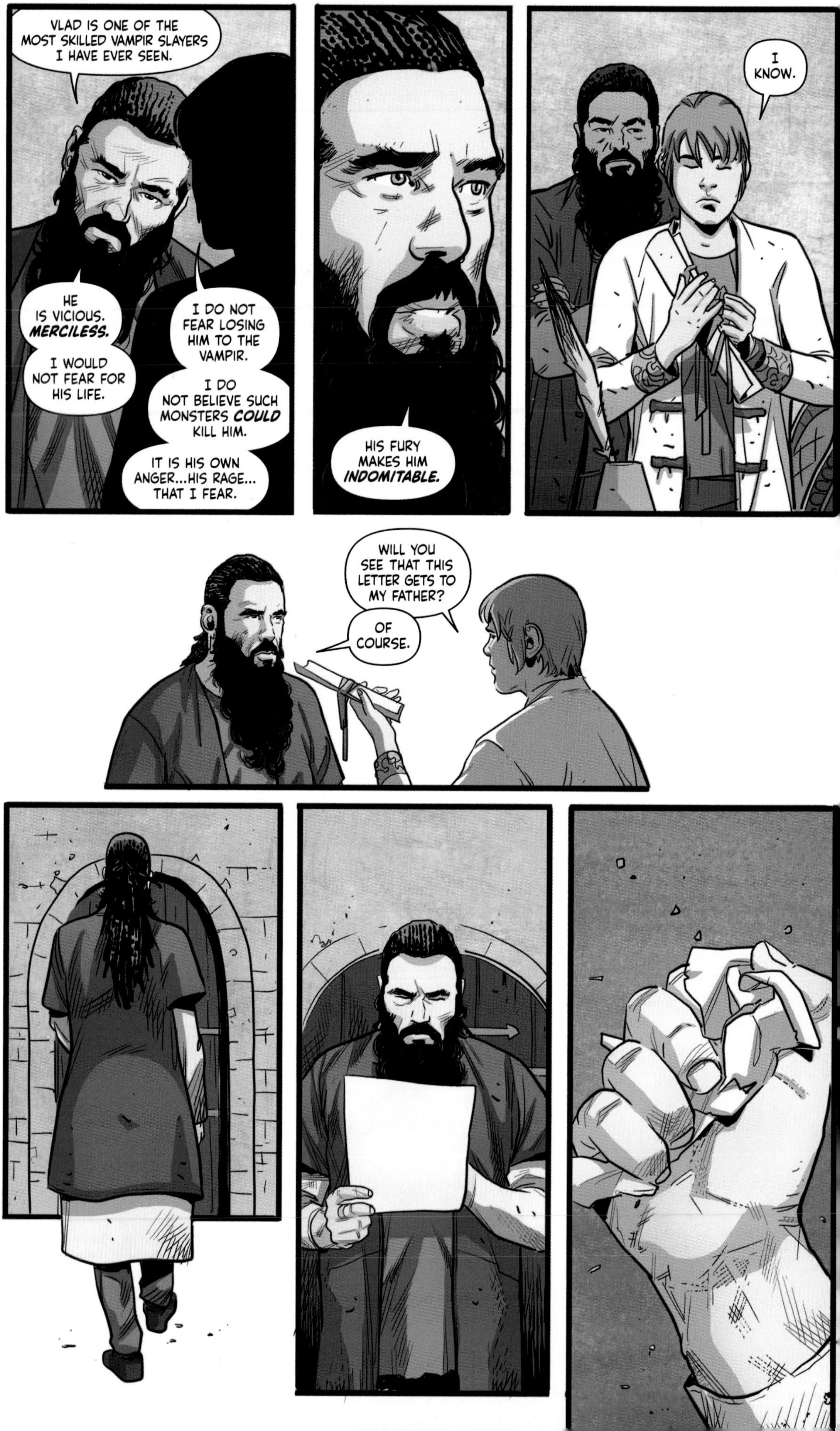
VLAD IS ONE OF THE MOST SKILLED VAMPIR SLAYERS I HAVE EVER SEEN.
HE IS VICIOUS. ***MERCILESS.***
I WOULD NOT FEAR FOR HIS LIFE.
I DO NOT FEAR LOSING HIM TO THE VAMPIR.
I DO NOT BELIEVE SUCH MONSTERS ***COULD*** KILL HIM.
IT IS HIS OWN ANGER...HIS RAGE... THAT I FEAR.
HIS FURY MAKES HIM ***INDOMITABLE.***
I KNOW.
WILL YOU SEE THAT THIS LETTER GETS TO MY FATHER?
OF COURSE.

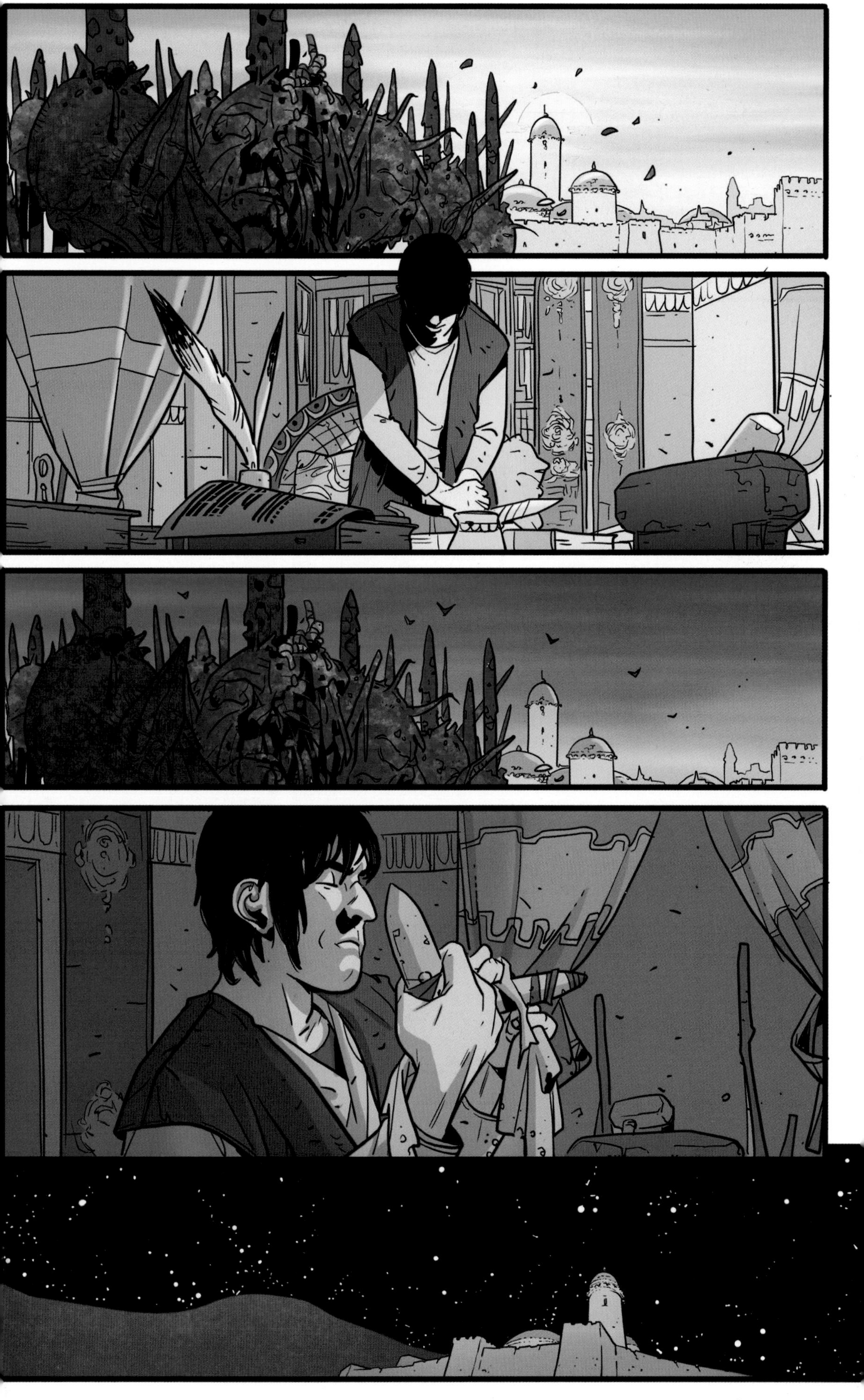

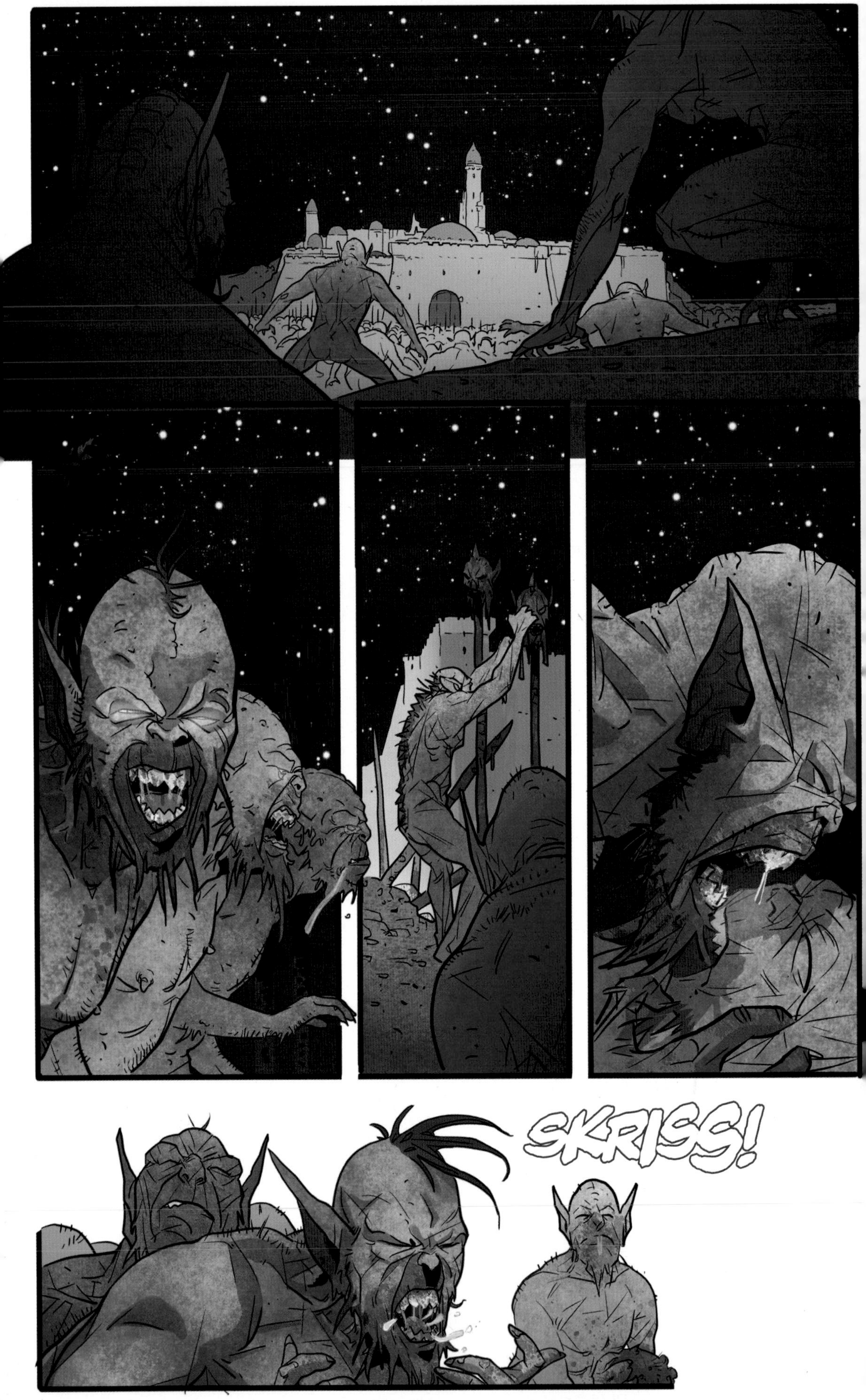
SKRISS!

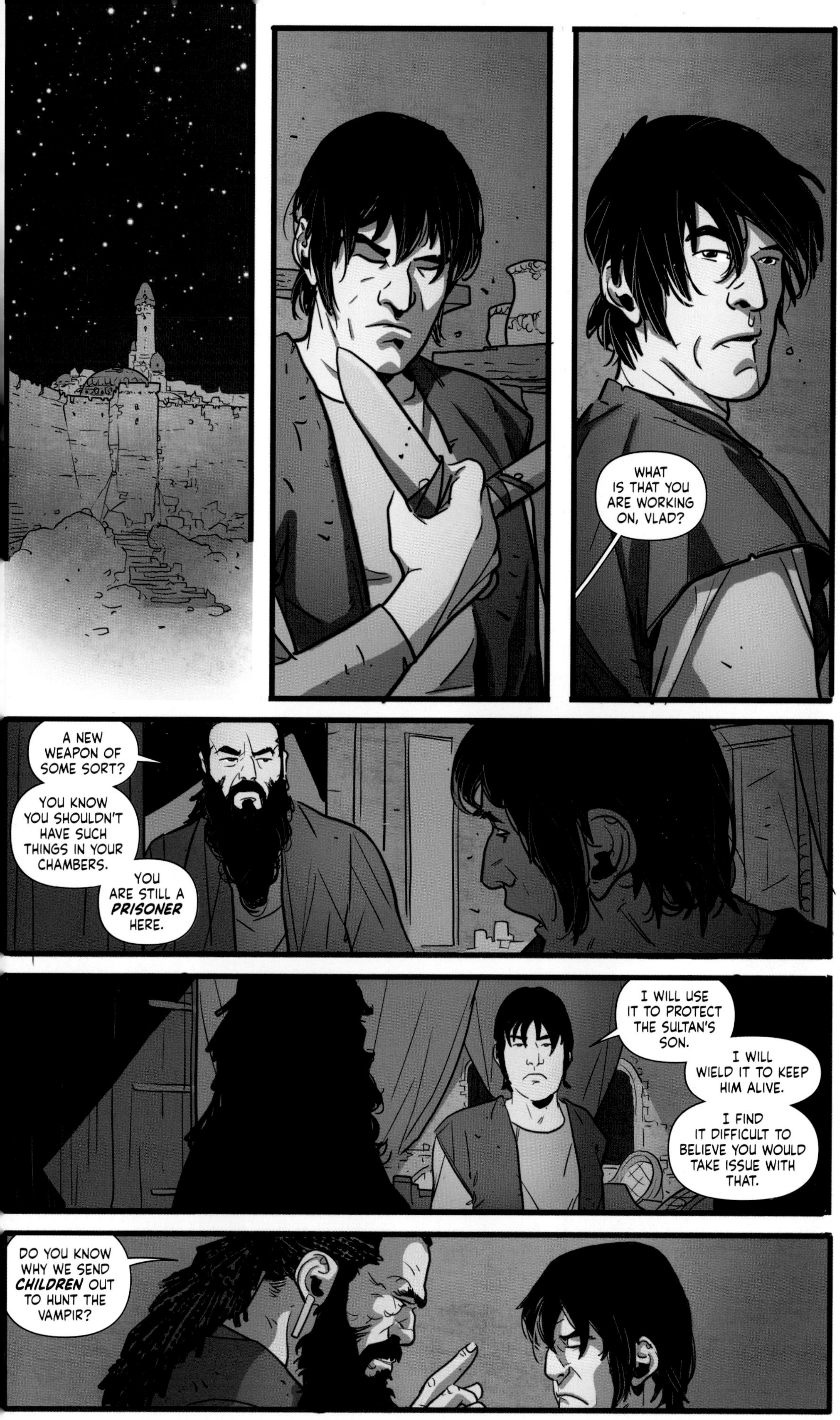
WHAT IS THAT YOU ARE WORKING ON, VLAD?
A NEW WEAPON OF SOME SORT?
YOU KNOW YOU SHOULDN'T HAVE SUCH THINGS IN YOUR CHAMBERS.
YOU ARE STILL A *PRISONER* HERE.
I WILL USE IT TO PROTECT THE SULTAN'S SON.
I WILL WIELD IT TO KEEP HIM ALIVE.
I FIND IT DIFFICULT TO BELIEVE YOU WOULD TAKE ISSUE WITH THAT.
DO YOU KNOW WHY WE SEND *CHILDREN* OUT TO HUNT THE VAMPIR?

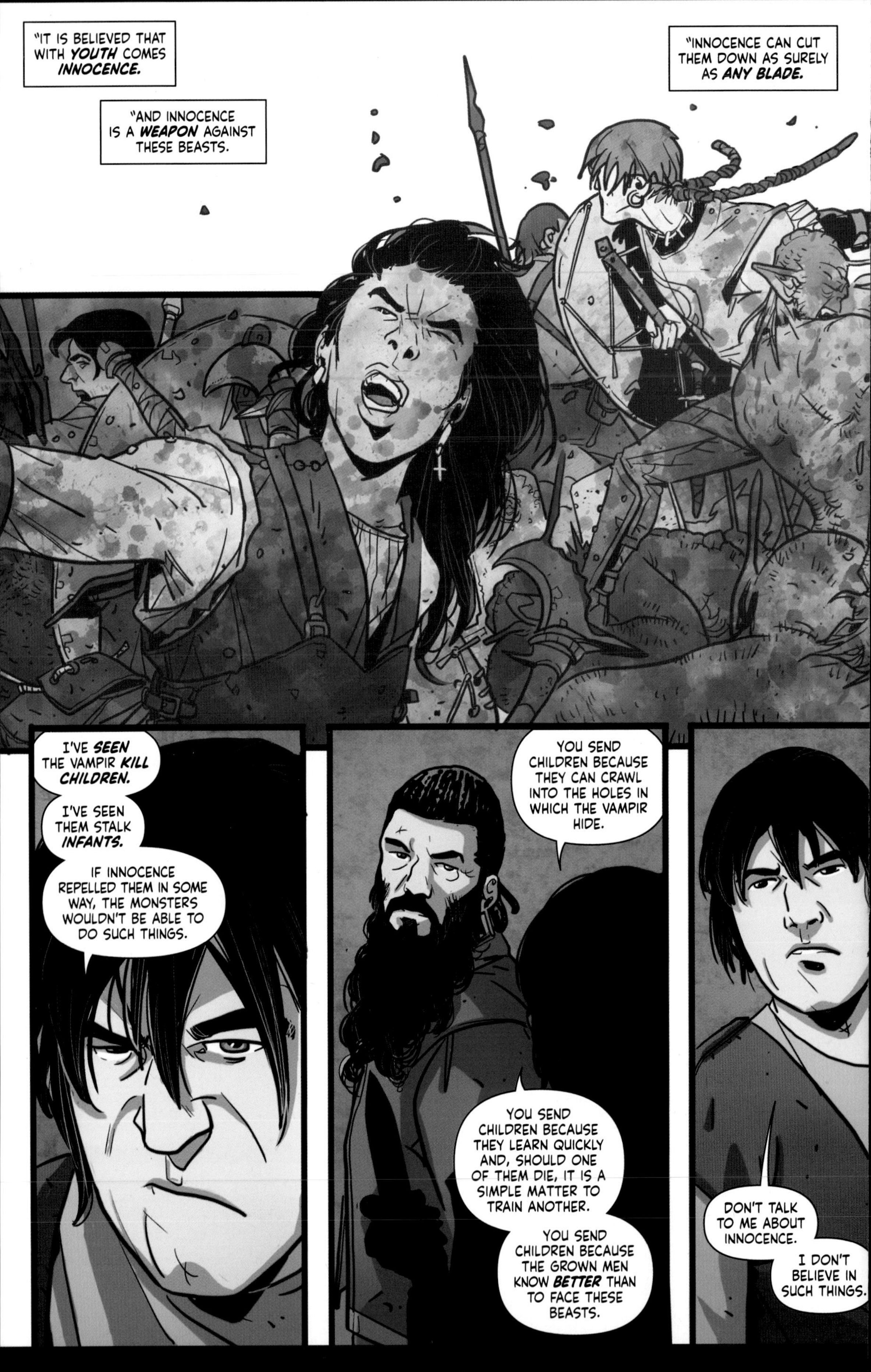
"IT IS BELIEVED THAT WITH YOUTH COMES INNOCENCE.
"AND INNOCENCE IS A WEAPON AGAINST THESE BEASTS.
"INNOCENCE CAN CUT THEM DOWN AS SURELY AS ANY BLADE.
I'VE SEEN THE VAMPIR KILL CHILDREN.
I'VE SEEN THEM STALK INFANTS.
IF INNOCENCE REPELLED THEM IN SOME WAY, THE MONSTERS WOULDN'T BE ABLE TO DO SUCH THINGS.
YOU SEND CHILDREN BECAUSE THEY CAN CRAWL INTO THE HOLES IN WHICH THE VAMPIR HIDE.
YOU SEND CHILDREN BECAUSE THEY LEARN QUICKLY AND, SHOULD ONE OF THEM DIE, IT IS A SIMPLE MATTER TO TRAIN ANOTHER.
YOU SEND CHILDREN BECAUSE THE GROWN MEN KNOW BETTER THAN TO FACE THESE BEASTS.
DON'T TALK TO ME ABOUT INNOCENCE.
I DON'T BELIEVE IN SUCH THINGS.

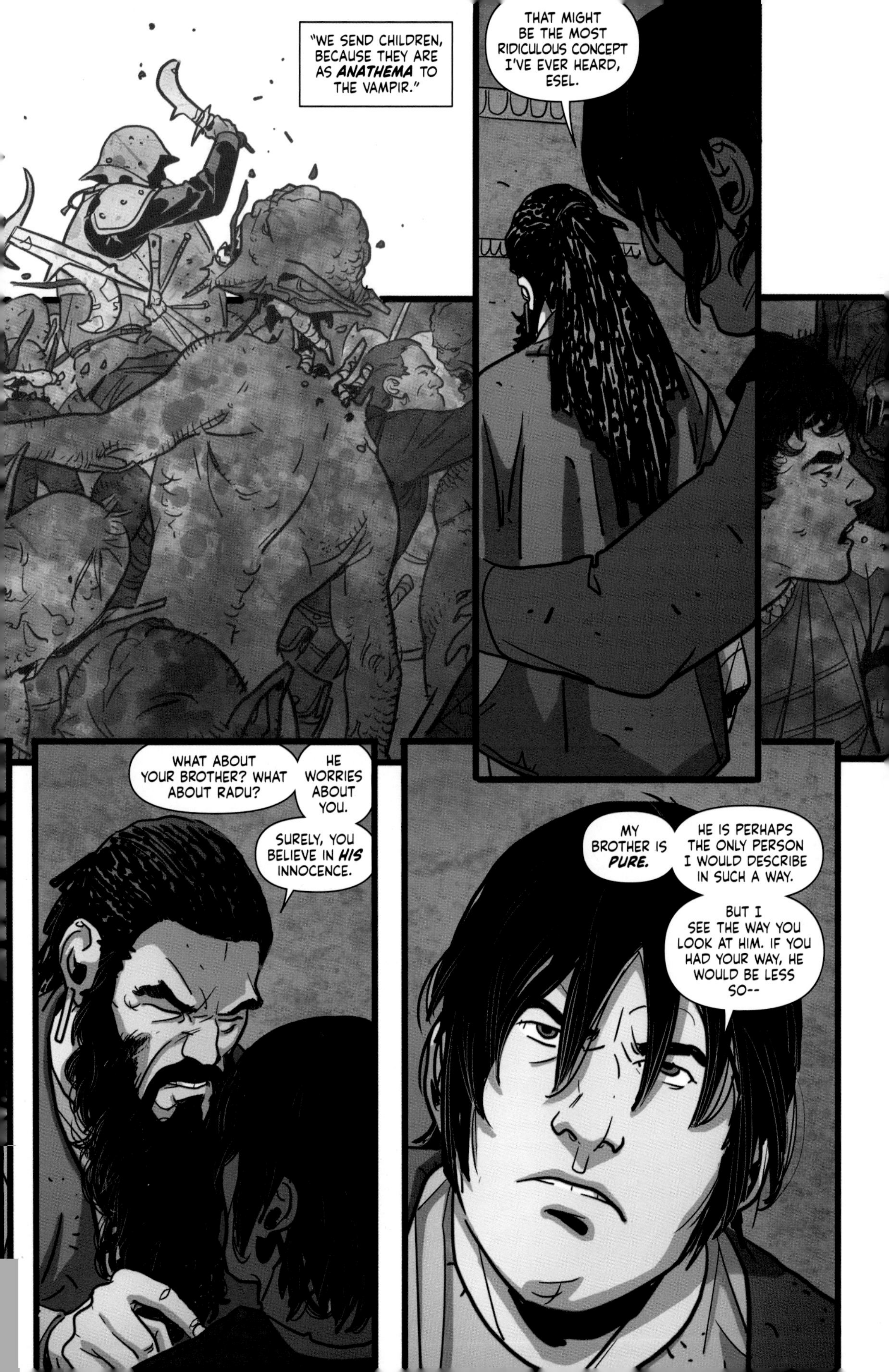
"WE SEND CHILDREN, BECAUSE THEY ARE AS ANATHEMA TO THE VAMPIR."
THAT MIGHT BE THE MOST RIDICULOUS CONCEPT I'VE EVER HEARD, ESEL.
WHAT ABOUT YOUR BROTHER? WHAT ABOUT RADU?
HE WORRIES ABOUT YOU.
SURELY, YOU BELIEVE IN HIS INNOCENCE.
MY BROTHER IS PURE.
HE IS PERHAPS THE ONLY PERSON I WOULD DESCRIBE IN SUCH A WAY.
BUT I SEE THE WAY YOU LOOK AT HIM. IF YOU HAD YOUR WAY, HE WOULD BE LESS SO--

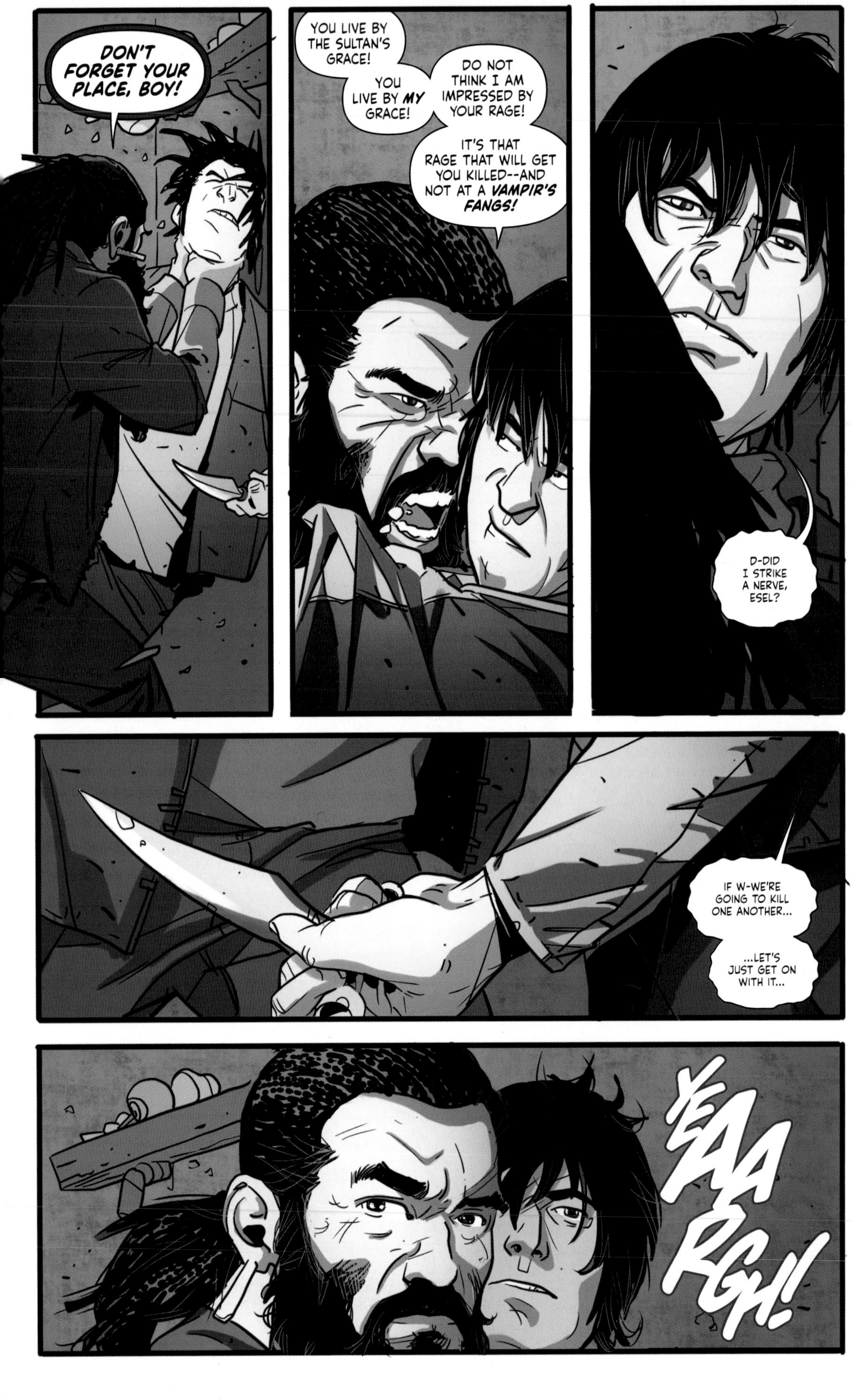
DON'T FORGET YOUR PLACE, BOY!
YOU LIVE BY THE SULTAN'S GRACE!
YOU LIVE BY MY GRACE!
DO NOT THINK I AM IMPRESSED BY YOUR RAGE!
IT'S THAT RAGE THAT WILL GET YOU KILLED--AND NOT AT A VAMPIR'S FANGS!
D-DID I STRIKE A NERVE, ESEL?
IF W-WE'RE GOING TO KILL ONE ANOTHER...
...LET'S JUST GET ON WITH IT...
YEAARGH!

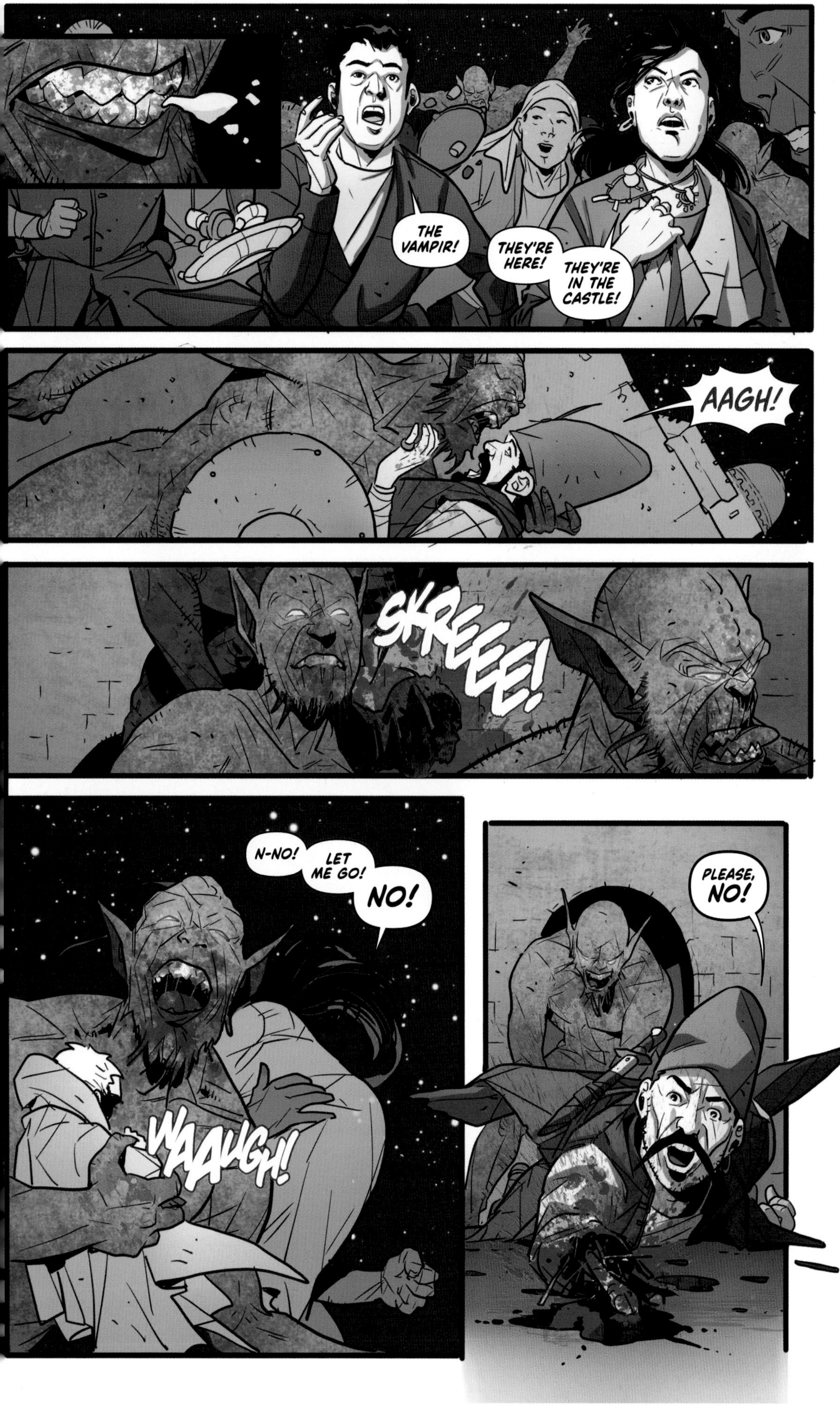
THE VAMPIR!
THEY'RE HERE!
THEY'RE IN THE CASTLE!
AAGH!
SKREEEE!
N-NO!
LET ME GO!
NO!
WAAUGH!
PLEASE, NO!

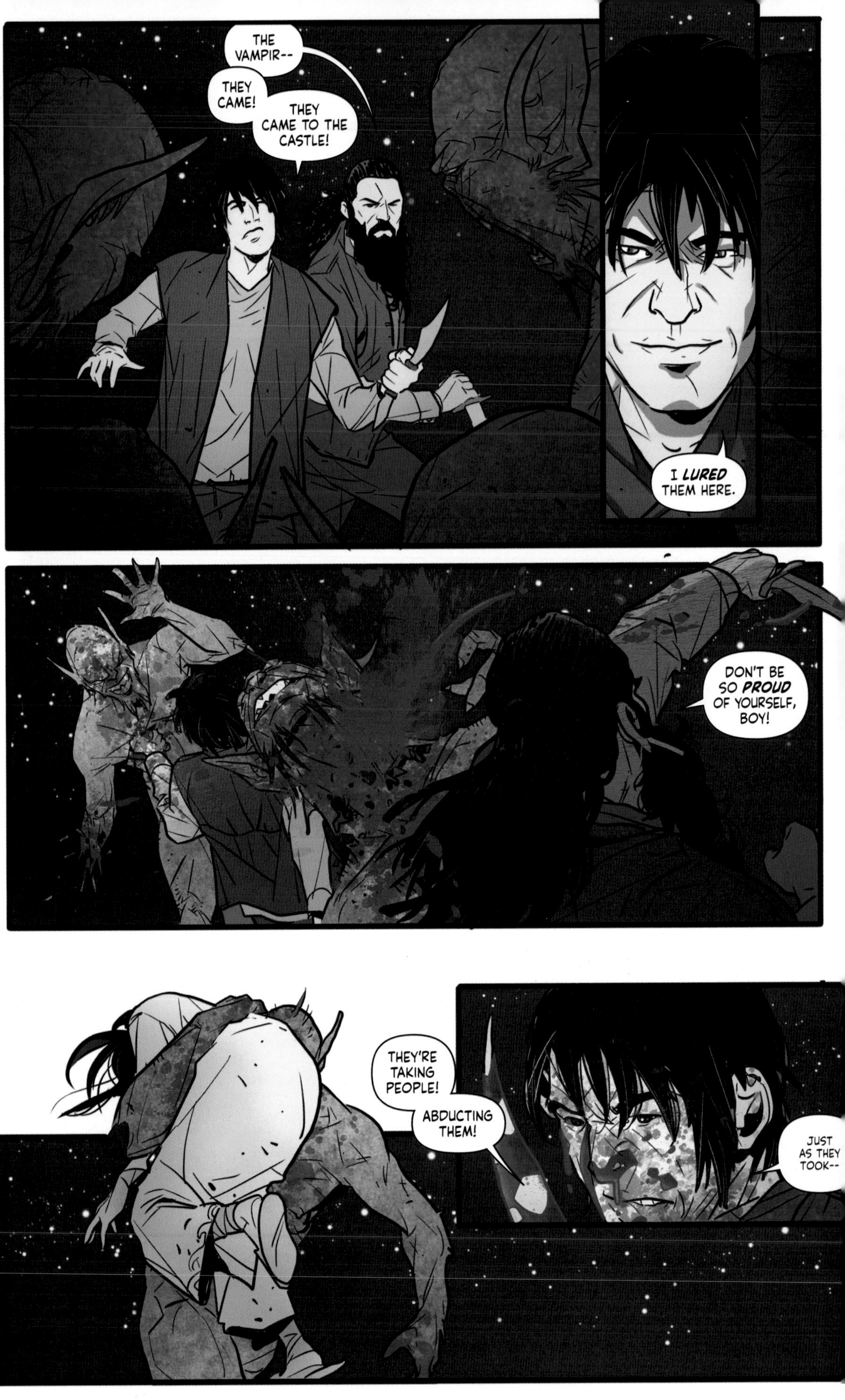
THE VAMPIR--
THEY CAME!
THEY CAME TO THE CASTLE!
I LURED THEM HERE.
DON'T BE SO PROUD OF YOURSELF, BOY!
THEY'RE TAKING PEOPLE!
ABDUCTING THEM!
JUST AS THEY TOOK--

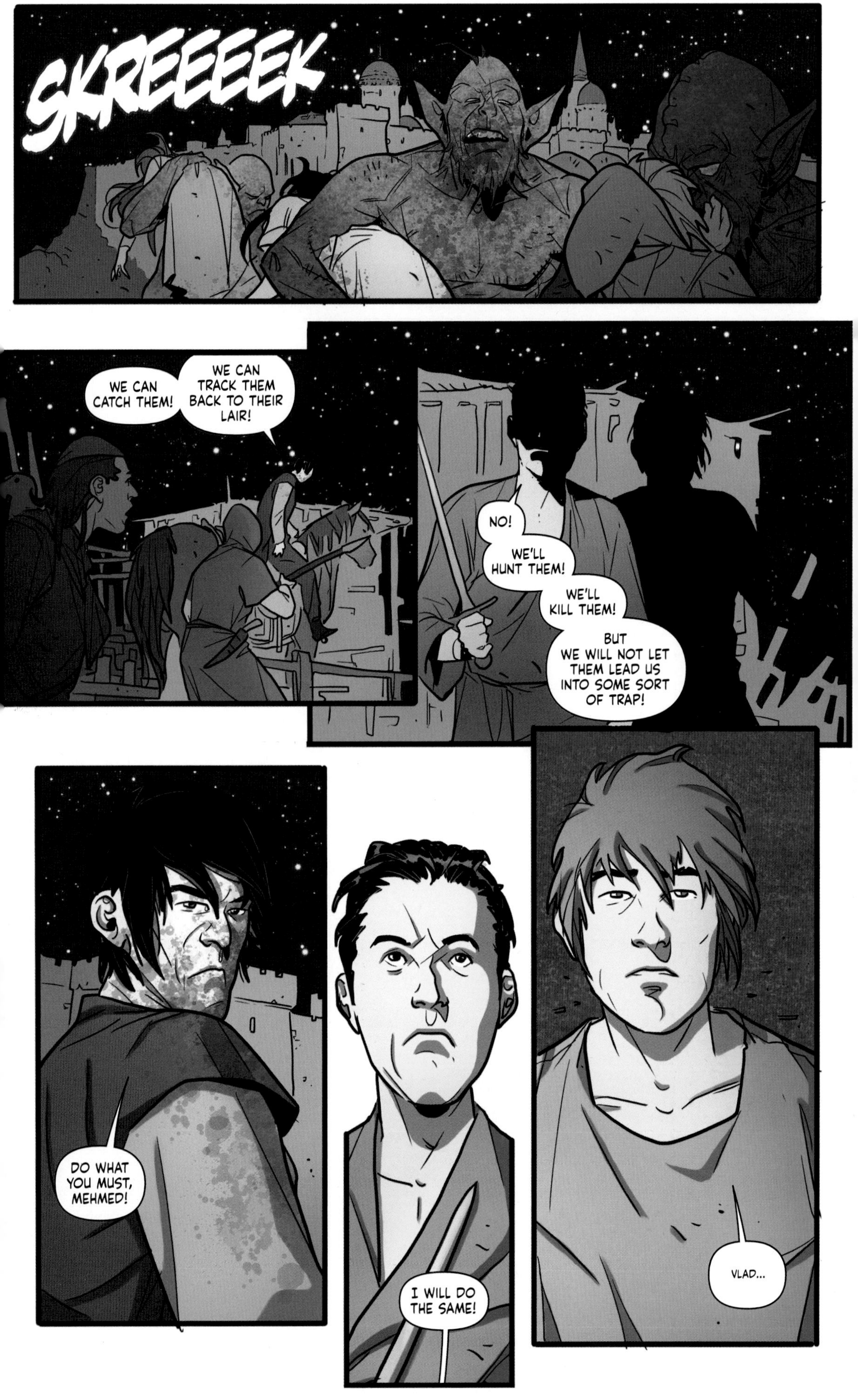
SKREEEEEK
WE CAN CATCH THEM!
WE CAN TRACK THEM BACK TO THEIR LAIR!
NO!
WE'LL HUNT THEM!
WE'LL KILL THEM!
BUT WE WILL NOT LET THEM LEAD US INTO SOME SORT OF TRAP!
DO WHAT YOU MUST, MEHMED!
I WILL DO THE SAME!
VLAD...

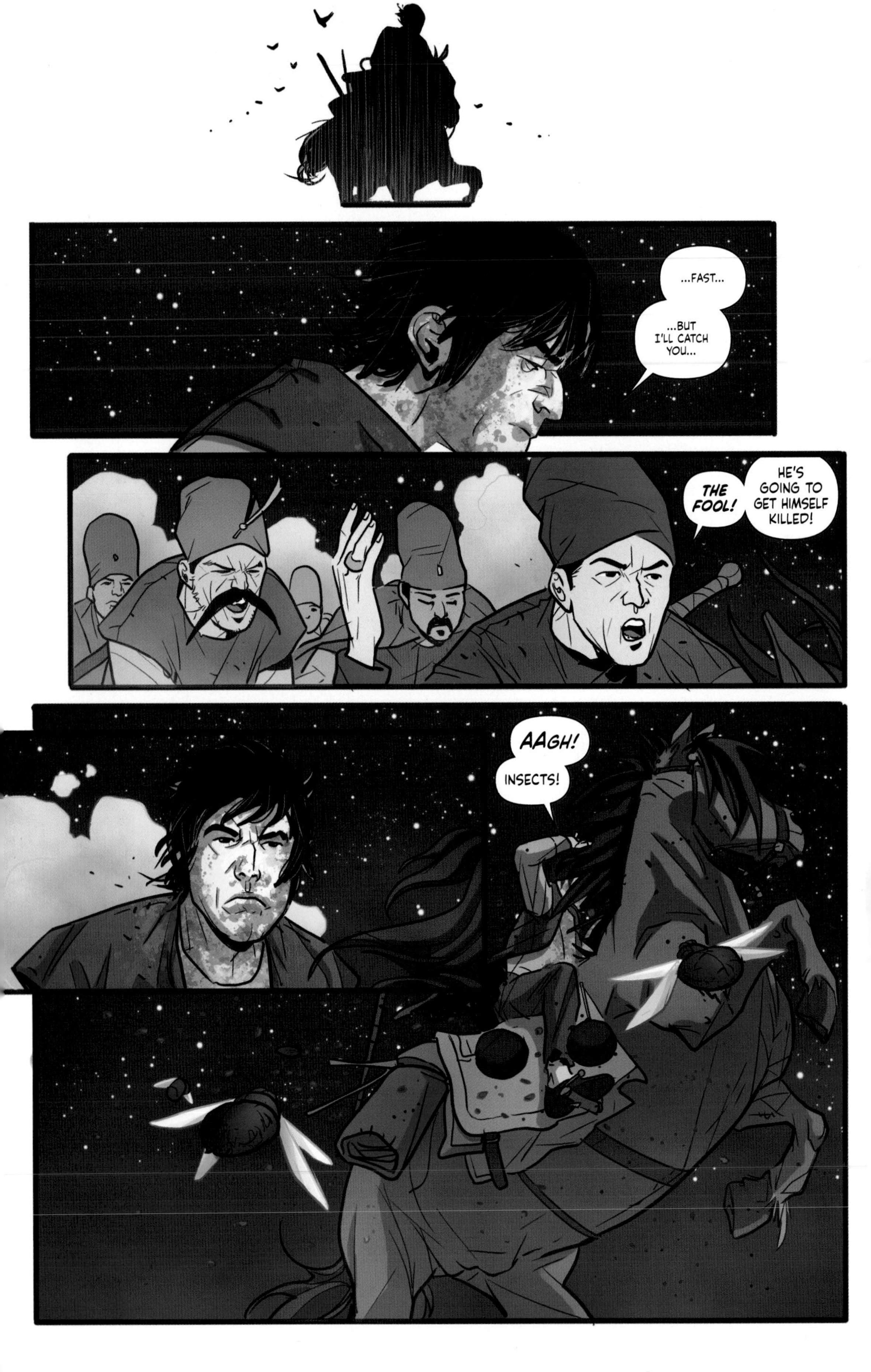
...FAST...
...BUT I'LL CATCH YOU...
THE FOOL!
HE'S GOING TO GET HIMSELF KILLED!
AAGH!
INSECTS!

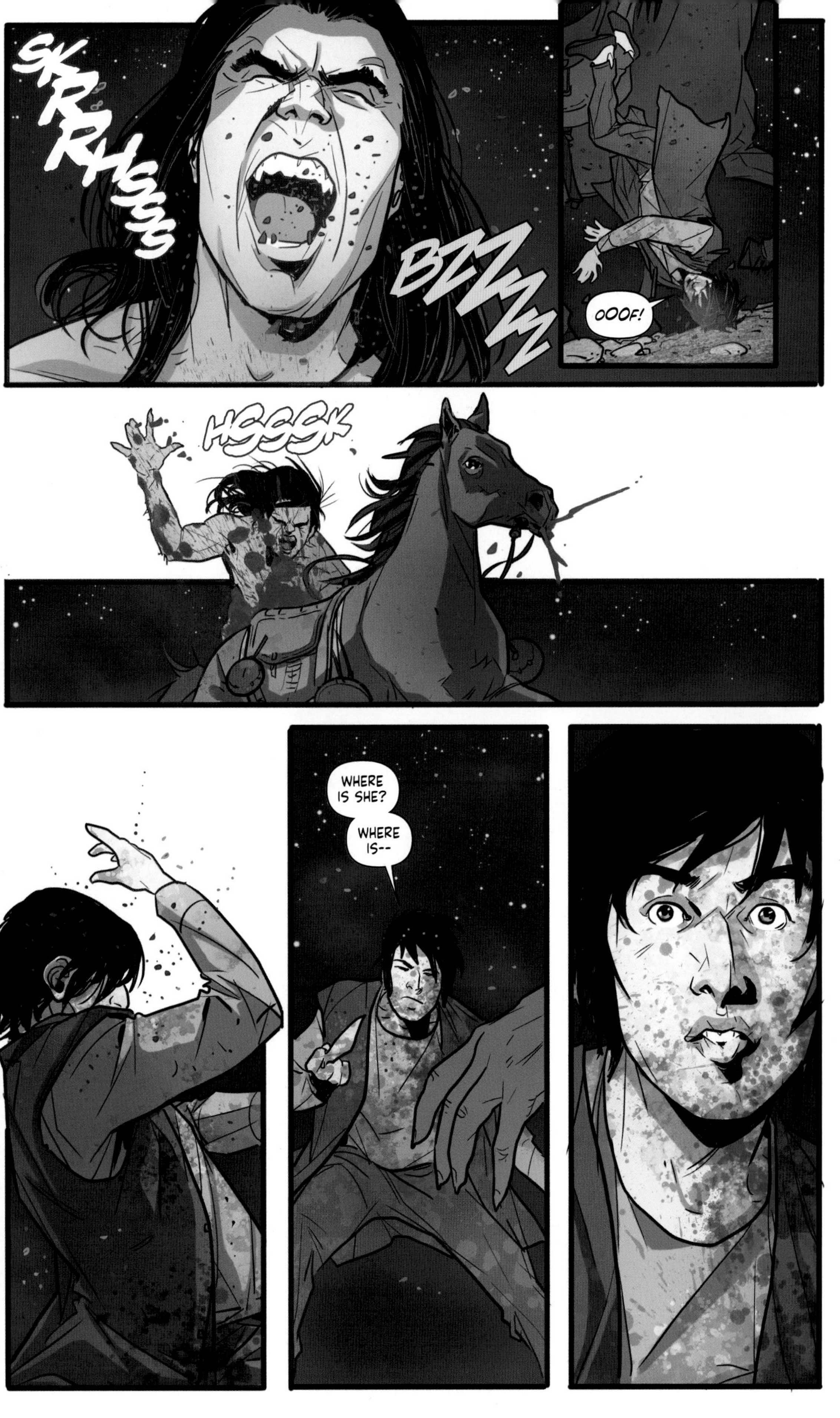
SKRRHSSSS
BZZMMM
OOOF!
HSSSK
WHERE IS SHE?
WHERE IS--

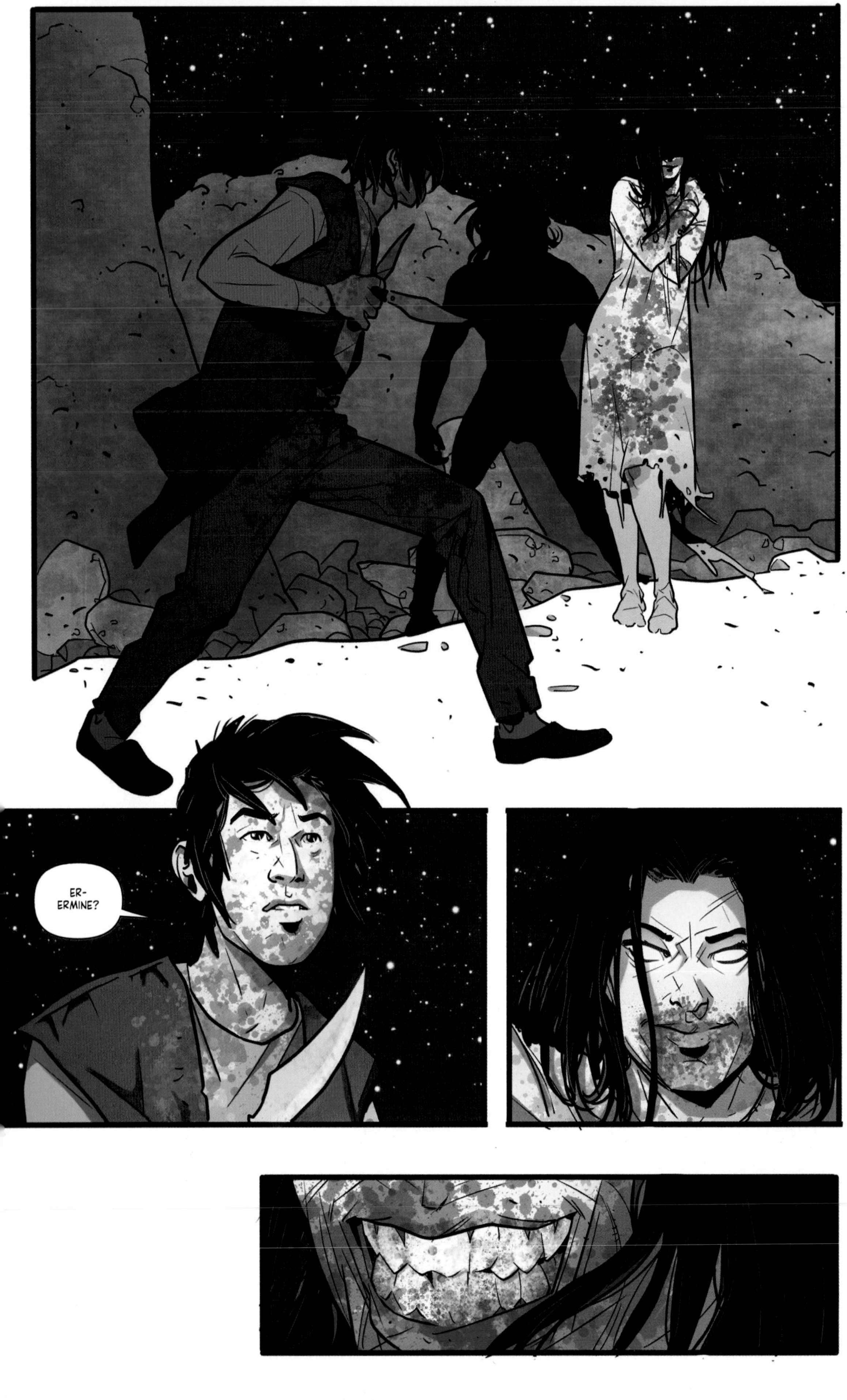
ER-
ERMINE?

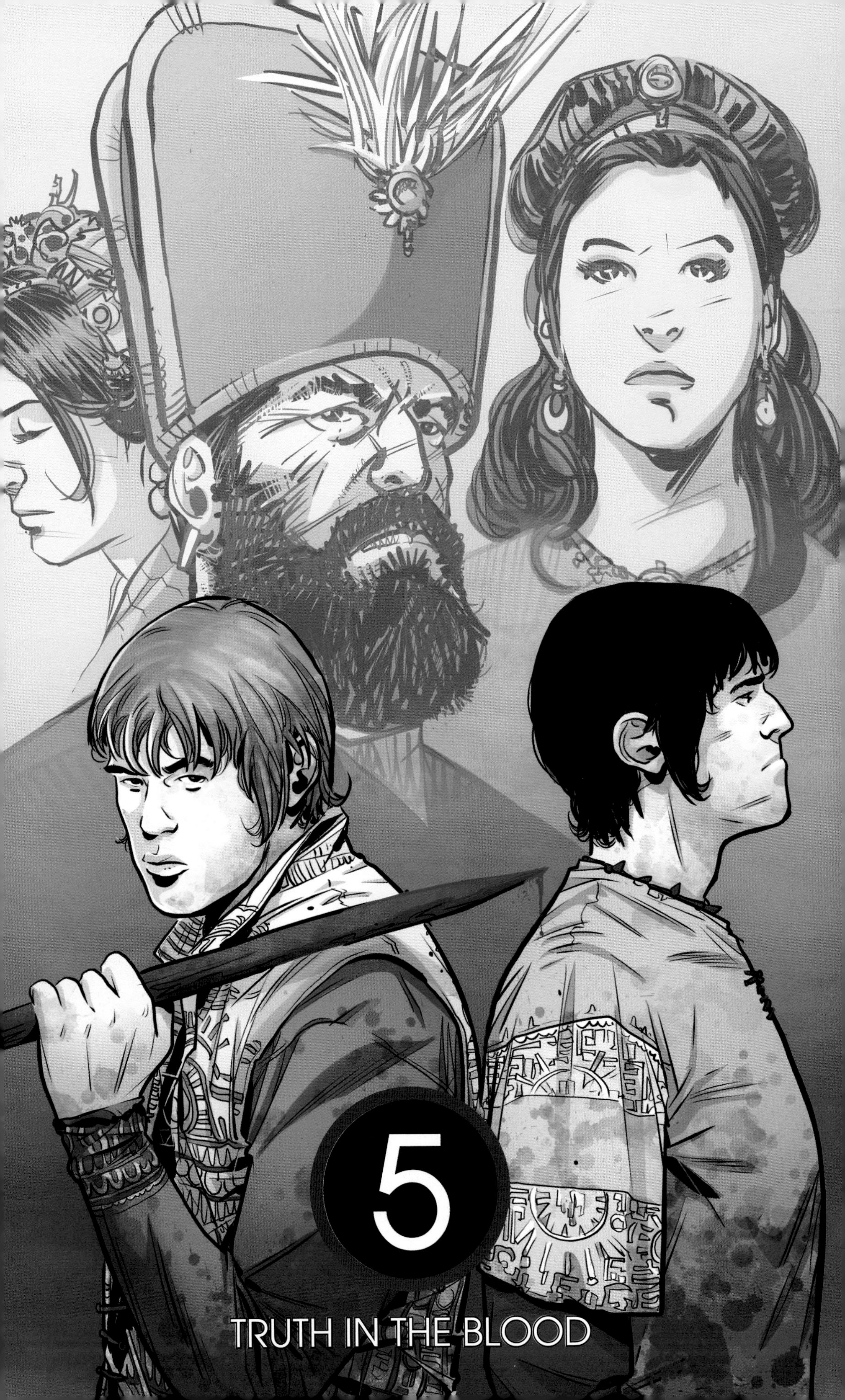
5
TRUTH IN THE BLOOD

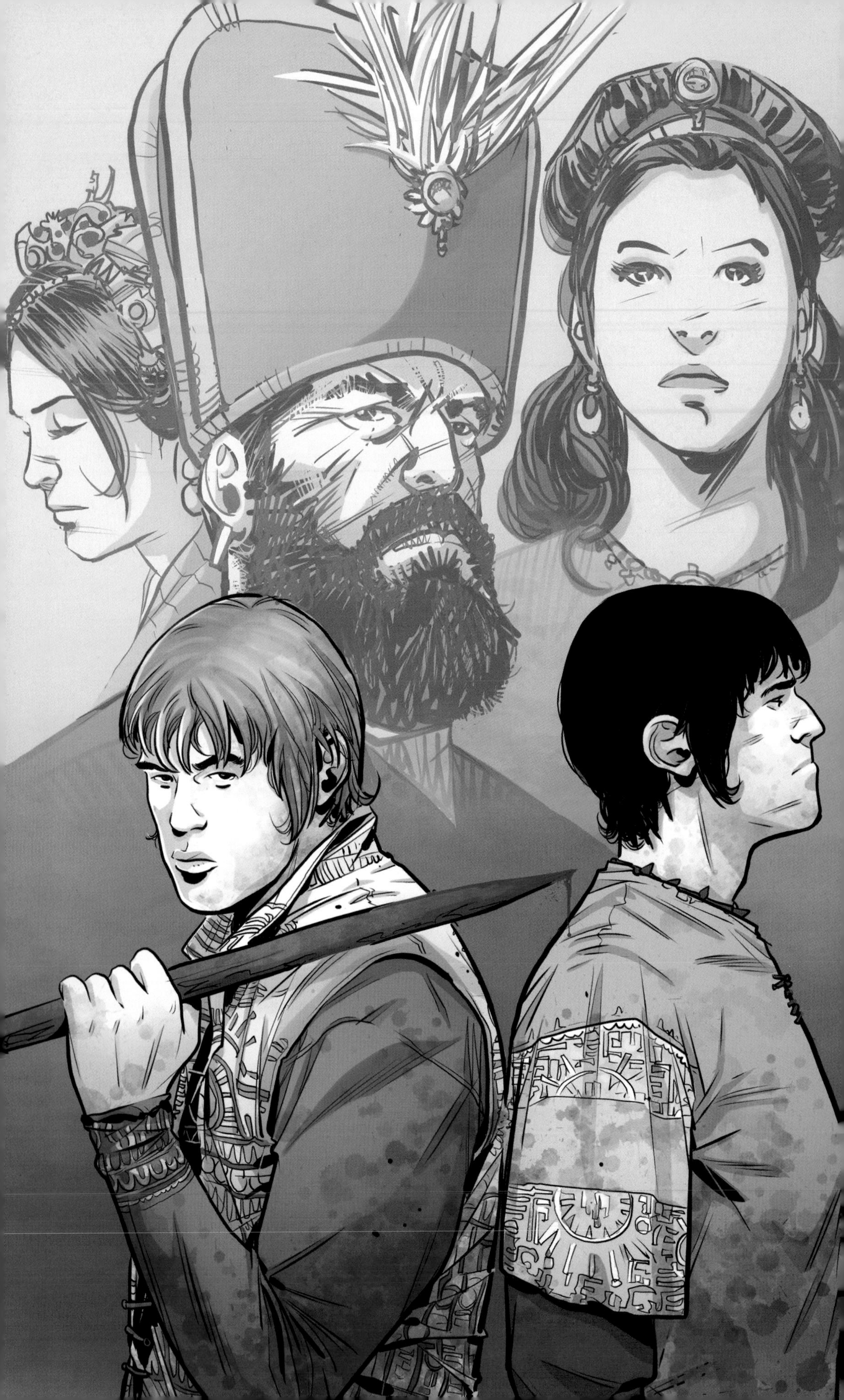

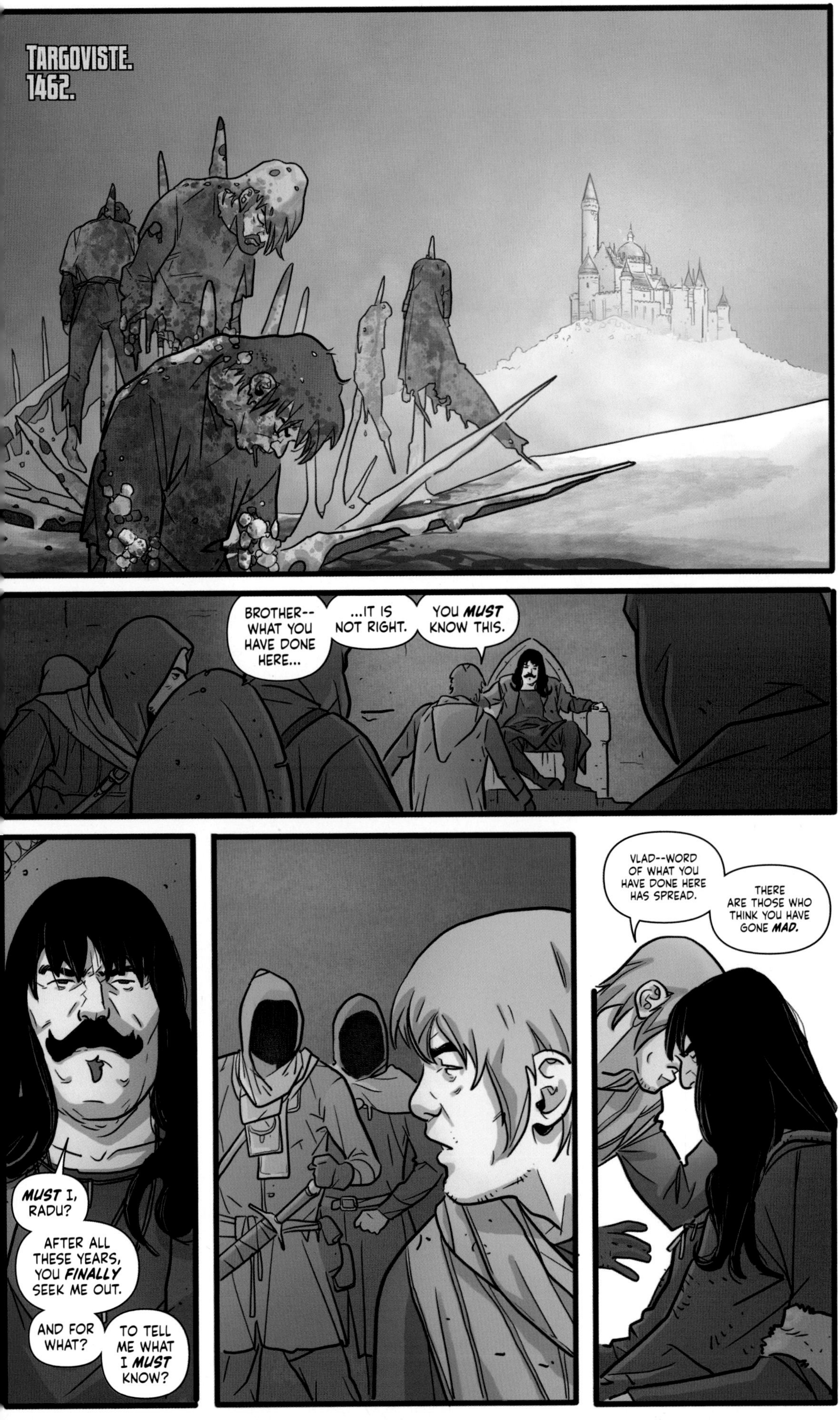
TARGOVISTE. 1462.
BROTHER-- WHAT YOU HAVE DONE HERE...
...IT IS NOT RIGHT.
YOU MUST KNOW THIS.
MUST I, RADU?
AFTER ALL THESE YEARS, YOU FINALLY SEEK ME OUT.
AND FOR WHAT?
TO TELL ME WHAT I MUST KNOW?
VLAD--WORD OF WHAT YOU HAVE DONE HERE HAS SPREAD.
THERE ARE THOSE WHO THINK YOU HAVE GONE MAD.

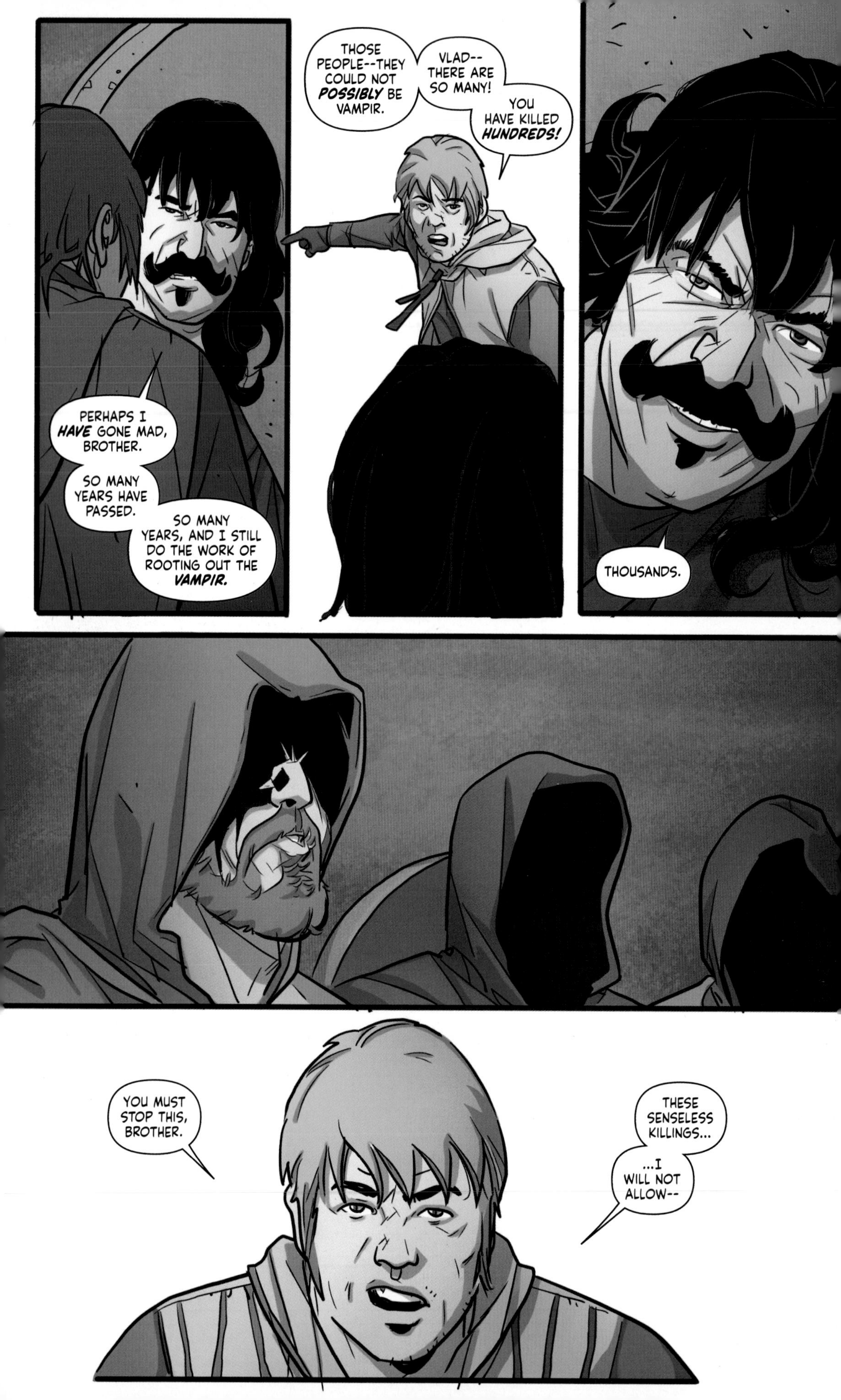

THOSE PEOPLE--THEY COULD NOT POSSIBLY BE VAMPIR.
VLAD-- THERE ARE SO MANY!
YOU HAVE KILLED HUNDREDS!
PERHAPS I HAVE GONE MAD, BROTHER.
SO MANY YEARS HAVE PASSED.
SO MANY YEARS, AND I STILL DO THE WORK OF ROOTING OUT THE VAMPIR.
THOUSANDS.
YOU MUST STOP THIS, BROTHER.
THESE SENSELESS KILLINGS...
...I WILL NOT ALLOW--

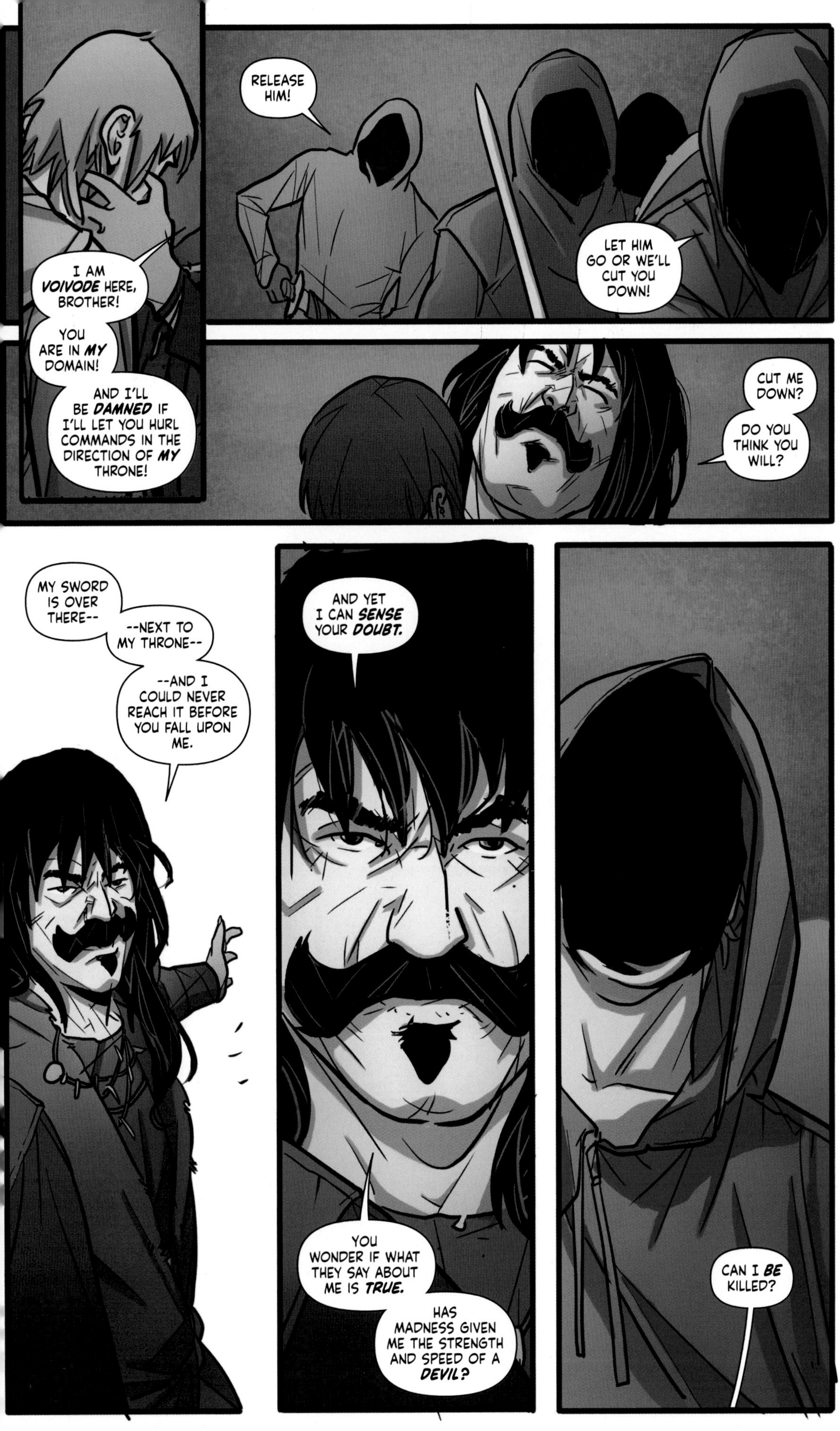
RELEASE HIM!
I AM VOIVODE HERE, BROTHER!
YOU ARE IN MY DOMAIN!
AND I'LL BE DAMNED IF I'LL LET YOU HURL COMMANDS IN THE DIRECTION OF MY THRONE!
LET HIM GO OR WE'LL CUT YOU DOWN!
CUT ME DOWN?
DO YOU THINK YOU WILL?
MY SWORD IS OVER THERE--
--NEXT TO MY THRONE--
--AND I COULD NEVER REACH IT BEFORE YOU FALL UPON ME.
AND YET I CAN SENSE YOUR DOUBT.
YOU WONDER IF WHAT THEY SAY ABOUT ME IS TRUE.
HAS MADNESS GIVEN ME THE STRENGTH AND SPEED OF A DEVIL?
CAN I BE KILLED?

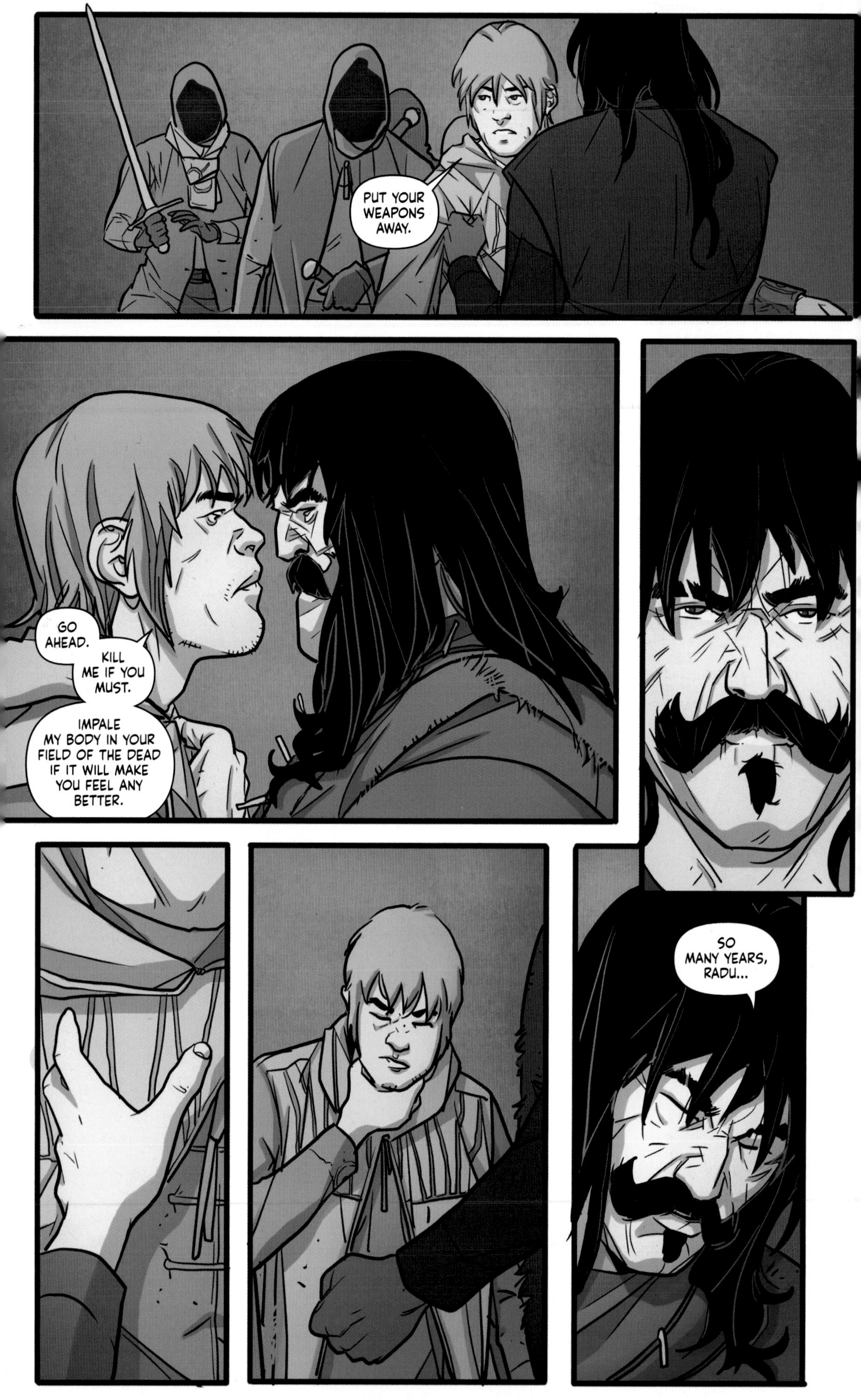
PUT YOUR WEAPONS AWAY.
GO AHEAD.
KILL ME IF YOU MUST.
IMPALE MY BODY IN YOUR FIELD OF THE DEAD IF IT WILL MAKE YOU FEEL ANY BETTER.
SO MANY YEARS, RADU...

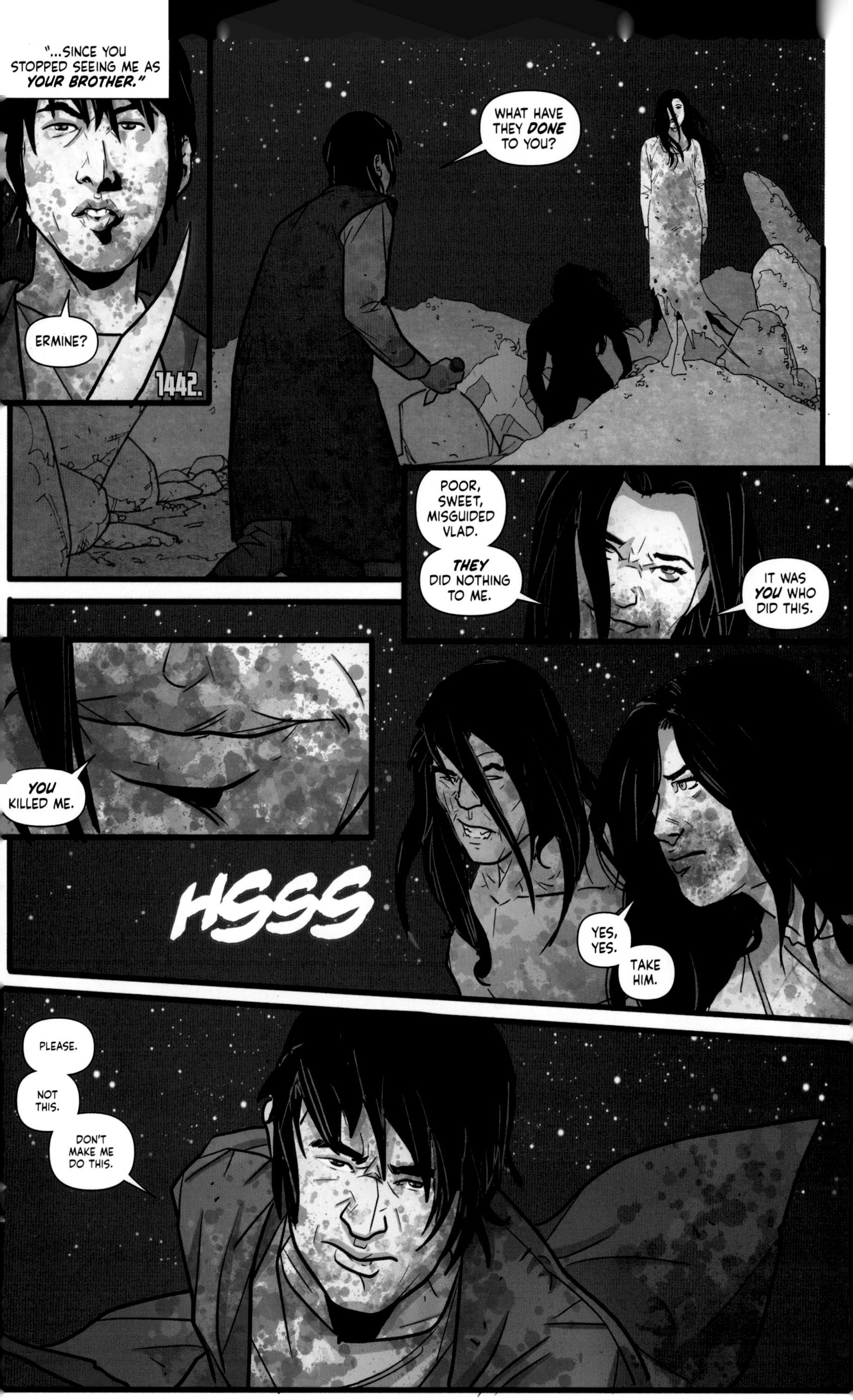
"...SINCE YOU STOPPED SEEING ME AS YOUR BROTHER."
ERMINE?
1442.
WHAT HAVE THEY DONE TO YOU?
POOR, SWEET, MISGUIDED VLAD.
THEY DID NOTHING TO ME.
IT WAS YOU WHO DID THIS.
YOU KILLED ME.
HSSS
YES, YES.
TAKE HIM.
PLEASE.
NOT THIS.
DON'T MAKE ME DO THIS.

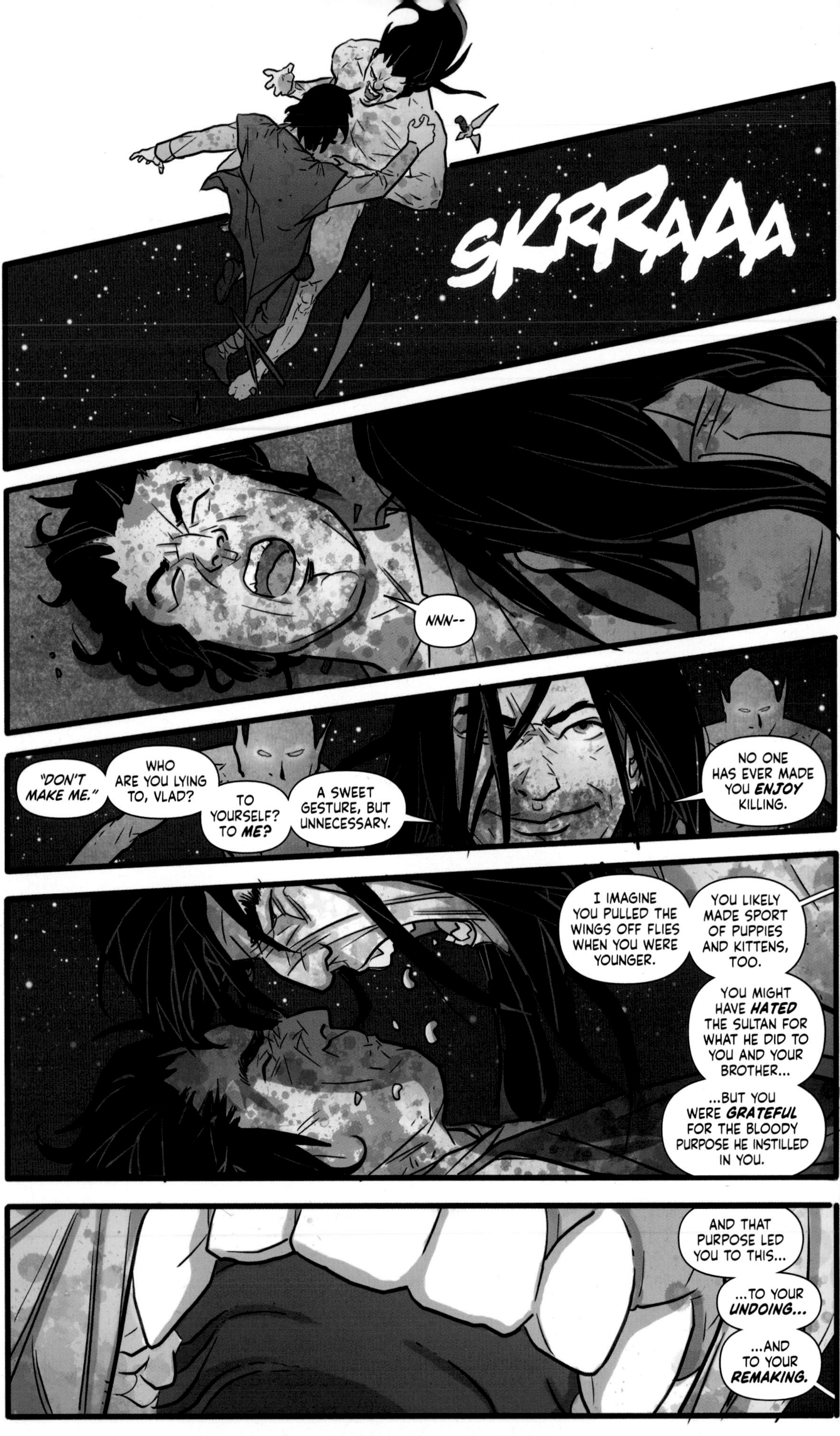
SKRRAAA
NNN--
"DON'T MAKE ME."
WHO ARE YOU LYING TO, VLAD?
TO YOURSELF? TO *ME?*
A SWEET GESTURE, BUT UNNECESSARY.
NO ONE HAS EVER MADE YOU *ENJOY* KILLING.
I IMAGINE YOU PULLED THE WINGS OFF FLIES WHEN YOU WERE YOUNGER.
YOU LIKELY MADE SPORT OF PUPPIES AND KITTENS, TOO.
YOU MIGHT HAVE *HATED* THE SULTAN FOR WHAT HE DID TO YOU AND YOUR BROTHER...
...BUT YOU WERE *GRATEFUL* FOR THE BLOODY PURPOSE HE INSTILLED IN YOU.
AND THAT PURPOSE LED YOU TO THIS...
...TO YOUR *UNDOING...*
...AND TO YOUR *REMAKING.*

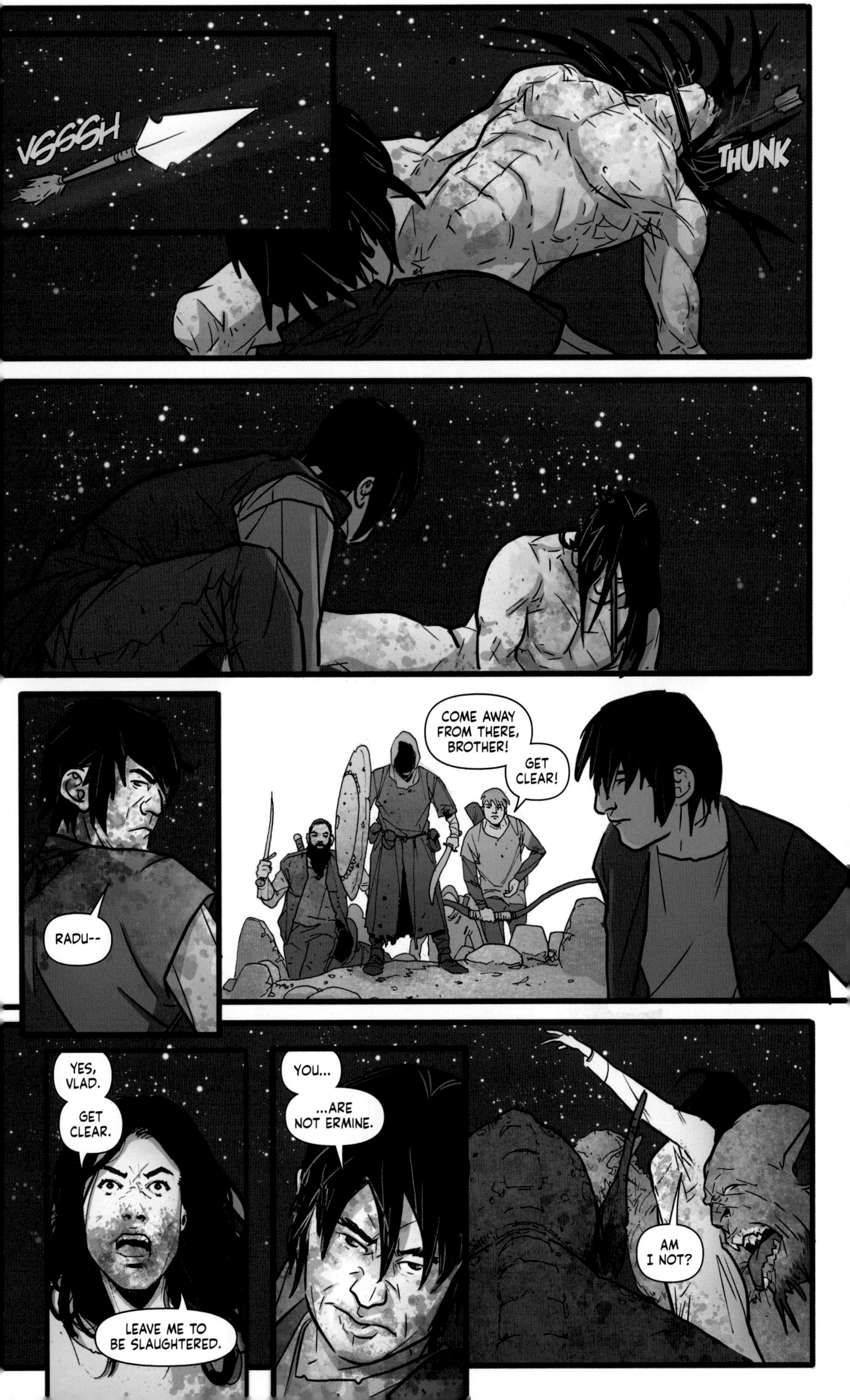
VSSSH
THUNK
RADU--
COME AWAY FROM THERE, BROTHER!
GET CLEAR!
YES, VLAD.
GET CLEAR.
LEAVE ME TO BE SLAUGHTERED.
YOU...
...ARE NOT ERMINE.
AM I NOT?

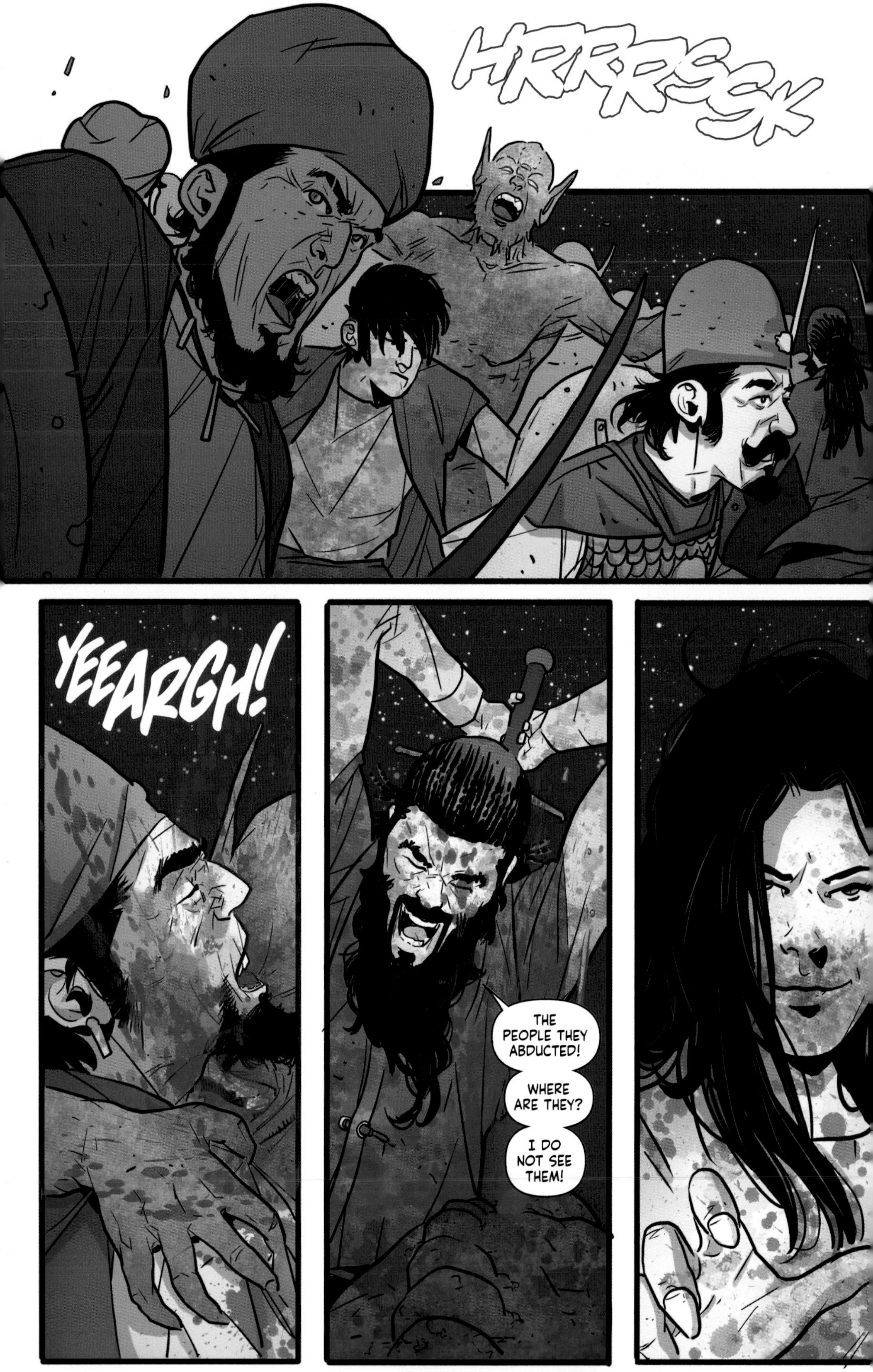
HRRRSSK
YEEARGH!
THE PEOPLE THEY ABDUCTED!
WHERE ARE THEY?
I DO NOT SEE THEM!

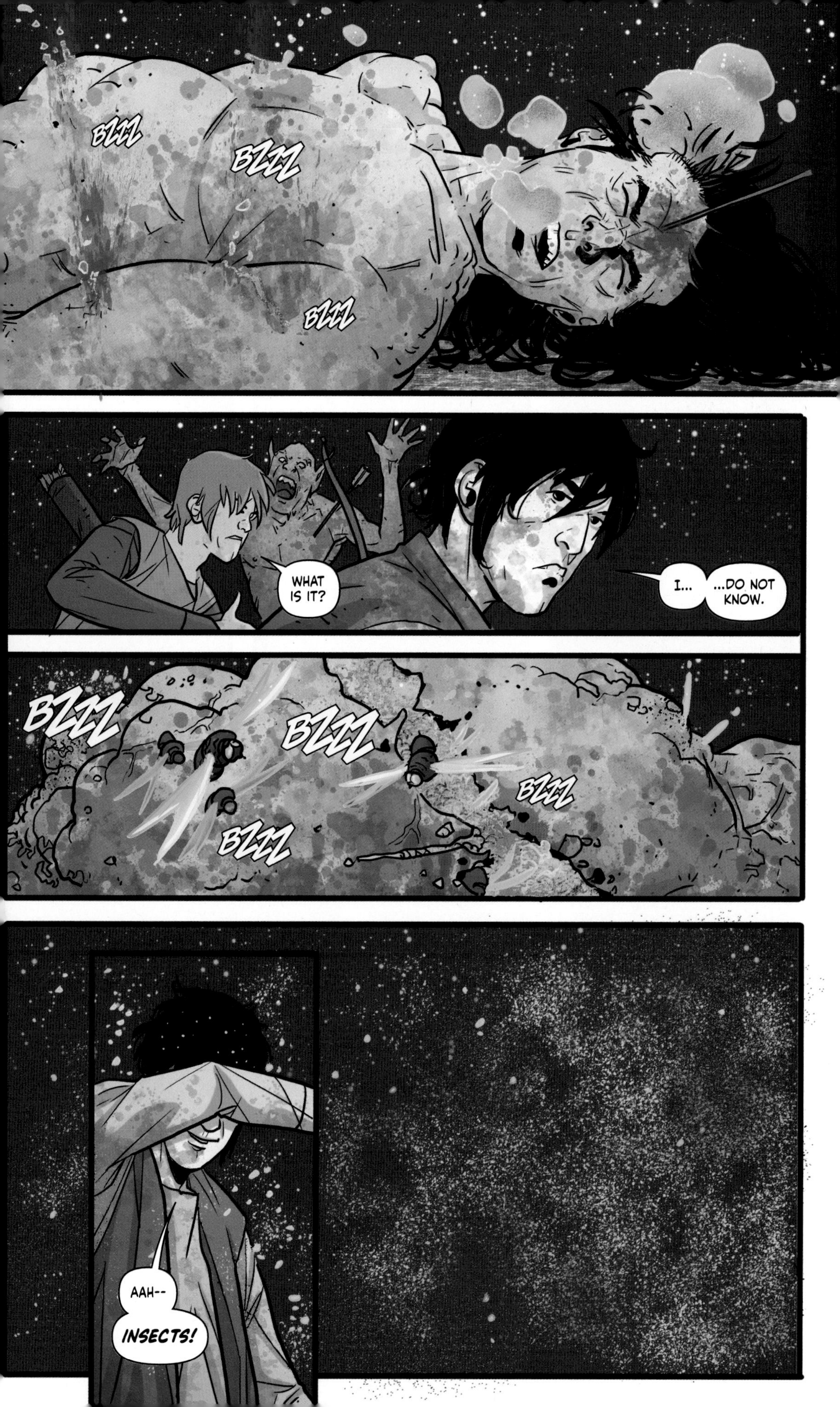
BZZZ
BZZZ
BZZZ
WHAT IS IT?
I...
...DO NOT KNOW.
BZZZ
BZZZ
BZZZ
BZZZ
AAH--
INSECTS!

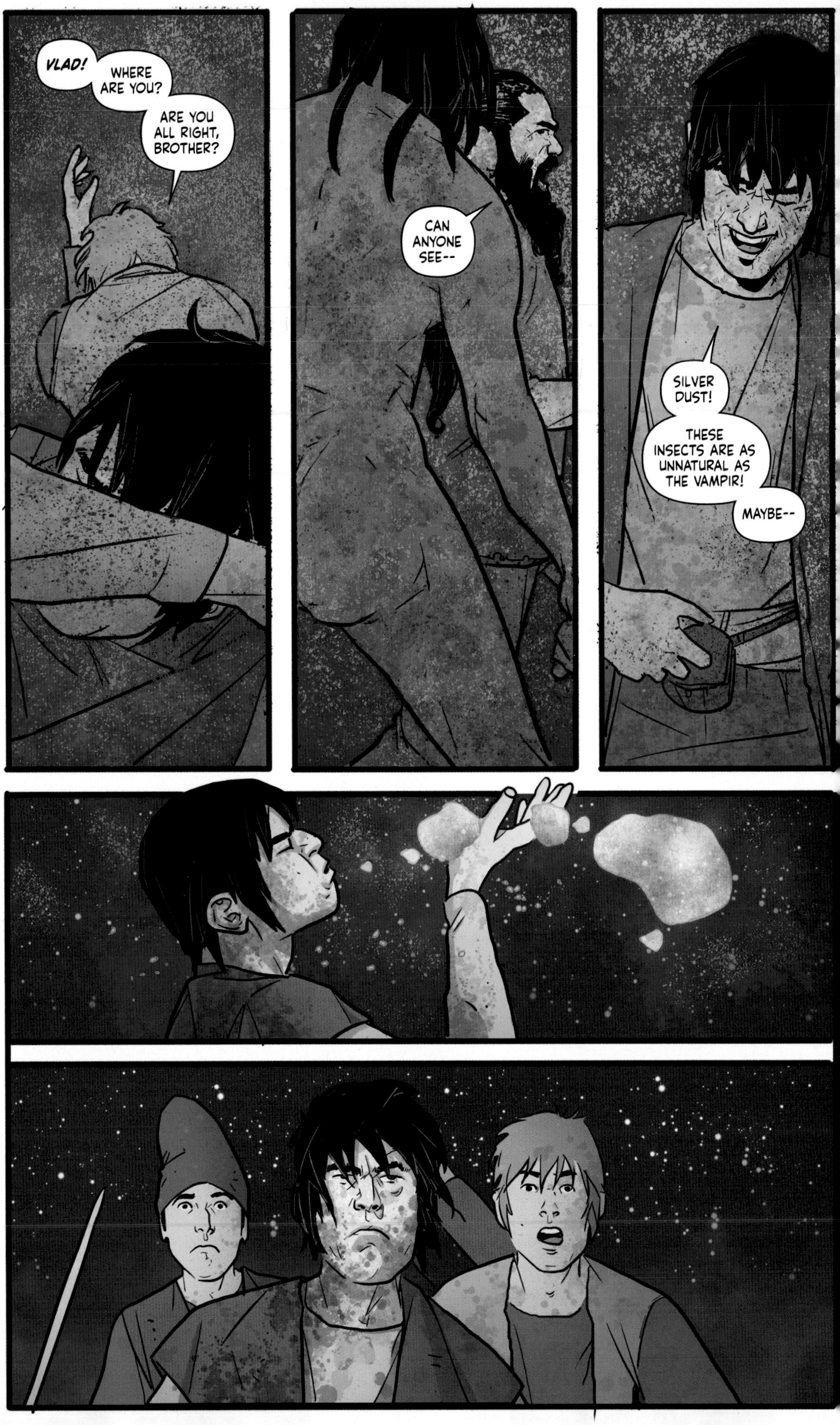
VLAD!
WHERE ARE YOU?
ARE YOU ALL RIGHT, BROTHER?
CAN ANYONE SEE--
SILVER DUST!
THESE INSECTS ARE AS UNNATURAL AS THE VAMPIR!
MAYBE--

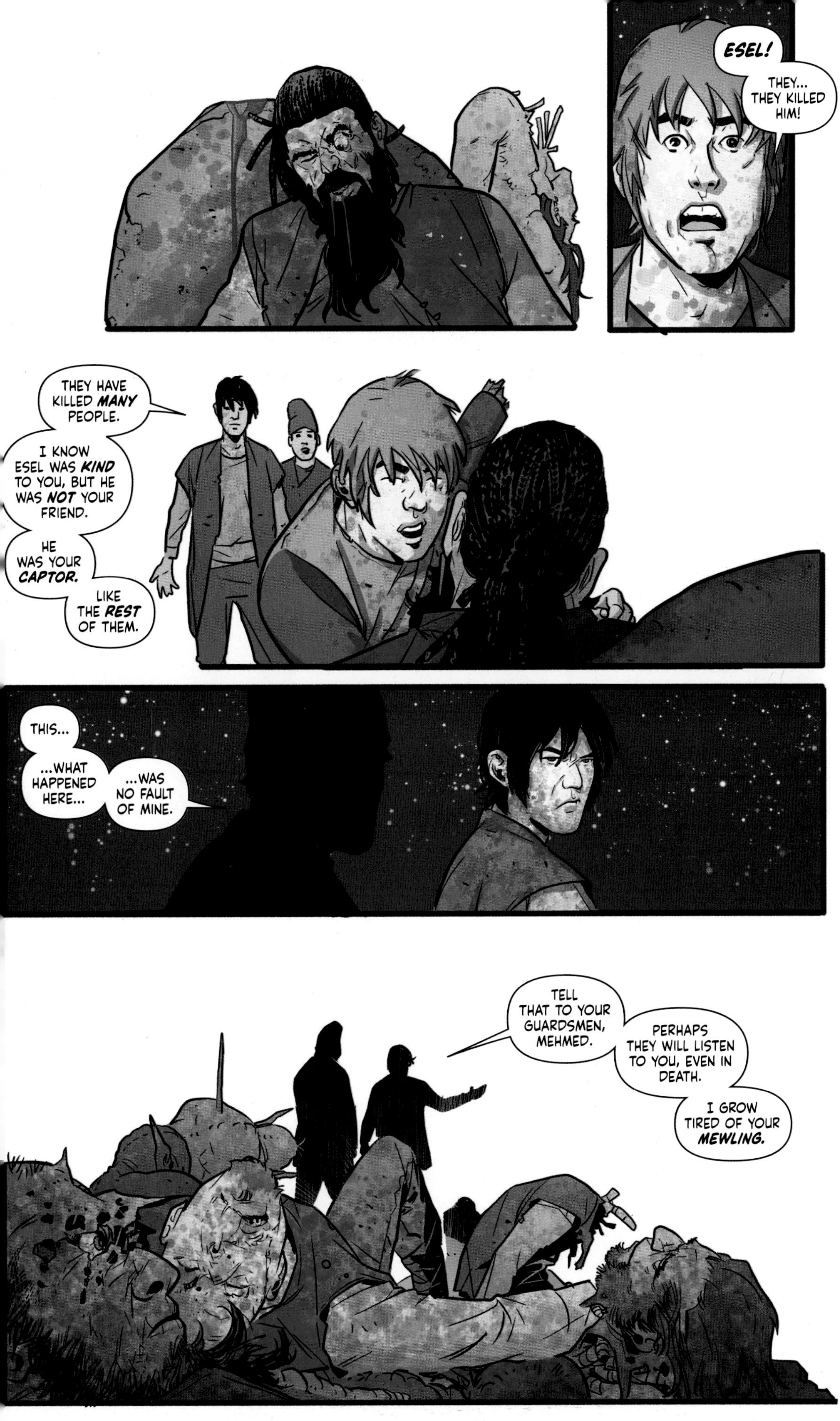
ESEL!
THEY... THEY KILLED HIM!
THEY HAVE KILLED MANY PEOPLE.
I KNOW ESEL WAS KIND TO YOU, BUT HE WAS NOT YOUR FRIEND.
HE WAS YOUR CAPTOR.
LIKE THE REST OF THEM.
THIS...
...WHAT HAPPENED HERE...
...WAS NO FAULT OF MINE.
TELL THAT TO YOUR GUARDSMEN, MEHMED.
PERHAPS THEY WILL LISTEN TO YOU, EVEN IN DEATH.
I GROW TIRED OF YOUR MEWLING.

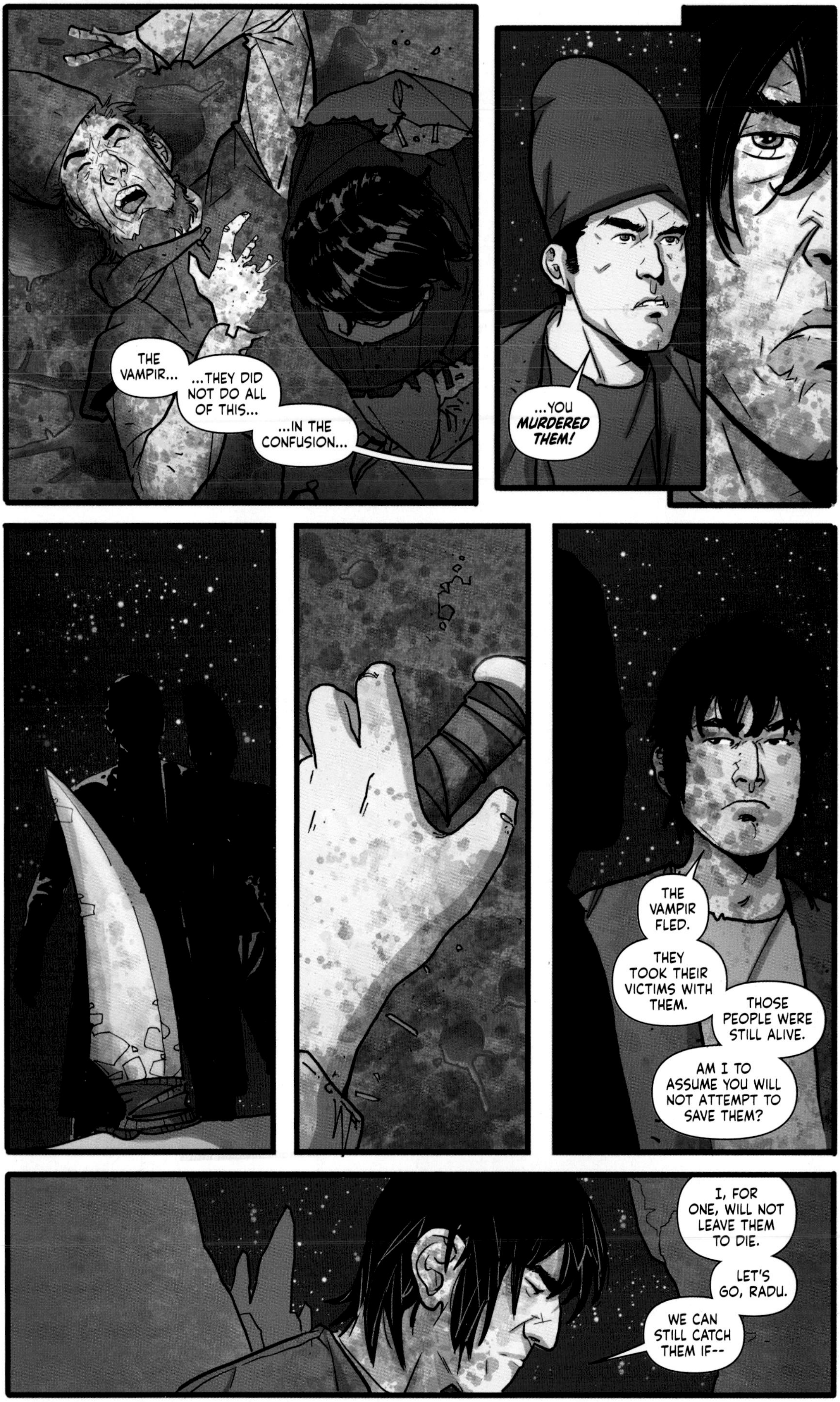
THE VAMPIR...
...THEY DID NOT DO ALL OF THIS...
...IN THE CONFUSION...
...YOU *MURDERED THEM!*
THE VAMPIR FLED.
THEY TOOK THEIR VICTIMS WITH THEM.
THOSE PEOPLE WERE STILL ALIVE.
AM I TO ASSUME YOU WILL NOT ATTEMPT TO SAVE THEM?
I, FOR ONE, WILL NOT LEAVE THEM TO DIE.
LET'S GO, RADU.
WE CAN STILL CATCH THEM IF--

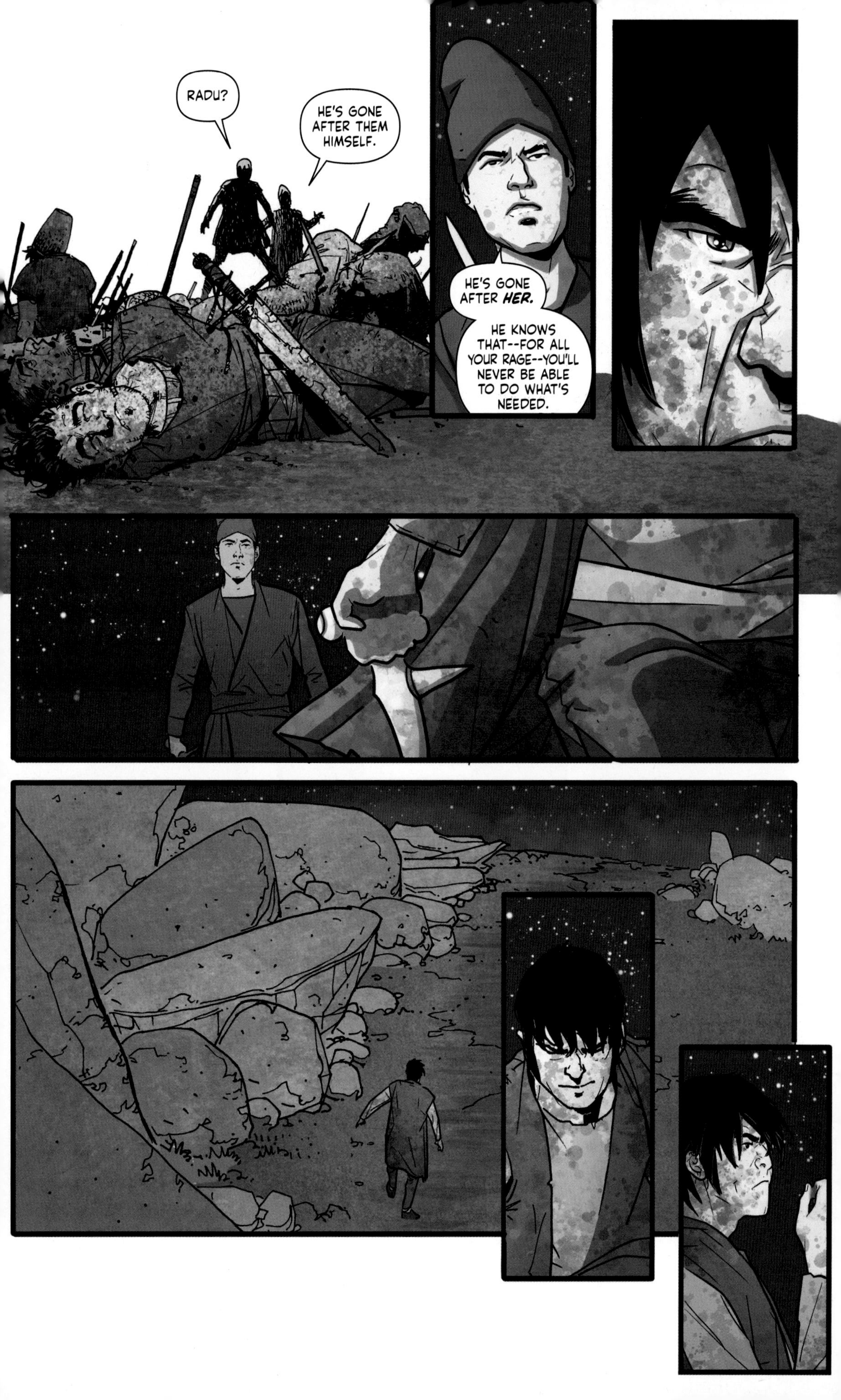
RADU?
HE'S GONE AFTER THEM HIMSELF.
HE'S GONE AFTER *HER.*
HE KNOWS THAT--FOR ALL YOUR RAGE--YOU'LL NEVER BE ABLE TO DO WHAT'S NEEDED.

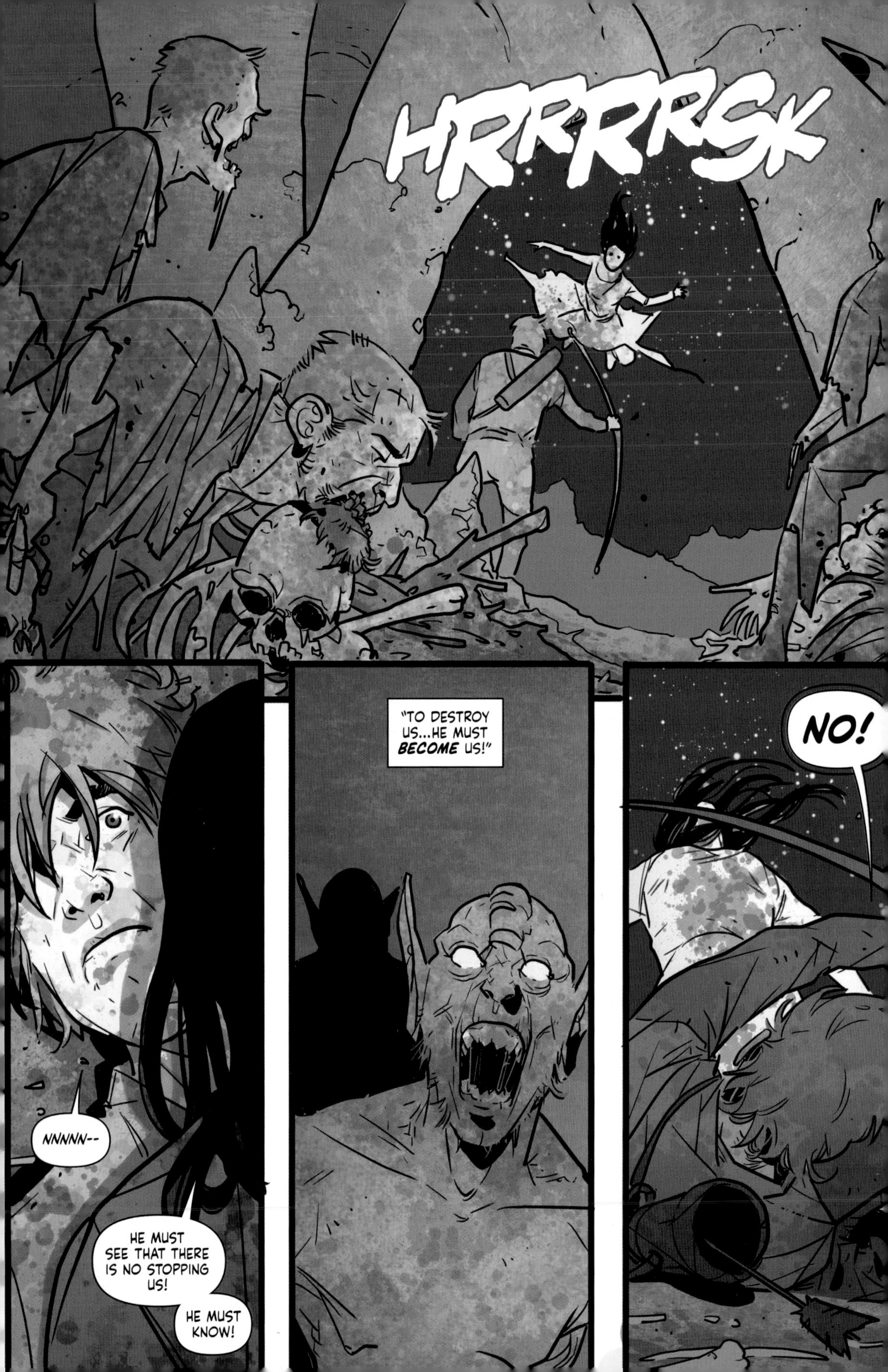
HRRRRSK
NNNNN--
HE MUST SEE THAT THERE IS NO STOPPING US!
HE MUST KNOW!
"TO DESTROY US...HE MUST *BECOME* US!"
NO!

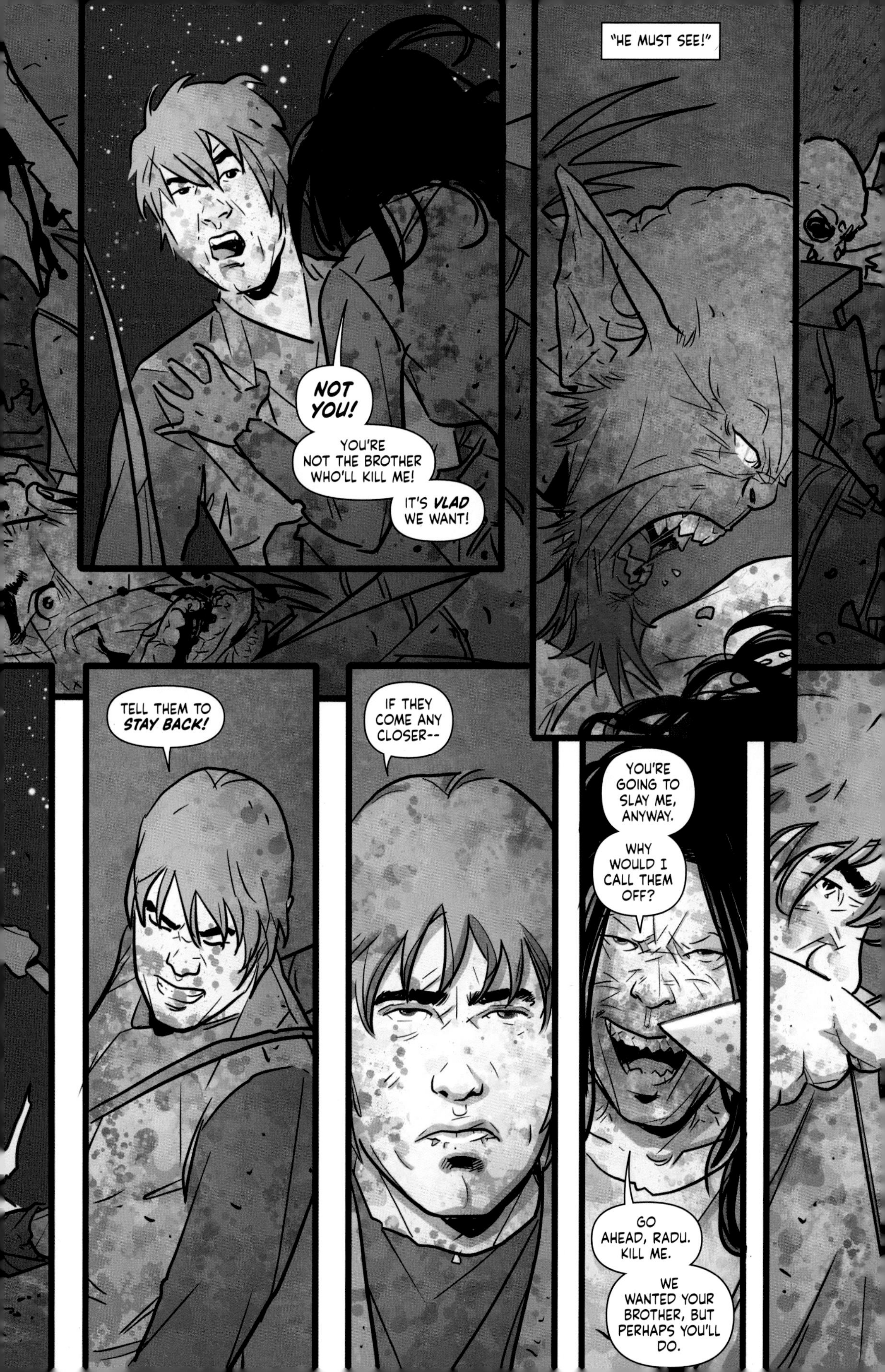
NOT YOU!
YOU'RE NOT THE BROTHER WHO'LL KILL ME!
IT'S VLAD WE WANT!
"HE MUST SEE!"
TELL THEM TO STAY BACK!
IF THEY COME ANY CLOSER--
YOU'RE GOING TO SLAY ME, ANYWAY.
WHY WOULD I CALL THEM OFF?
GO AHEAD, RADU. KILL ME.
WE WANTED YOUR BROTHER, BUT PERHAPS YOU'LL DO.

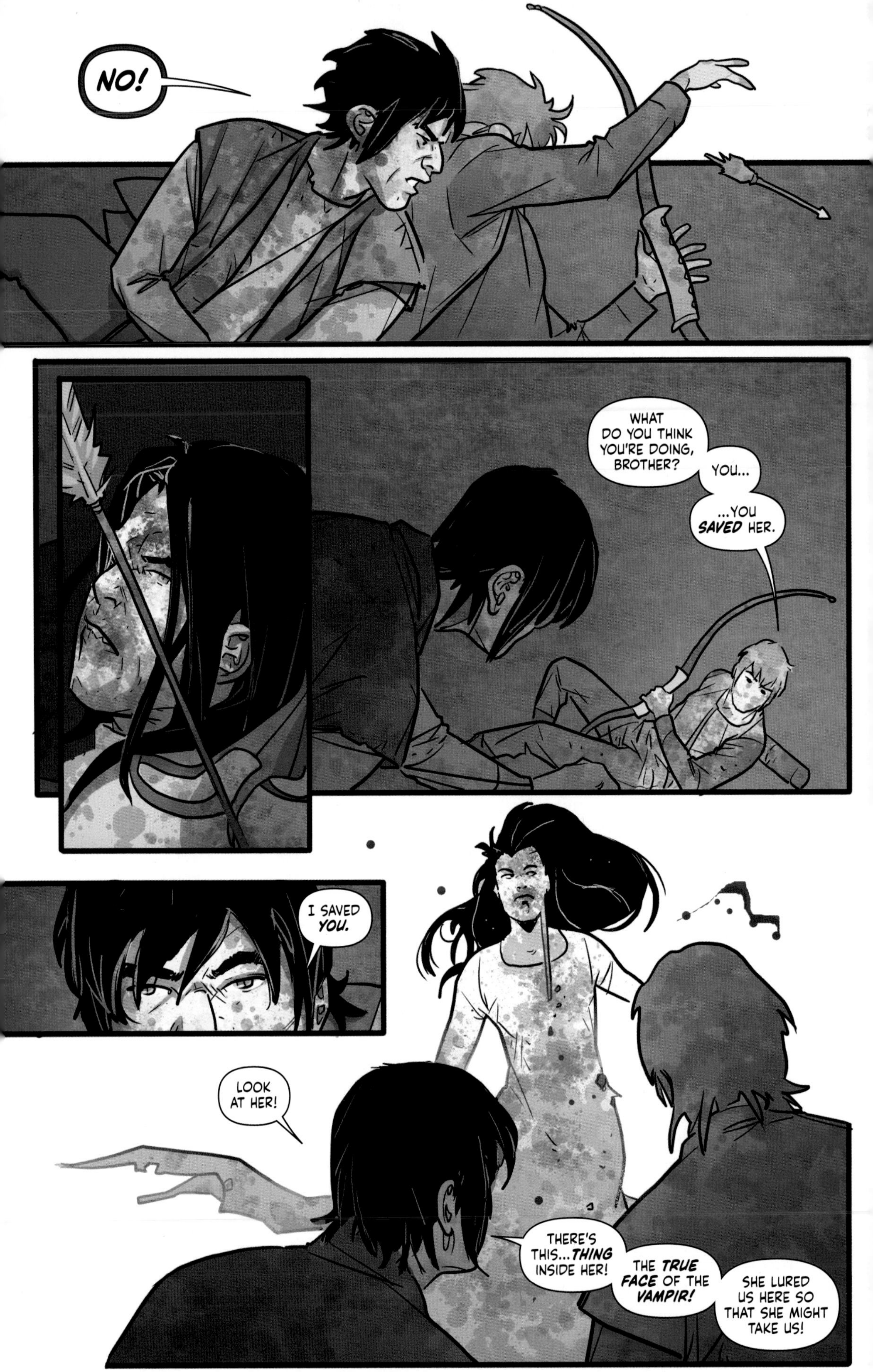
NO!
WHAT DO YOU THINK YOU'RE DOING, BROTHER?
YOU...
...YOU SAVED HER.
I SAVED YOU.
LOOK AT HER!
THERE'S THIS...THING INSIDE HER!
THE TRUE FACE OF THE VAMPIR!
SHE LURED US HERE SO THAT SHE MIGHT TAKE US!

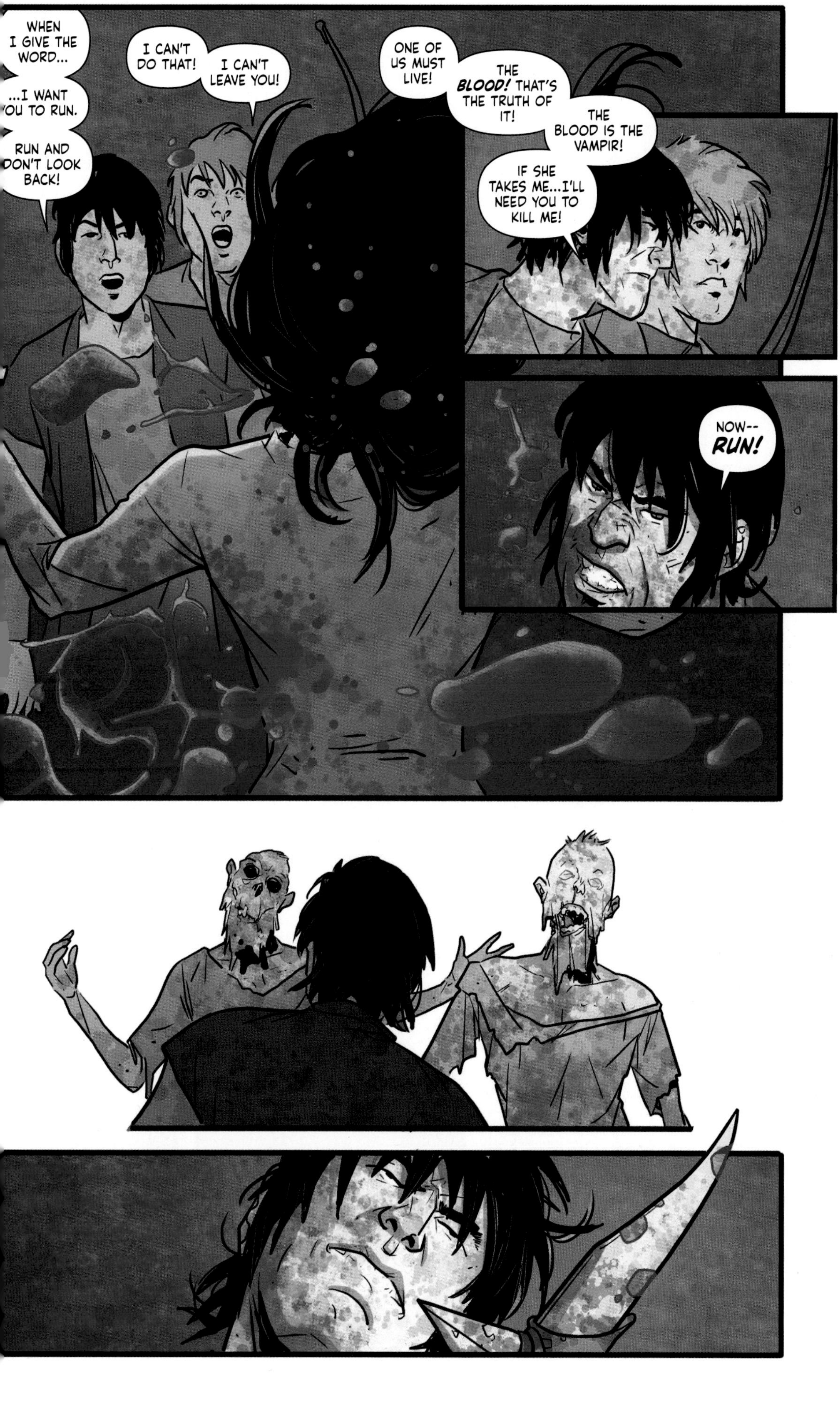
WHEN I GIVE THE WORD...
...I WANT YOU TO RUN.
RUN AND DON'T LOOK BACK!
I CAN'T DO THAT!
I CAN'T LEAVE YOU!
ONE OF US MUST LIVE!
THE BLOOD! THAT'S THE TRUTH OF IT!
THE BLOOD IS THE VAMPIR!
IF SHE TAKES ME...I'LL NEED YOU TO KILL ME!
NOW-- RUN!

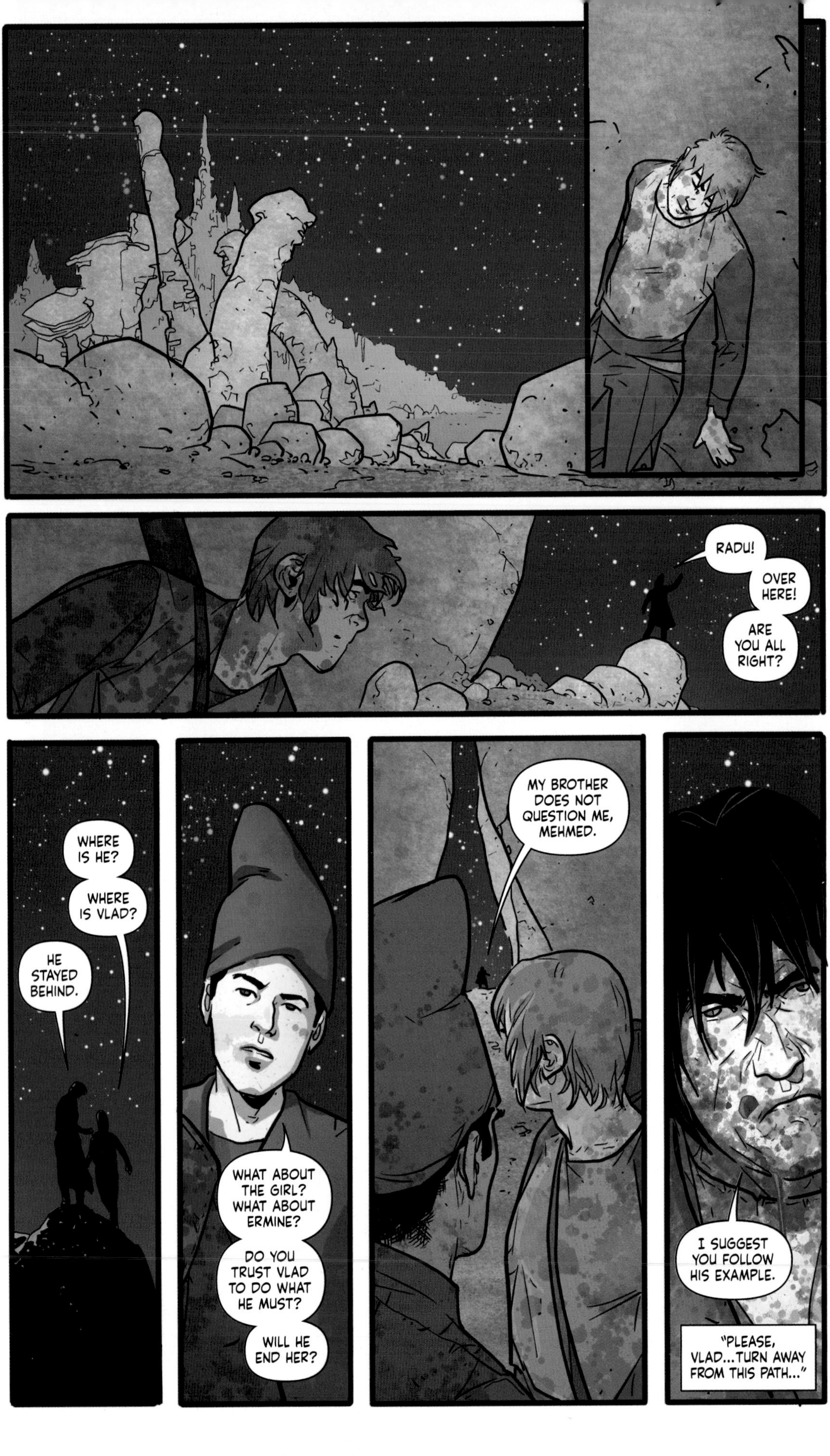
RADU!
OVER HERE!
ARE YOU ALL RIGHT?
WHERE IS HE?
WHERE IS VLAD?
HE STAYED BEHIND.
WHAT ABOUT THE GIRL? WHAT ABOUT ERMINE?
DO YOU TRUST VLAD TO DO WHAT HE MUST?
WILL HE END HER?
MY BROTHER DOES NOT QUESTION ME, MEHMED.
I SUGGEST YOU FOLLOW HIS EXAMPLE.
"PLEASE, VLAD...TURN AWAY FROM THIS PATH..."

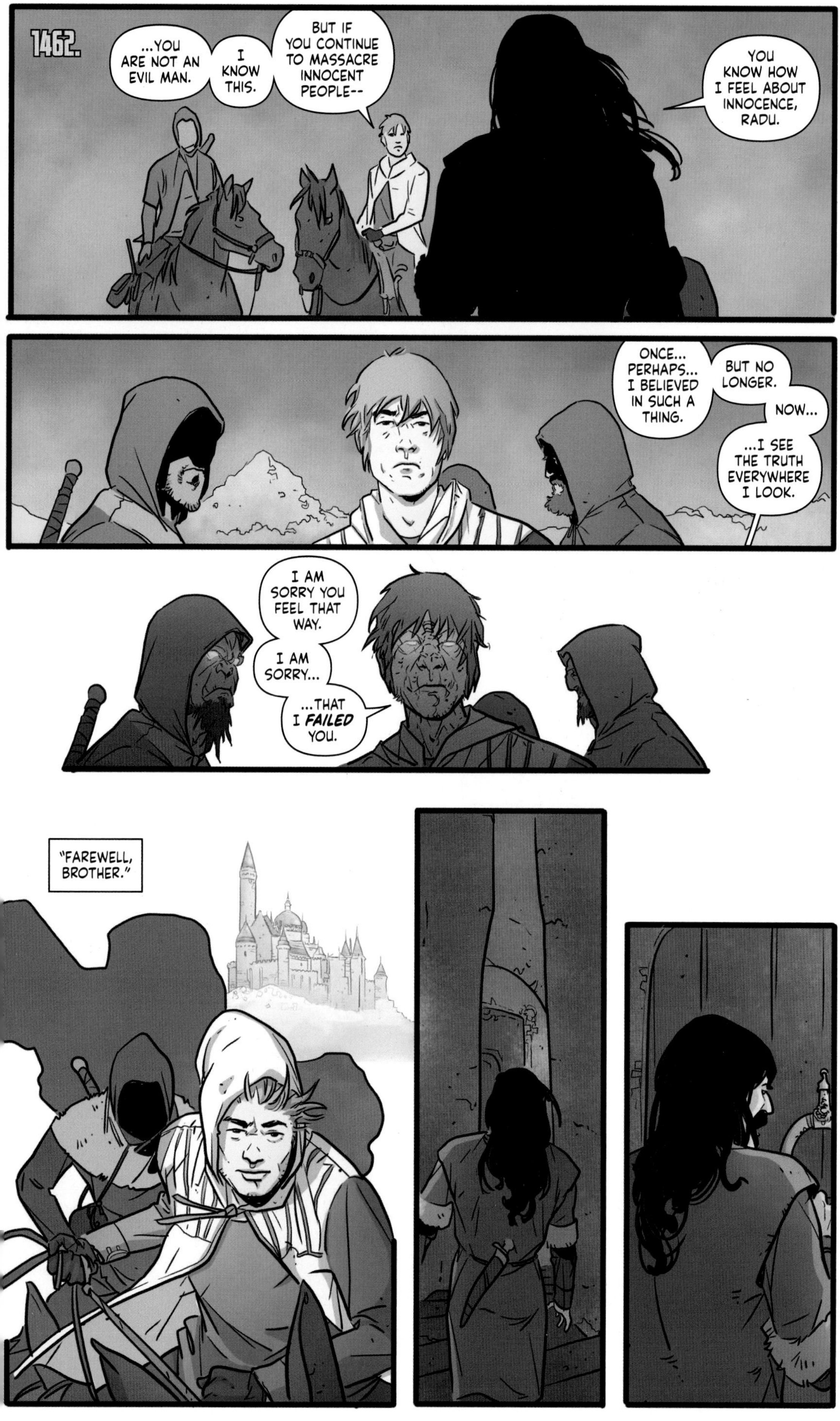
1462.
...YOU ARE NOT AN EVIL MAN.
I KNOW THIS.
BUT IF YOU CONTINUE TO MASSACRE INNOCENT PEOPLE--
YOU KNOW HOW I FEEL ABOUT INNOCENCE, RADU.
ONCE... PERHAPS... I BELIEVED IN SUCH A THING.
BUT NO LONGER.
NOW...
...I SEE THE TRUTH EVERYWHERE I LOOK.
I AM SORRY YOU FEEL THAT WAY.
I AM SORRY...
...THAT I *FAILED* YOU.
"FAREWELL, BROTHER."

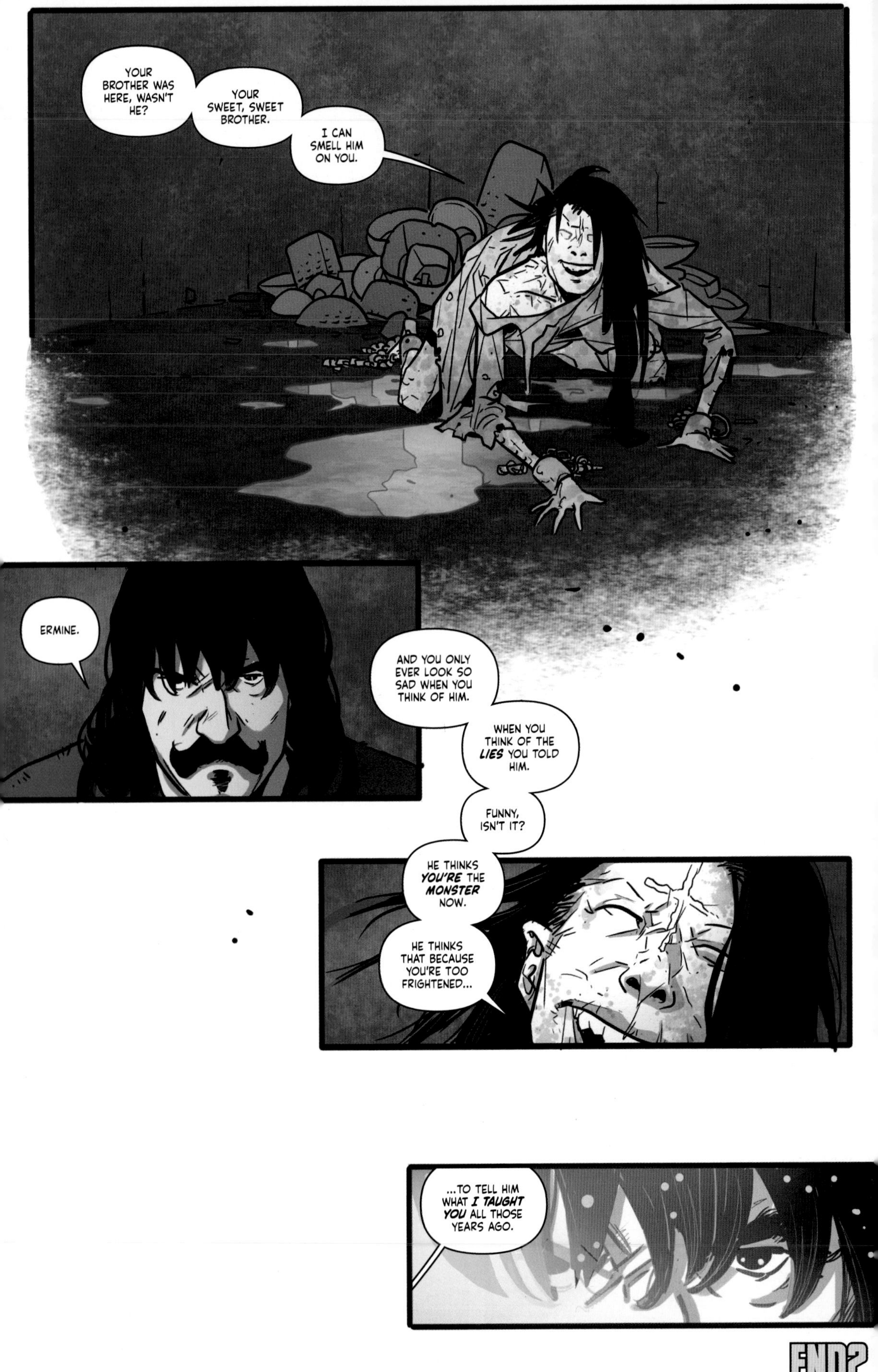
YOUR BROTHER WAS HERE, WASN'T HE?
YOUR SWEET, SWEET BROTHER.
I CAN SMELL HIM ON YOU.
ERMINE.
AND YOU ONLY EVER LOOK SO SAD WHEN YOU THINK OF HIM.
WHEN YOU THINK OF THE LIES YOU TOLD HIM.
FUNNY, ISN'T IT?
HE THINKS YOU'RE THE MONSTER NOW.
HE THINKS THAT BECAUSE YOU'RE TOO FRIGHTENED...
...TO TELL HIM WHAT I TAUGHT YOU ALL THOSE YEARS AGO.
END?

Issue 1
SZYMON KUDRANSKI
cover B

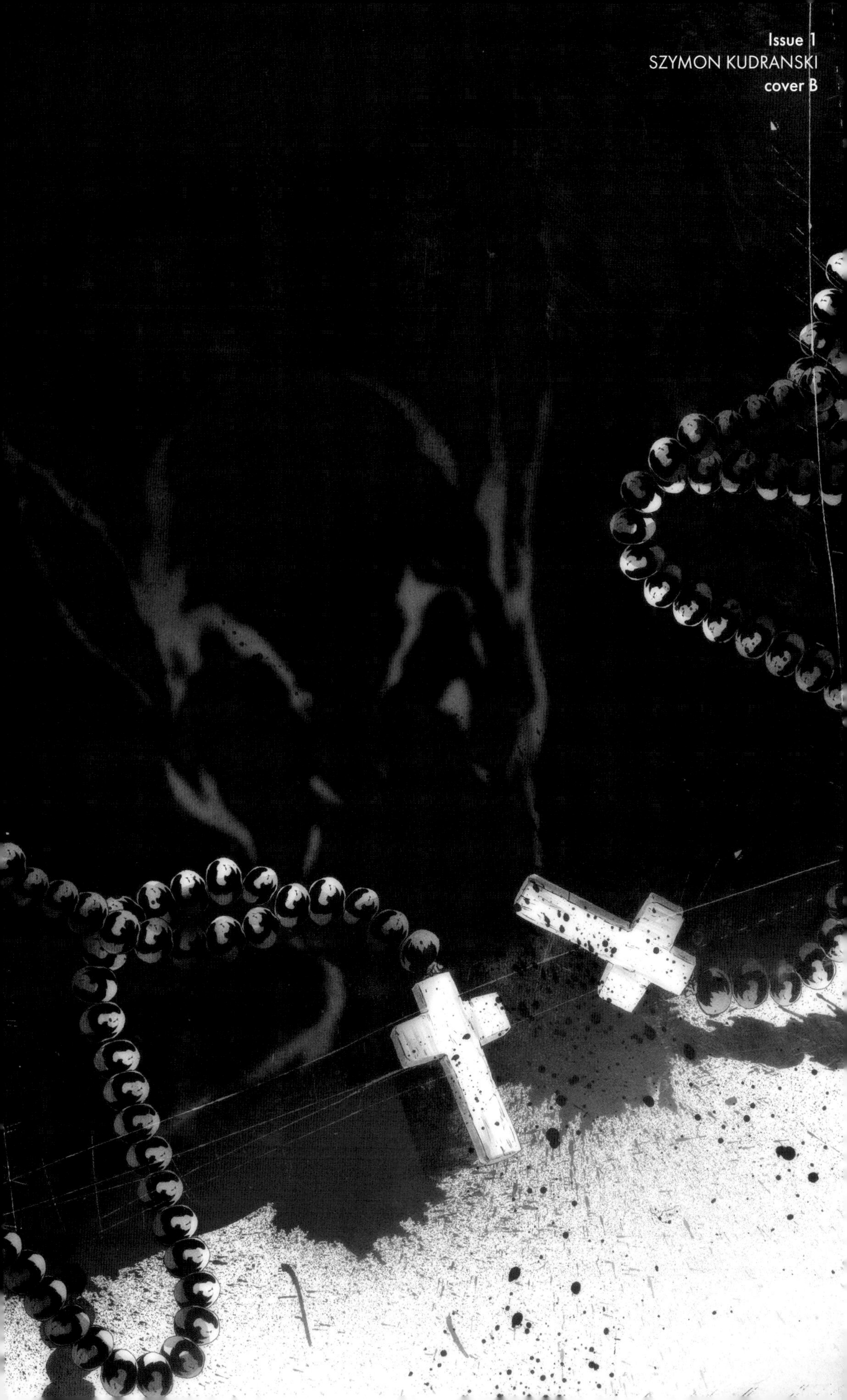

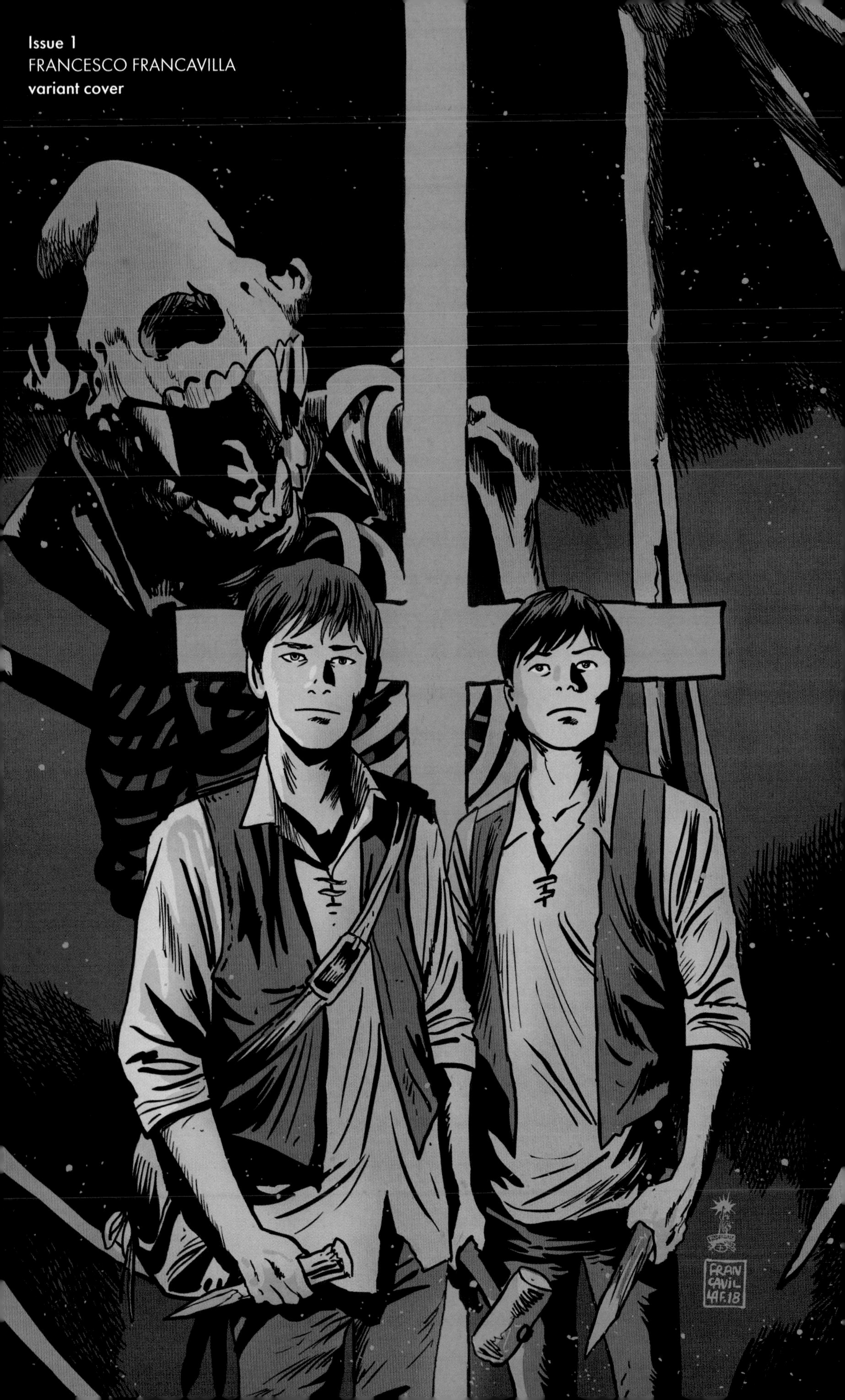
FRAN CAVIL LA F.18

Issue 1
FRANCESCO FRANCAVILLA
variant cover

Issue 1
MARCO RUDY
variant cover

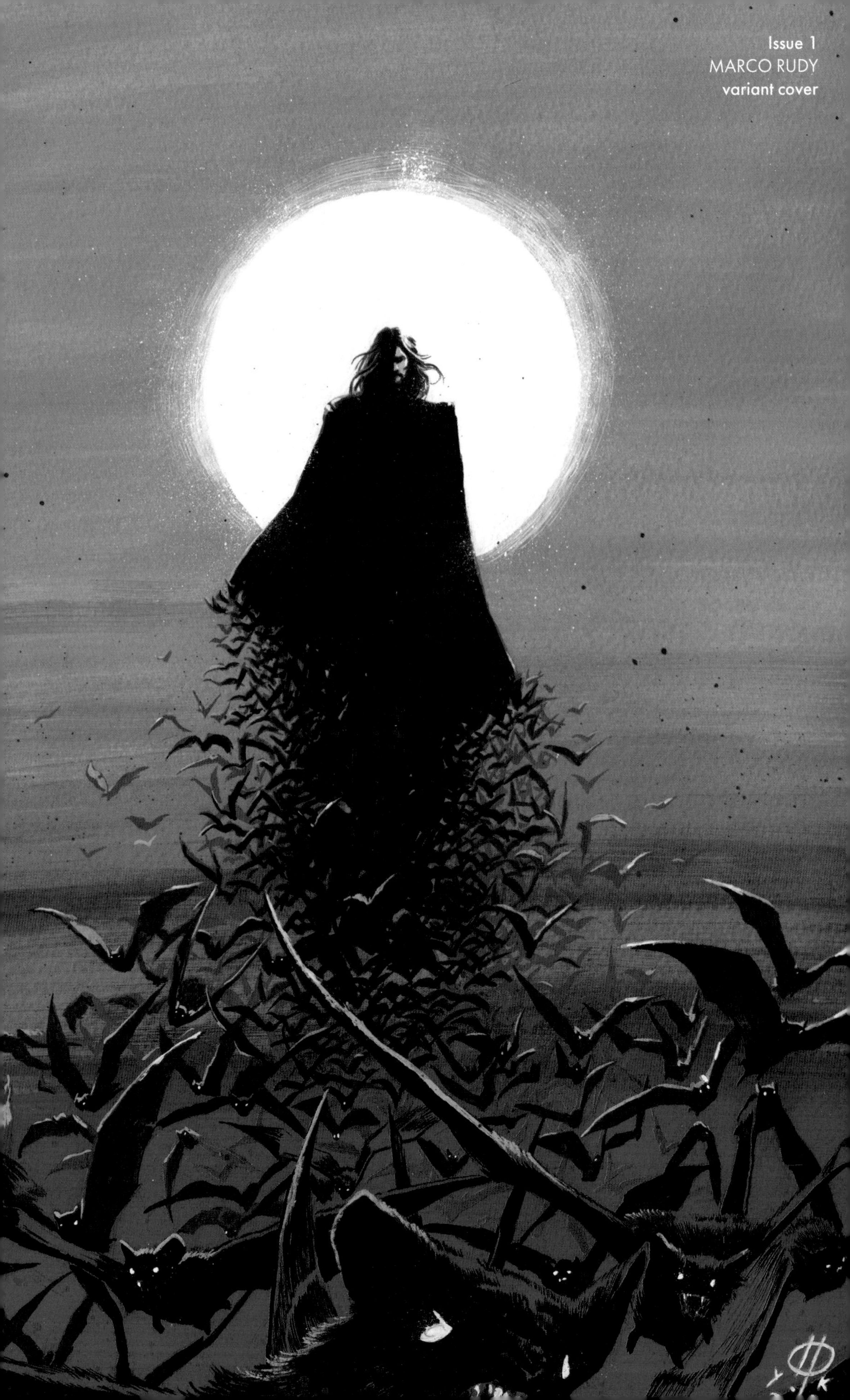

Issue 1
DALIBOR TALAJIĆ
variant cover

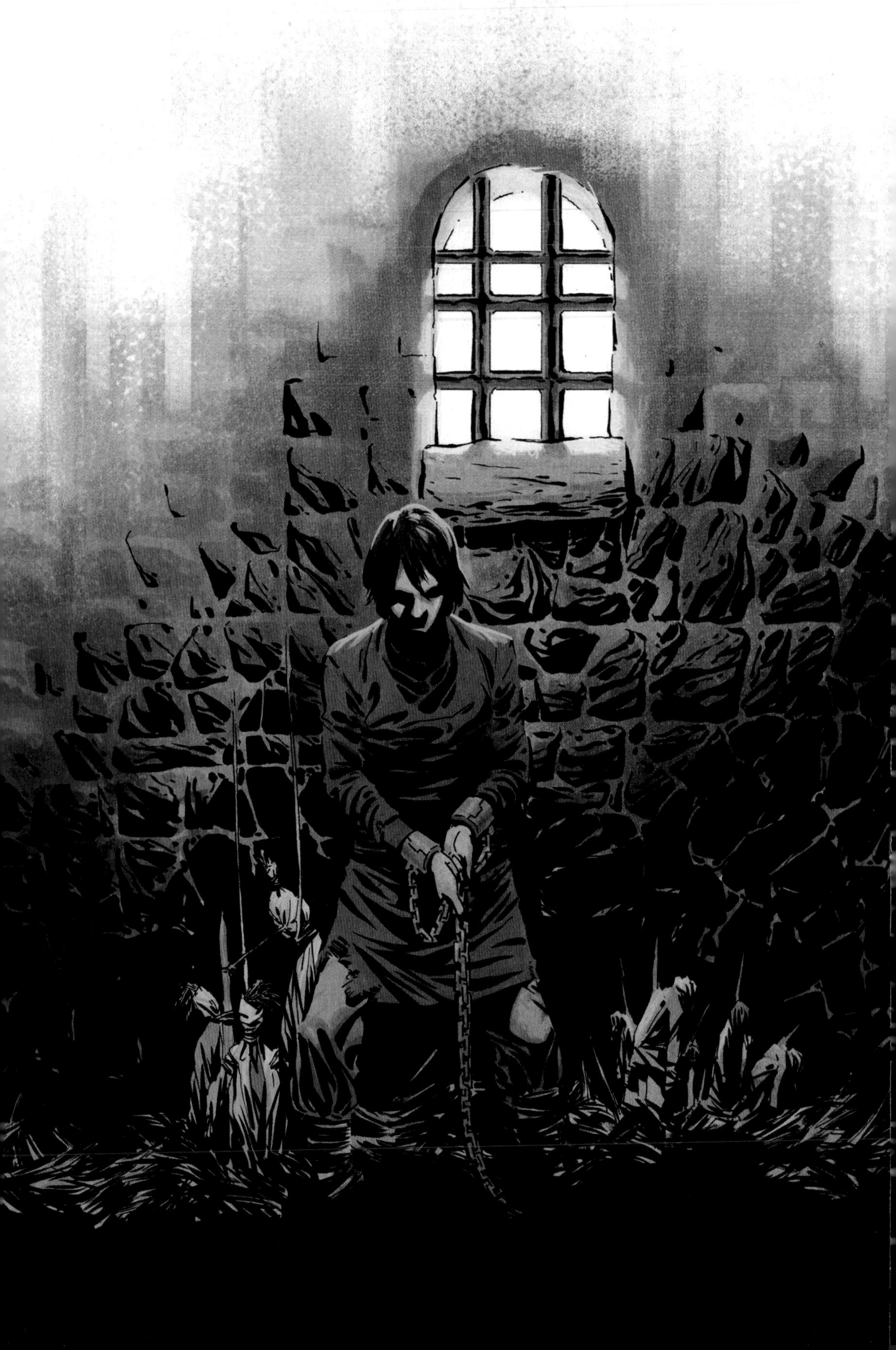

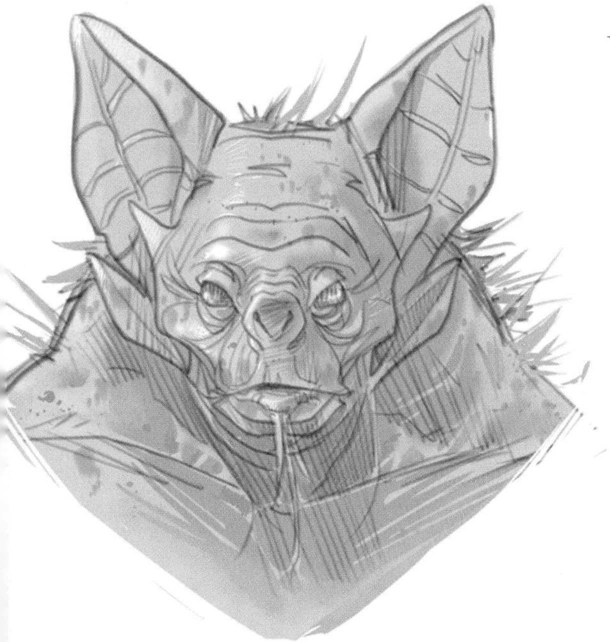

Brothers Dracul™
sketchbook

Artist Mirko Colak gives us a behind-the-scenes look at his sketchbook for BROTHERS DRACUL!

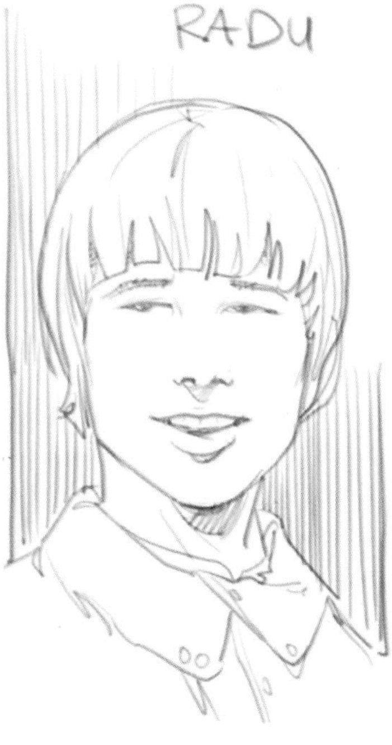
RADU

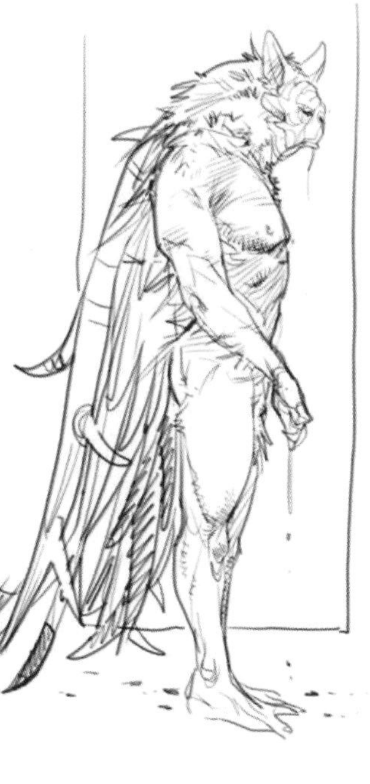

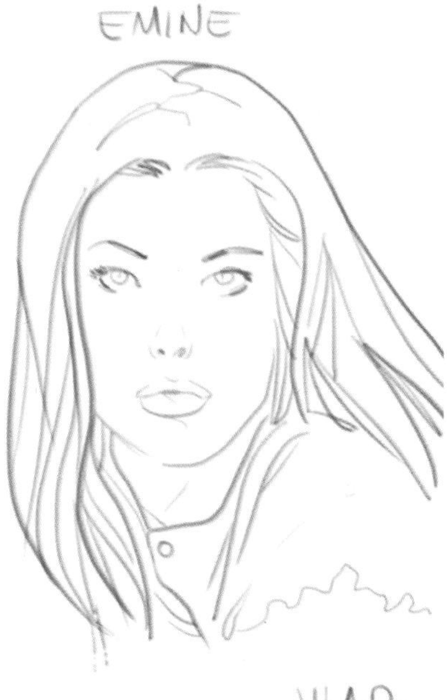
EMINE

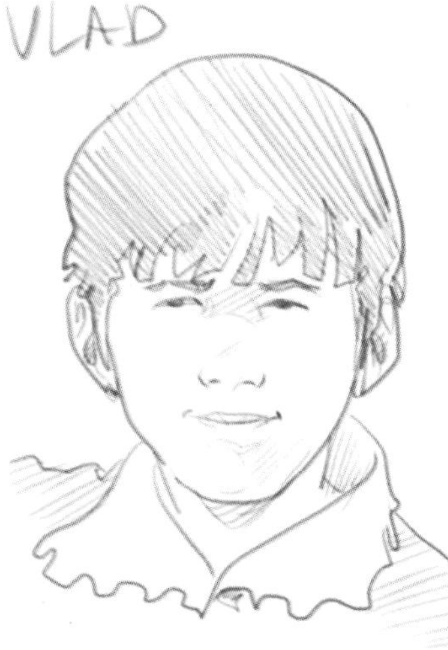
VLAD

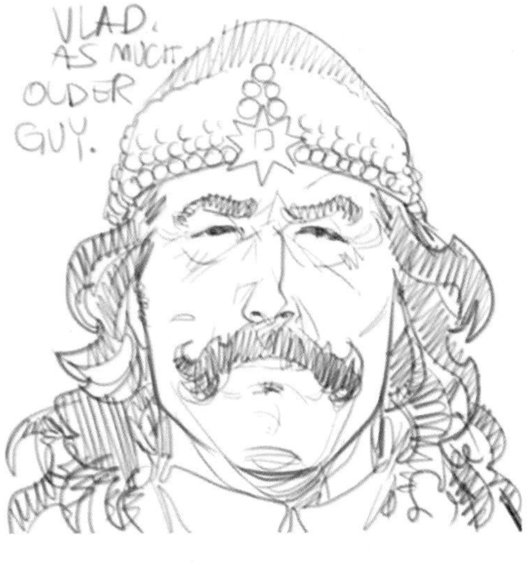
VLAD.
AS MUCH
OLDER
GUY.

ABOUT THE CREATORS OF

Brothers Dracul™

CULLEN BUNN
writer

@CullenBunn

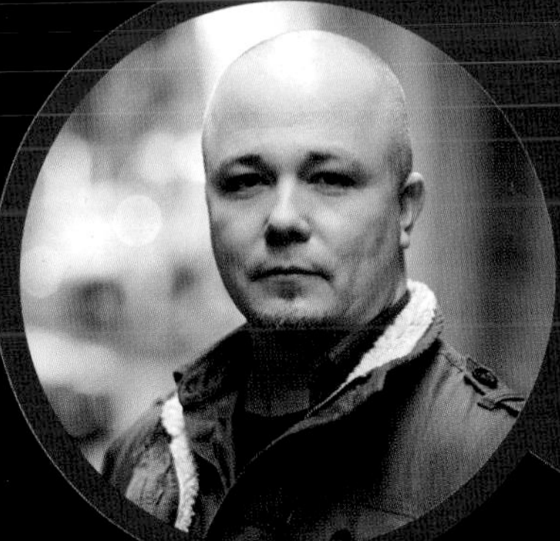

Cullen is the writer of such creator-owned comics as *The Sixth Gun, The Damned, Harrow County* and *Regression.* In addition, he writes *X-Men Blue, Monsters Unleashed* and numerous *Deadpool* comics for Marvel.

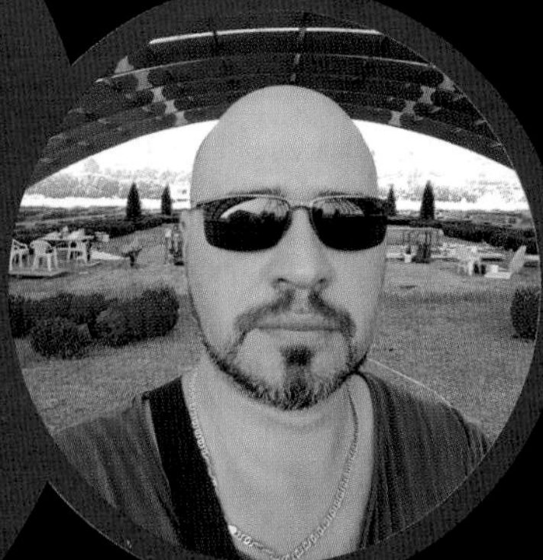

MIRKO COLAK
artist

@ColakMirko

Mirko has only recently hit the American comics scene, but European readers have had the pleasure of seeing his earlier artistic work in such Soliel publications as *Atlantide Experiment, Marie* and *Templier.* More recently, his intricate, masterful style has been seen in such comics as *Red Skull, Punisher, Spider-Man, The Avengers, Saucer Country, DeathStroke, Green Lantern, Red Hood* and *Turok.* To name a few.

MARIA SANTAOLALLA colorist

@MSantaolallart

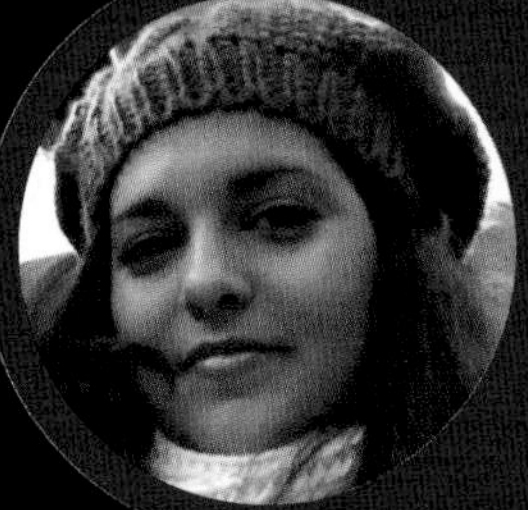

Born in Málaga, Spain, Maria initially studied tourism in college before realizing she wanted to be a comic book colorist. Being a dreamer and loving new challenges, Maria taught herself how to color, eventually earning professional work first at Fantasy Prone and later at IDW, where she colored *Back to the Future* and *Biff to the Future.* Now, she is excited to continue her collaboration with Cullen Bunn, Mirko Colak and AfterShock Comics!

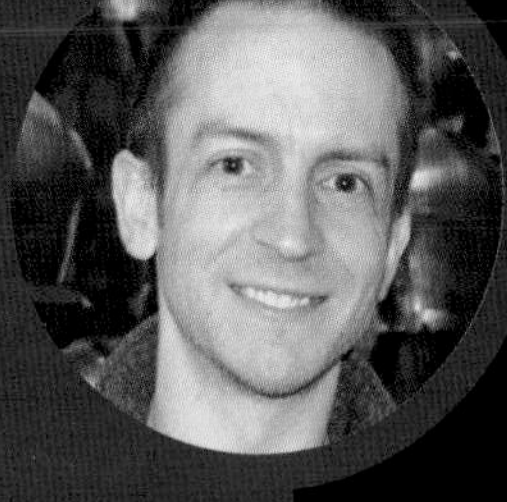

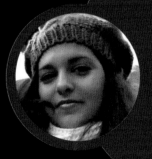

SIMON BOWLAND letterer

@SimonBowland

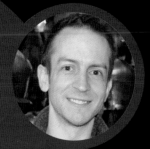

Simon has been lettering comics for over a decade and is currently working for DC, Image, Valiant, Dark Horse, Dynamite, 2000AD and IDW, amongst others. His debut AfterShock project was UNHOLY GRAIL. Born and bred in England, Simon still lives there today alongside his girlfriend and their tabby cat.